ADVANCE PI

China's Influence and American Interests

"China seeks to influence how we think about China. Diamond and Schell and their colleagues tell us what to look for, how to discern illicit coercion from legitimate public diplomacy, and practical steps for governments, universities, corporations, and other institutions to respond to this challenge while respecting our core American values."

—**George P. Shultz,** *former Secretary of State*

"This report is a model of thorough research, impeccable analysis, and compelling argument. But it must not be read passively. It is a call to action to those in industry, academia, think tanks, local government and law enforcement who must take responsibility for protecting our nation and our citizens from a sophisticated and pernicious form of aggression."

—**H. R. McMaster,** *retired US Army general and former National Security Adviser*

"This book is a wake-up call and serves as an important contribution to meaningfully starting—and advancing—a discussion in the United States about the Chinese Communist Party's influence operations. Policymakers must recognize that democracy is a national security issue and develop effective means that are consistent with our values to counter authoritarian tools of malign influence."

— **Laura Rosenberger,** *director of the Alliance for Securing Democracy and former National Security Council Director for China and Korea*

China's Influence &
American Interests

China's Influence & American Interests

PROMOTING CONSTRUCTIVE VIGILANCE

Report of the Working Group on
Chinese Influence Activities in the United States

REVISED EDITION

Co-Chairs

LARRY DIAMOND
Senior Fellow
The Hoover Institution
Stanford University

ORVILLE SCHELL
Arthur Ross Director
Center on US-China
Relations
Asia Society

HOOVER INSTITUTION PRESS
STANFORD UNIVERSITY   STANFORD, CALIFORNIA

www.hoover.org

Hoover Institution Press Publication No. 702
Hoover Institution at Leland Stanford Junior University,
Stanford, California 94305-6003

First printing 2019
25 24 23 22 21 20 19   10 9 8 7 6 5 4 3 2 1

Manufactured in the United States of America

Cataloging-in-Publication data available from the Library of Congress.

ISBN 978-08179-2285-6 (paperback)
ISBN 978-08179-2286-3 (epub)
ISBN 978-08179-2287-0 (mobi)
ISBN 978-08179-2288-7 (PDF)

♾ This paper meets the requirements of ANSI/NISO Z39.48-1992 (Permanence of Paper).

CONTENTS

LIST OF ABBREVIATIONS

CAFFC	Chinese People's Association for Friendship with Foreign Countries
CAFIU	Chinese Association for International Understanding
CAIFC	China Association for International Friendly Contact
CASS	Chinese Academy of Social Sciences
CCP	Chinese Communist Party
CCP/ID	Chinese Communist Party International Liaison Department
CCPPNR	China Council for Promotion of Peaceful National Reunification
CCTV	China Central Television
CFIIS	China Foundation for International Strategic Studies
CFIUS	Committee on Foreign Investment in the United States
CGCC	China General Chamber of Commerce
CGTN	China Global Television Network
CICIR	China Institutes of Contemporary International Relations
CICWS	China Institute of Contemporary World Studies
CIIS	China Institute of International Studies
CIISS	China Institute of International and Strategic Studies
CIs	Confucius Institutes
CMC	Central Military Commission
CPIFA	Chinese People's Institute of Foreign Affairs

CPPCC	Chinese People's Political Consultative Conference
CPS/NAA	Central Party School/National Administration Academy
CRI	China Radio International
CSCPA	China Strategic Culture Promotion Association
CSSA	Chinese Students and Scholars Association
CUSEF	China-US Exchange Foundation
FALSG	Foreign Affairs Leading Small Group
FAO	Foreign Affairs Office
FARA	Foreign Agent Registration Act
LSG	Leading Small Group
MECEA	Mutual Education and Cultural Exchange Act
OCAO	Overseas Chinese Affairs Office
PRC	People's Republic of China
SAFEA	State Administration of Foreign Experts Affairs
SCIO	State Council Information Office
TTP	Thousand Talents Plan/Program
UFLSG	United Front Leading Small Group
UFWD	United Front Work Department

FOREWORD

In February 2018 twenty-three American and ten foreign academics, diplomats, journalists, and think tank members met at the Annenberg Foundation Trust's Sunnylands estate in Southern California to launch a project to map the challenges posed by the People's Republic of China's growing quest—in what Beijing propagandists call a "discourse war," *huayuzhan* (话语战)—to influence civic discussions in societies outside the sovereign borders of China. Over the following months, participants in our Working Group on Chinese Influence Activities in the United States researched and drafted eight chapters assessing the nature and extent of China's influence-seeking activities in different sectors of American society, while our international associates contributed overviews of these efforts in eight other developed countries. The draft papers were discussed in several follow-up meetings and initially released as a report in November 2018. Following the release, we made modest revisions in response to new information and some specific concerns that were subsequently raised. This book represents the final version of our working group report.

As we stress repeatedly in our Introduction, every country has the right to promote its policies, values, and achievements abroad, so long as they do so through internationally accepted means of open engagement and persuasion, what is often referred to as "soft power" or "public diplomacy." But increasingly, policy makers, analysts, and civic leaders in the world's democracies find themselves confronting a very different form of power projection by the People's Republic of China (PRC). This entails efforts to advance the interest of the Chinese Communist Party by shaping, even constraining, policy discourse abroad in ways that are sometimes overt, but that also covertly disguise the origin and intent of the influence-seeking activity.

We want to briefly respond here at the outset to some of the criticisms that have been raised since the initial release of our working group report. One group worries that the report does not distinguish clearly enough between legitimate and illegitimate influence activities. As we noted in our original draft, and now in this final book, it is crucial to make a distinction between traditional soft-power activities and more subterranean and subversive "sharp power" projections. In the pages that follow, our concern with the PRC's ostensible soft-power activities in the United States—its surging media presence, the growing number of visits and exchanges of all kinds, the expansion of philanthropic activities—is not the rising scale of them, but their all-too-often covert and nonreciprocal nature. As we stress in our Policy Principles, it should no longer be acceptable that scholars, journalists, diplomats, and public officials from the People's Republic of China be afforded unfettered access to American society while reciprocal access is severely constrained or denied to American counterparts in China. It is here that the political question of what has been happening internally within China has relevance to our own foreign policy.

Although it was beyond the scope of our work to document in detail the political trajectory of the People's Republic of China, it is critical to understand that under Communist Party general secretary Xi Jinping China has become increasingly authoritarian and marked by rising levels of ideological indoctrination and control; diminishing tolerance for dissent; new crackdowns on human-rights lawyers; an unprecedented new assault on the rights of the Uighur and other Muslim minorities; and the emergence of a new surveillance state set on compiling digital profiles of every Chinese citizen with a "social credit score" that will double as a political loyalty index determining access to a wide range of services and privileges in Chinese life. For readers of this report, it is critical to remember that the PRC remains a Leninist regime in which the Communist Party not only reigns supreme over the state at home but also now presides over a vast and lavishly resourced bureaucracy to project global influence, through so-called "united front" ties, to willing or ill-informed constituencies around the world.

We share with our critics the goal of building a healthy relationship between the world's two superpowers that is based as much as possible on cooperation rather than conflict. But as we repeatedly argue in this book, this can only be possible with a rebalancing of the relationship toward greater transparency, reciprocity, and fairness. Such a rebalancing will require, in part, pushing back against nontransparent forms of intrusion, such as PRC efforts to vet which topics relating to US-China relations are open for discussion, which Americans can participate in scholarly delegations and conferences in China (or even in the United States), and what topics writers and journalists may cover without being treated in a punitive way. For example, when pluralism of perspectives largely disappears in the Chinese-language media within the United States, that development reduces the quality of the democratic experience for an important sector of American society, and thus the issue becomes a legitimate US national interest that must be addressed.

The same is true for the effects of other kinds of influence activities documented in this report. When foreign students and scholars have good reason to fear that their statements and comments—even in the classroom—may be monitored by some of their peers and reported back to authorities of their home government, which places little value on freedom of expression, societal freedoms in the United States are undermined. When American scholars and researchers concede that they engage in some degree of self-censorship in order to avoid losing access to Chinese visas, archives, libraries, institutions, officials, and society, *that* is an impact on academic freedom in the United States. When a think tank shies away from overt criticism of China for fear of jeopardizing its Beijing branch office or generous flows of financing, *that* is an impact on American public discourse. When US corporations are pressured to refer to Taiwan in their commercial activity only in a way that strictly adheres to PRC insistence that Taiwan is a province of the PRC, *that* impinges on their freedom to operate globally, as well as their freedom of expression in the United States. We believe that the sum total of the PRC's influence-seeking activities in the United States and other societies (including but not limited to the eight case studies in our Appendix) represents an ambitious new project to *control* the narrative about China and to shape the policies and thinking of other societies toward China, and that a worrisome portion of these efforts involves illegitimate methods. A posture of informed, responsible, and balanced vigilance now will hopefully contain the potential for much more worrisome levels of untoward influence down the road.

Finally, as we have stated explicitly and repeatedly in our report—including in our Afterword—we reject casting general aspersions on Chinese Americans or Chinese nationals who are studying and doing business in the United States. Chinese Americans constitute a vital and treasured portion of the extraordinary cultural mosaic of American society and have come to constitute an important element of American exceptionalism. American Chinese are just as "American" as any other ethnic or nationality group in the United States, and their extraordinary achievements in business, science, the arts, philanthropy, and public affairs place them among the most successful and admired of all American nationality groups. It goes without saying that we oppose any efforts, past or future, to single them out as a group for investigation or discrimination, and this report notes examples of what we believe to constitute prosecutorial overreach.

Any American of any ethnicity or national origin could, for financial, ideological, or personal reasons, become an agent of covert influence of an adversarial power. Any concern about whether an American citizen or resident is acting inappropriately must therefore be judged on a case-by-case basis and strictly based on evidence. And American democracy will always be stronger when no ethnic group has its loyalty as a group to this country called into question.

However, as our report documents, the Chinese Communist Party views the situation quite differently: the "united front" influence bureaucracy in the PRC considers the whole worldwide Chinese diaspora as "overseas compatriots," *huaqiao tongbaomen* (侨同胞们) owing a measure of loyalty to "the Chinese Motherland," *zhongguode zuguo* (中国的祖国).

Consequently, the Communist authorities treat people of Chinese ethnic origin as a special priority in the PRC's global influence-seeking activities. This creates a situation that we cannot wish away, a racial targeting that many ethnically Chinese citizens of the United States and other democratic societies worry about and deserve protection from. It is *their* rights as American citizens—including their right to a wide range of information of sources in Chinese and freedom from pressure or intimidation by agents of foreign governments such as the PRC—that are highlighted in this report. This does not mean that Chinese Americans who advocate for more constructive relations with the PRC, or who may align themselves with certain PRC policies, are doing so because they have been inappropriately "influenced." But in the context of an increasingly adversarial bilateral relationship, China's efforts to influence them, especially covertly, are a legitimate subject of research, discussion, and concern, which is what we have sought to do with this volume.

We do not advocate or support a new Cold War with China, nor do we hope for a diminution in ties between the two countries or a diminished flow of graduate students, even in "sensitive" STEM fields (science, technology, engineering, and mathematics). If the United States wants to maintain its global technological leadership, we believe a far better approach to the issue of tech transfer (addressed in chapter 8 of this book) is to carefully vet foreign graduate student applicants for undisclosed ties to PRC intelligence and security agencies, and then not only welcome the overwhelming majority of Chinese (and other foreign) applicants, but *encourage* them to stay on after their studies are completed to become citizens.

For the foreseeable future, China will be the United States' principal competitor for global power and influence. International peace and security require that the relationship between these two superpowers remain as constructive as possible. But any healthy relationship must be built on transparency, reciprocity, fairness, and balance. That is the promise that has motivated our working group, our initial report, and now this book.

ACKNOWLEDGMENTS

This working group was jointly convened by the Hoover Institution at Stanford University and the Center on US-China Relations at the Asia Society in New York. These co-conveners have also been assisted, financially and logistically, by The Annenberg Foundation Trust at Sunnylands. We are grateful to each of these institutions for their support of our work, and to Thomas Gilligan, director of the Hoover Institution, and Ambassador David Lane, president of The Annenberg Foundation Trust at Sunnylands, for their personal support of this project. We also thank the latter two institutions, as well as the China Policy Program of the Elliott School of International Affairs at George Washington University, for supporting and hosting meetings of the working group.

This report has been a collaborative effort among a group of American scholars and policy practitioners who have spent long careers studying and engaging with China, Asia more broadly, and a wide variety of political systems around the world. Each participant also has an abiding interest in protecting and strengthening democratic institutions in the United States and elsewhere in the world. While different participants took the lead in drafting particular chapters of the report, each chapter was reviewed and contributed to by a number of participants in what became a truly collective and collaborative research effort. Our general findings and policy principles represent a broad—though not necessarily complete—consensus of the working group participants.

This working group grew out of the task force on US-China Relations (chaired by Susan Shirk and Orville Schell), and we thank the Carnegie Corporation of New York and the Henry Luce Foundation for their support of the task force. Although the two efforts share many members in common, they are separate and distinct endeavors.

We present this report as the collective product of discussions and research among a group of distinguished American specialists on China and US foreign affairs. It analyzes the growing challenge posed by China's influence-seeking activities in the United States across a number of important sectors of American public life. However, as we note throughout the report, these influence activities are not confined to the United States. Indeed, they appear in different forms and to different degrees in a large number of other democratic societies around the world (in some cases more deeply than in the United States). We therefore have opted to include in an appendix short summary reports on China's influence activities (and the resulting national responses) in eight other countries.

We owe a particular debt of thanks to Kyle Hutzler, an MBA student at Stanford University with significant experience in China. His superior organizational skills and uncomplaining capacity for prodigious work contributed enormously to the coordination of our work throughout the project. We could not have produced this report without him.

We would also like to thank Barbara Arellano and Alison Petersen at the Hoover Institution Press for their dedicated assistance in producing, editing, and publishing this report, as well as Laura Chang at the Center on US-China Relations at the Asia Society for her assistance in helping to coordinate the project.

Finally, we would like to thank all of the working group participants for their generous contributions of time and effort. None were remunerated for their contributions, and everyone participated and contributed out of their professional and national sense of responsibility.

LARRY DIAMOND   ORVILLE SCHELL
The Hoover Institution   *Center on US-China Relations*
Stanford University   *Asia Society*

October 24, 2018

POLICY PRINCIPLES FOR CONSTRUCTIVE VIGILANCE

The members of this working group seek a productive relationship between the People's Republic of China (PRC) and the United States. To this end, and in light of growing evidence of China's interference in various sectors of American government and society, we propose three broad principles that should serve as the basis for protecting the integrity of American institutions inside the United States while also protecting basic core American values, norms, and laws.

Transparency

Transparency is a fundamental tenet and asset of democracy, and the best protection against the manipulation of American entities by outside actors.

- American nongovernmental organizations (NGOs) should play an important role in investigating and monitoring illicit activities by China and other foreign actors. They should as well seek to inform themselves about the full range of China's influence activities and the distinctions between legitimate and illegitimate influence efforts.
- Congress should perform its constitutional role by continuing to investigate, report on, and recommend appropriate action concerning China's influence activities in the United States. It should

update relevant laws and regulations regarding foreign influence, and adopt new ones, to strengthen transparency in foreign efforts to exert influence.

- Executive branch agencies should similarly investigate and publicize, when appropriate, findings concerning these activities, with a view to promoting healthy and responsible vigilance among American governmental and nongovernmental actors.
- The US media should undertake careful, fact-based investigative reporting of China's influence activities, and it should enhance its knowledge base for undertaking responsible reporting.
- Faculty governance is the key to preserving academic freedom in American universities. All gifts, grants, endowments, and cooperative programs, including Confucius Institutes, should be subjected to the usual procedures of faculty oversight.
- US governmental and nongovernmental sectors should disclose financial and other relationships that may be subject to foreign influence.

Integrity

Foreign funding can undermine the independence of American institutions, and various types of coercive and covert activities by China (and other countries) directly contradict core democratic values and freedoms, which must be protected by institutional vigilance and effective governance.

- Openness and freedom are fundamental elements of American democracy and intrinsic strengths of the United States and its way of life. These values must be protected against corrosive actions by China and other countries.
- Various institutions—but notably universities and think tanks—need to enhance sharing and pooling of information concerning China's activities, and they should promote more closely coordinated collective action to counter China's inappropriate activities and pressures. This report recommends that American institu-

tions within each of the above two sectors (and possibly others) formulate and agree to a "Code of Conduct" to guide their exchanges with Chinese counterparts.

- When they believe that efforts to exert influence have violated US laws or the rights of American citizens and foreign residents in the United States, US institutions should refer such activities to the appropriate law enforcement authorities.

- Rigorous efforts should be undertaken to inform the Chinese American community about potentially inappropriate activities carried out by China. At the same time, utmost efforts must be taken to protect the rights of the Chinese American community, as well as protecting the rights of Chinese citizens living or studying in the United States.

- Consideration should be given to establishing a federal government office that American state and local governments and nongovernmental institutions could approach—on a strictly voluntary basis—for advice on how best to manage Chinese requests for engagement and partnership. This office could also provide confidential background on the affiliations of Chinese individuals and organizations to party and state institutions.

- All American institutions—governmental and nongovernmental— that deal with Chinese actors (and other potential sources of inappropriate foreign influence) should review their oversight and governance practices and codify and exemplify best standards of practice and due diligence.

Reciprocity

American institutions are deflected from their purpose of increasing US-China understanding, and become distorted as one-way channels of Chinese influence, when they are denied access to China on a basis that is reciprocal with the access Chinese institutions are granted here.

- The asymmetry of scholarly research access is the most glaring example of the lack of reciprocity. A whole variety of normal

scholarly activities—including access to archives and certain libraries, fieldwork, conducting surveys, and interviewing officials
or average citizens—has been cut off for American researchers in
China while Chinese enjoy all of these academic opportunities in
the United States. Individually and collectively, universities and
other sectors of American democratic life should insist on greater
reciprocity of access.

- US government public diplomacy activities are heavily circumscribed in China, while NGOs have encountered an increasingly
difficult environment in which to carry out their work. More reasonable reciprocity for US public diplomacy efforts in China, rela-
tive to China's activities in the United States, should be addressed
in negotiations between the two countries. In addition, this report
recommends enhanced American efforts to promote independent
news and information, and democratic ideas, through US global
broadcasting and efforts to counter disinformation.

- The US government should actively promote and protect opportunities for American actors to operate in China.

Introduction

For three and a half decades following the end of the Maoist era, China adhered to Deng Xiaoping's policies of "reform and opening to the outside world" and "peaceful development." After Deng retired as paramount leader, these principles continued to guide China's international behavior in the leadership eras of Jiang Zemin and Hu Jintao. Admonishing Chinese to "keep your heads down and bide your time," these party leaders sought to emphasize that China's rapid economic development and its accession to "great power" status need not be threatening to either the existing global order or the interests of its Asian neighbors. However, since party general secretary Xi Jinping came to power in 2012, the situation has changed. Under his leadership, China has significantly expanded the more assertive set of policies initiated by his predecessor Hu Jintao. These policies not only seek to redefine China's place in the world as a global player, but they also have put forward the notion of a "China option" (中国方案) that is claimed to be a more efficient developmental model than that of liberal democracy.

While Americans are well acquainted with China's quest for influence through the projection of diplomatic, economic, and military power, we are less aware of the myriad ways Beijing has more recently been seeking cultural and informational influence, some of which could undermine our democratic processes. These include efforts to penetrate and sway—through various methods that former Australian prime minister Malcolm Turnbull summarized as "covert, coercive or corrupting"—a range of groups and institutions, including the Chinese American community, Chinese students in the United States, and American civil society organizations, academic institutions, think tanks, and media.[1]

Some of these efforts fall into the category of normal public diplomacy as pursued by many other countries. But others involve the use of coercive or corrupting methods to pressure individuals and groups and thereby interfere in the functioning of American civil and political life.

It is important not to exaggerate the threat of Beijing's new initiatives. China has not sought to interfere in a national election in the United States or to sow confusion or inflame polarization in our democratic discourse the way Russia has done. For all the tensions in the relationship, there are deep historical bonds of friendship, cultural exchange, and mutual inspiration between the two societies, which we celebrate and wish to nurture. And it is imperative that Chinese Americans— who feel the same pride in American citizenship as do other American ethnic communities—not be subjected to the kind of generalized suspicion or stigmatization that could lead to racial profiling or a new era of McCarthyism.

Yet, with increased challenges in the diplomatic, economic, and security domains, China's influence activities have collectively helped throw the crucial relationship between the PRC and the United States into a worrisome state of imbalance and antagonism. (Throughout this book, we use "the PRC," "China" and "Beijing" interchangeably to refer to the Chinese Communist Party and the government apparatus of the People's Republic of China, and not to Chinese society at large or the Chinese people as a whole.) Not only are the values of China's authoritarian system anathema to those held by most Americans, but there is also a growing body of evidence that the Chinese Communist Party views the American ideals of freedom of speech, press, assembly, religion, and association as direct challenges to its defense of its own form of one-party rule.[2]

Both the United States and China have derived substantial benefit as the two nations have become more economically and socially intertwined. The value of combined US-China trade ($635.4 billion, with a $335.4 US deficit) far surpasses that between any other pair of countries.[3] More than

350,000 Chinese students currently study in US universities (plus 80,000 more in secondary schools). Moreover, millions of Chinese have immigrated to the United States seeking to build their lives with more economic, religious, and political freedom, and their presence has been an enormous asset to American life.

However, these virtues cannot eclipse the reality that in certain key ways China is exploiting America's openness in order to advance its aims on a competitive playing field that is hardly level. For at the same time that China's authoritarian system takes advantage of the openness of American society to seek influence, it impedes legitimate efforts by American counterpart institutions to engage Chinese society on a reciprocal basis. This disparity lies at the heart of this project's concerns.

China's influence activities have moved beyond their traditional united front focus on diaspora communities to target a far broader range of sectors in Western societies, ranging from think tanks, universities, and media to state, local, and national government institutions. The PRC seeks to promote views sympathetic to the government, its policies, and Chinese society and culture; to suppress alternative views; and to co-opt key American players to support China's foreign policy goals and economic interests.

Normal acts of public diplomacy, such as visitor programs, cultural and educational exchanges, paid media inserts, and government lobbying are accepted methods used by many governments to project soft power. They are legitimate in large measure because they are transparent. But this report details a range of more assertive and opaque "sharp power" activities that China has stepped up within the United States in an increasingly active manner.[4] These exploit the openness of our democratic society to challenge, and sometimes even undermine, core American freedoms, norms, and laws.

Except for Russia, no other country's effort to influence American politics and society is as extensive and well-funded as the PRC's. The ambition of China's activity in terms of its breadth, depth of investment of financial resources, and intensity requires far greater scrutiny than it has so far received, because China is intervening more resourcefully and forcefully across a wider range of sectors than Russia. By undertaking activities that have become more organically embedded in the pluralistic fabric of American life, it has gained a far wider and potentially longer-term impact.

Summary of Findings

This report, written and endorsed by a group of this country's leading China specialists and students of one-party systems, is the result of more than a year of research and represents an attempt to document the extent of Beijing's expanding influence operations inside the United States. While there have been many excellent reports documenting specific examples of China's influence seeking,[5] this effort attempts to come to grips with the issue as a whole and features an overview of the Chinese party-state united front apparatus responsible for guiding overseas influence activities. It also includes individual chapters on different sectors of American society that have been targeted by Beijing. The appendices survey China's quite diverse influence activities in other democratic countries around the world.

Among the Report's Findings

- The Chinese Communist party-state leverages a broad range of party, state, and nonstate actors to advance its influence-seeking objectives, and in recent years it has significantly accelerated both its investment in and the intensity of these efforts. While many of the activities described in this report are state-directed, there is no single institution in China's party-state that is wholly responsible, even though the "United Front Work Department" has become a synecdoche for China's influence activities, and the State Council Information Office and CCP Central Committee Foreign Affairs Commission have oversight responsibilities (see Appendix 1: "China's Influence Operations Bureaucracy").[6] Because of the pervasiveness of the party-state, many nominally independent actors— including Chinese civil society, academia, corporations, and even religious institutions—are also ultimately beholden to the government and are frequently pressured into service to advance state interests. The main agencies responsible for foreign influence operations include the party's United Front Work Department, the Central Propaganda Department, the International Liaison Department, the State Council Information Office, the All-China Federation of Overseas Chinese, and the Chinese People's Association for Friendship with Foreign Countries. These organizations and others are bolstered by various state agencies such as the Ministry of Foreign Affairs and the Overseas Chinese Affairs Office of the State Council, which in March 2018 was merged into the United Front Work Department, reflecting that department's increasing power.

- In American federal and state politics, China seeks to identify and cultivate rising politicians. Like many other countries, Chinese entities employ prominent lobbying and public relations firms and cooperate with influential civil society groups. These activities complement China's long-standing support of visits to China by members of Congress and their staffs. In some rare instances Beijing has used private citizens and companies to exploit loopholes in US regulations that prohibit direct foreign contributions to elections.

- On university campuses, Confucius Institutes (CIs) provide the Chinese government with access to US student bodies. Because CIs have had positive value in exposing students and communities to Chinese language and culture, this report does not generally oppose them. But it does recommend that more rigorous university oversight and standards of academic freedom and transparency be exercised over CIs. With the direct support of the Chinese embassy and consulates, Chinese Students and Scholars Associations (CSSAs) sometimes report on and compromise the academic freedom of other Chinese students and American faculty on American campuses. American universities that host events deemed politically offensive by the Chinese Communist Party and government have been subject to increasing pressure, and sometimes even to retaliation, by diplomats in the Chinese embassy and its six consulates as well as by CSSA branches. Although the United States is open to Chinese scholars studying American politics or history, China restricts access to American scholars and researchers seeking to study politically sensitive areas of China's political system, society, and history in its country.

- At think tanks, researchers, scholars, and other staffers report regular attempts by Chinese diplomats and other intermediaries to influence their activities within the United States. At the same time that China has begun to establish its own network of think tanks in the United States, it has been constraining the number and scale of American think-tank operations in China. It also restricts the access to China and to Chinese officials of American think-tank researchers and delegations.

- In business, China often uses its companies to advance strategic objectives abroad, gaining political influence and access to critical infrastructure and technology. China has made foreign companies' continued access to its domestic market conditional on their compliance with Beijing's stance on Taiwan and Tibet. This report documents how China has supported the formation of dozens of local Chinese chambers of commerce in the United States that appear to have ties to the Chinese government.

- In the American media, China has all but eliminated the plethora of independent Chinese-language media outlets that once served Chinese American communities. It has co-opted existing Chinese-language outlets and established its own new outlets. State-owned Chinese media companies have also established a significant foothold in the English-language market, in print, radio, television, and online. At the same time, the Chinese government has severely limited the ability of US and other Western media outlets to conduct normal news-gathering activities within China, much less to provide news feeds directly to Chinese listeners, viewers, and readers in China, by limiting and blocking their Chinese-language websites and forbidding distribution of their output within China itself.

- Among the Chinese American community, China has long sought to influence—even silence—voices critical of the PRC or supportive of Taiwan by dispatching personnel to the United States to pressure these individuals and while also pressuring their relatives in China. Beijing also views Chinese Americans as members of a worldwide Chinese diaspora that presumes them to retain not only an interest in the welfare of China but also a loosely defined cultural, and even political, allegiance to the so-called Motherland. Such activities not only interfere with freedom of speech within the United States but also risk generating suspicion of Chinese Americans, even though those who accept Beijing's directives are a very small minority.

• In the technology sector, China is engaged in a multifaceted effort to misappropriate technologies it deems critical to its economic and military success. Beyond economic espionage, theft, and the forced technology transfers that are required of many joint venture partnerships, China also captures much valuable new technology through its investments in US high-tech companies and through its exploitation of the openness of American university labs. This goes well beyond influence-seeking to a deeper and more disabling form of penetration. The economic and strategic losses for the United States are increasingly unsustainable, threatening not only to help China gain global dominance of a number of the leading technologies of the future but also to undermine America's commercial and military advantages.

• Around the world, China's influence-seeking activities in the United States are mirrored in different forms in many other countries. To give readers a sense of the variation in China's influence-seeking efforts abroad, this report also includes summaries of the experiences of eight other countries, including Australia, Canada, France, Germany, Japan, New Zealand, Singapore, and the United Kingdom.

Toward Constructive Vigilance

In weighing policy responses to influence seeking in a wide variety of American institutions, the working group has sought to strike a balance between passivity and overreaction, confidence in our foundations and alarm about their possible subversion, and the imperative to sustain openness while addressing the unfairness of contending on a series of uneven playing fields. Achieving this balance requires that we differentiate constructive from harmful forms of interaction and carefully gauge the challenge, lest we see threats everywhere and overreact in ways that both undermine our own principles and unnecessarily damage the US-China relationship.

The chapters that follow lodge recommendations under three broad headings. The first two, promoting "transparency" and "integrity," are hardly controversial in the face of the existing challenge, and they elicited little debate among the working group. Sunshine is the best disinfectant against any manipulation of American entities by outside actors, and we should shine as much light as possible on China's influence seeking over organizations and individuals if it is covert, coercive, or corrupting. We should also shore up the vitality of our institutions and our own solidarity against Chinese divide-and-conquer tactics. Defending the integrity of American democratic institutions requires standing up for our principles of openness and freedom, more closely coordinating responses within institutional sectors, and also better informing both governmental and nongovernmental actors about the potentially harmful influence activities of China and other foreign actors.

It was in the third category, promoting "reciprocity," where the working group confronted the most difficult choices. In a wide range of fields, the Chinese government severely restricts American platforms and access while Chinese counterparts are given free rein in our society. Can this playing field be leveled and greater reciprocity be attained without lowering our own standards of openness and fairness? Since complaints and démarches by the US government and private institutions have not produced adequate results, is it possible to get Chinese attention by imposing reciprocal restrictions that do not undermine our own principles of openness?

The working group, not always in unanimity, settled on a selective approach. We believe that in certain areas the only practical leverage resides in tit-for-tat retaliation. This would not be an end in itself but a means to compel a greater reciprocity. The Chinese government respects firmness, fairness summons it, and American opinion compels it.

Each chapter of this report offers its own recommendations for responding to China's influence-seeking activities in ways that will enhance the transparency of relationships, defend the integrity of American democratic institutions, and grant American individuals and institutions greater access in China that equates with the degree of access afforded to Chinese counterparts in the United States.

Our recommendations urge responses to China's challenge that will promote greater transparency, integrity, and reciprocity. We believe that a new emphasis on such "constructive vigilance" is the best way to begin to protect our democratic traditions, institutions, and nation, and to create a fairer and more reciprocal relationship that will be the best guarantor of healthier ties between the United States and China.

CHAPTER ONE

Congress

During past presidential administrations, the US Congress has generally served as a brake on executive initiatives to "engage" China at the expense of other US interests that members have historically valued, such as maintaining good relations with Taiwan, interacting with the Tibetan government in exile, and expressing support for human rights. When President Donald Trump assumed office in 2017 and actively began courting Chinese President Xi Jinping, first at Mar-a-Lago and then at the Beijing summit, Congress took a wait-and-see posture. But as his own ardor for a partnership with Xi cooled and his administration became disenchanted with the idea of finding an easy new "engagement" policy, momentum began to shift. Soon Congress was working toward one of the most significant reevaluations of US policy toward China since the start of normalization fifty years ago. And with the White House increasingly skeptical about the prospects of winning President Xi's cooperation, a series of new initiatives began issuing forth from both the administration and Congress, suggesting a rapidly changing landscape for US-China relations.

What was telling was that this tidal shift now emanated not from Congress alone—where it had strong bipartisan support—but also from the White House and National Security Council, the Pentagon, the Office of the US Trade Representative, the Department of the Treasury, and even the Department of State. As sentiment shifted away from hopes of finding common ways to collaborate, a spate of new US policy initiatives began appearing that suggested a sea change. Congress passed the 2019 National Defense Authorization Act, which sought to bolster US defenses against both Chinese military threats and China's influence-seeking operations inside the United States. Congress also passed the Foreign Investment Risk Review Modernization Act of 2018, which empowered CFIUS (the Committee on Foreign Investment in the United States) to expand its oversight of foreign direct investment from China. At the same time, members of Congress also began expressing ever more strenuous opposition to Chinese nonreciprocal practices in trade and investment, such as putting whole sectors of the Chinese economy out-of-bounds to American investors; using Chinese companies to buy into sensitive high-tech areas of the US economy through mergers and acquisitions; and making the transfer of American advanced technology to Chinese partners the price of American companies being given access to Chinese markets. Congressional concern rose over Beijing's continued expansion into and militarization of the South China Sea; the predatory lending practices that can be involved in President Xi Jinping's signature Belt and Road Initiative; and Beijing's continued persecution of Taiwan and opposition to US support for the island.

This chapter reviews highlights of the Chinese government's efforts to influence the US Congress since the start of the normalization process in 1972. As suggested above, because it has viewed such "engagement" as too often taking place at the expense of more important interests, Congress has usually been more wary than the White House of allowing hopes for more positive US-China relations to determine our policy. At times, such as during the passage of the Taiwan Relations Act in 1979 and in reaction to the Chinese crackdown around Tiananmen Square in 1989, Congress has actively resisted the White House and sought to turn American policy in directions both the Chinese leadership and the US administration have opposed. However, often Congress has played a somewhat passive role, especially in recent years. Still, the control it formally exercises over US government budget outlays, legislation, and the approval of appointments of senior administration officials makes Congress not only important in the formation of US-China policy but also a prime target for Chinese influence efforts.

The review that follows provides historical background to the contemporary US concerns about Chinese government efforts to influence American leaders and public opinion. The record over the past four decades shows some success in Chinese efforts to win influence over congressional opinion. However, more often than not, whatever positive results they have won have not lasted in the face of enduring differences between the two countries.

Congressional Visits to China, 1972–1977

President Nixon's second term featured the Watergate scandal, which forced his resignation in 1974 and resulted in a lull in high-level communication with China. This circumstance gave more prominence to the reports issued by the approximately eighty members of Congress who traveled to China in the period between President Nixon's visit in 1972 and the start of the Carter administration in January 1977. The visits of these congressional delegations—including (repeatedly) top leaders from both parties—were by far the most active channel of high-level communications between the United States and the PRC during this time. And most of the members who went to China wrote reports that were published as official documents. At the time, these congressional reports, as well as the media's coverage of their visits, became important vehicles through which American congressional leaders voiced their views and opinions on domestic Chinese politics and on Sino-American relations, both of which were having an increasingly important impact on American interests in Asia and the world.

By and large, these American visitors were pleased by the post-1972 developments in US-China relations, seeing them as likely to be both a source of strategic leverage against the Soviet Union and a stabilizing influence in Asian affairs. The government in Beijing was seen as preoccupied with domestic affairs, no longer opposed to the presence of American forces in East Asia, and anxious to work with the United States and other noncommunist countries to offset Soviet pressure against China. The Americans saw the Taiwan question as the main impediment to improved bilateral relations, but they differed on how the United States should deal with the problem. Although most members of Congress accepted the Ford administration's cautious approach to China as wise, many were circumspect about the merits of China's political, economic, social, and value systems, then experiencing the last turmoil of the Cultural Revolution and the decline and death of Mao Zedong in 1976.

These congressional visits to China seemed to help the Chinese government improve its standing with Congress and favorably influence American public opinion. The resulting reports show how granting these delegations access to China's leaders and elements of Chinese society that Beijing wished to highlight proved an effective strategy of calming tensions. And the costs for Beijing were limited to modest in-country expenses, since the members usually traveled as official congressional delegations on US government aircraft.

One notable feature of this historical episode was the remarkable role played by Senate Majority Leader Mike Mansfield (D-MT). Senator Mansfield was widely consulted in Washington as an Asian affairs expert, meaning his observations arguably had more influence than those of other members. He visited China three times during this period, publishing separate reports with detailed assessments of various issues of concern to Americans at the time. In the main, his reports conveyed information and opinions that conformed with Chinese interests. The convergence with Chinese interests was not surprising given the senator's long-standing determination to develop constructive US relations with China going back to his service in China as a marine in the 1920s and during World War II, and reinforced by his strong opposition to the US war in Vietnam. The details in the reports offering strongly positive views of developments in Maoist China meshed well with the recollections of Mansfield's senior aide and secretary of the Senate, Frank Valeo, an Asian affairs specialist, who also recounted the senator's repeated private efforts to make contact with Chinese premier Zhou Enlai to enable Mansfield's visiting China in the period prior to Henry Kissinger's breakthrough in a secret visit to China in July 1971.

Unlike many other members favoring a more cautious pace of normalization with China and sustained ties with Taiwan, Senator Mansfield urged the United States to promptly end ties with Taiwan and accept Beijing's conditions for normal diplomatic relations, warning that to do otherwise would lead to dangerous friction in Sino-American relations and instability in Asia. Senator Mansfield portrayed China as a power with fundamentally peaceful motives in international affairs and placed much of the blame on the United States for past Sino-American conflicts in Asia. He also contradicted those members who worried that China's leadership change could lead to internal struggles affecting China's international and domestic policies. He insisted that such skepticism was unwarranted, because what he called the Maoist system had been effectively inculcated among the Chinese people. Some members complained that the limited itinerary for congressional visits that was furnished by the Chinese hosts did not provide a basis for any meaningful assessment of conditions there. Despite the fact that many congressional visitors questioned how durable China's Maoist regime was and how lasting China's cooperation with the United States would actually prove to be, Mansfield countered that he had had enough opportunity during his three visits to the PRC to move about and obtain enough information through on-the-spot observation and talks with PRC leaders to conclude that it was no passing phenomenon. So, while many members thought the PRC's system of indoctrination and control to be repressive politically, economically, and socially—an affront to the human rights and dignity of its people—voices like Mansfield's served to mute the criticism, maintaining that the country's political, economic, and social system was uniquely well suited to the Chinese people.

Influence Efforts after Establishing Official Relations, 1979–1988

As the Carter administration began moving toward full diplomatic recognition of the PRC, it withheld many of the details about its plans from Congress. One of the largest unresolved issues was the fate of Taiwan, in which Congress took a special interest. The United States had already dropped recognition of Taiwan at the United Nations, and now many in Congress worried that the United States would move to completely abandon the island. In response, Congress passed the Taiwan Relations Act in 1979, which underlined the importance of the United States keeping an ongoing relationship with Taiwan and continuing to provide weapons for its defense.

After formal diplomatic relations were reestablished, China responded in the 1980s by expanding the size and capacity of its Washington embassy staff dedicated to dealing with Congress. Chinese officials lobbying Congress viewed with dismay the rise of pro-Taiwan independence groups among Taiwanese Americans, such as the Formosan Association for Public Affairs, which demonstrated an ability to promote their agenda despite the fact that the United States had broken ties with Taiwan. Beijing would go on to borrow a page from the Nationalist government's playbook by beefing up a diplomatic arm capable of building closer relations with important congressional members and staffers.[1] Since then, the Chinese government has welcomed numerous US delegations composed of both congressional members and staffers. The main host in China for such delegations has been the Chinese People's Institute of Foreign Affairs (CPIFA).[2] Founded in December 1949, this organization focuses on international issues and foreign policy research and on conducting international exchanges of officials and expanding people-to-people diplomatic activities. This institute also works to establish contacts with foreign political activists, diplomats, and other distinguished individuals while organizing public lectures and symposia on academic subjects and international policy affairs.

CPIFA is a so-called united front organization, similar to those found in the former Soviet Union and other Leninist states that seek to opportunistically build alliances wherever they can. Such organizations, or GONGOs ("government-organized nongovernmental organizations"), carry out government-directed policies and cooperative initiatives with influential foreigners without being perceived as a formal part of the Chinese government. CPIFA's experience in dealing with foreign visitors is broad. Between 1972 and 2002, it hosted more than four thousand leading Americans in China. Being well connected with the Chinese government's State Council and the Ministry of Foreign Affairs, it is positioned to organize meetings with high-level officials when the party deems it in its interest to do so. The funding arrangements for congressional staff delegations visiting China usually provide for their travel to be paid by the US side, so as to avoid falling victim to ethics committees and overseers or violating rules regarding conflicts of interest and foreign lobbying. CPIFA often assumed in-country expenses.

The staff delegation trips to China were welcomed and sought after by congressional staff and congressional support agency personnel, mainly from the Congressional Research Service of the Library of Congress, which had a growing interest in China and the issues it posed for US policy. The trips generally came twice per year and involved meetings with Chinese government officials and others responsible for key foreign affairs and domestic issues of interest to Congress. The exchanges in these meetings were generally cordial and substantive, although the trips also included sightseeing and visits to parts of China of interest.

In the United States, there have been a number of counterpart groups that have facilitated congressional exchanges. Among them are the Washington, DC–based US-Asia Institute (USAI), which has played a leading role in managing the congressional staff delegations side since 1985.[3] The National Committee on US-China Relations undertook a pilot congressional staff delegation visit to China in 1976 and resumed involvement with such exchanges again during the past decade.[4] In the 1980s, the Asia-Pacific Exchange Foundation (also known as the Far East Studies Institute) also managed a number of congressional staff delegations to China, while the US-Asia Institute has, since 1985, coordinated over 120 such delegations and exchanges to China. These visits have been carried out in cooperation with the Chinese People's Institute of Foreign Affairs (CPIFA) and the Better Hong Kong Foundation (BHKF). But the National People's Congress (NPC) has perhaps hosted the most trips, taking more than a thousand congressional staff members to China. Over these trips, members have traveled to nearly every corner of China, including Xinjiang and Tibet. In their discussions, they have covered a wide range of themes important to the US-China relationship. Staffers participating in such trips have clearly advanced their understanding of Chinese developments.

Congress and Turmoil in US-China Relations, 1989–2001

The number of the congressional staff delegations to China slowed following the collapse of congressional support for engagement with China after the Tiananmen crackdown in 1989. Congressional anger and the impulse to punish the Chinese government overrode past interest in constructive engagement. As a result, Beijing began relying more heavily on the US business community and its organizations, notably the Emergency Committee for American Trade, to persuade Congress not to end the most-favored-nation tariff treatment for Chinese imports. The Chinese embassy and various lobbyists who were, or at least claimed to be, supported by the Chinese government also tried to limit the damage by seeking to convince congressional members that conditions in China were much better than those depicted in American media at the time.[5]

Based on the reputation of its past efforts, the US-Asia Institute, presumably with the encouragement of its Chinese counterparts, strove to resume the staff dialogues and attracted a wide range of senior staff and support personnel, including some of those working for the harshest congressional critics of China's crackdown. One trip in December 1989 featured very heated debates with Chinese officials, especially after it was announced that national security advisor Brent Scowcroft and deputy secretary of state Lawrence Eagleburger were also in Beijing for talks with Chinese leaders and that the two had made an earlier secret trip in July, soon after the crackdown. As the Bush administration had publicly promised Congress that all such contacts would end, the staff delegates' anger at and criticism of China's repression was compounded by their harsh reaction to the Bush administration's actions.

As US-China relations continued during a tumultuous post-Tiananmen crackdown period, Congress played important roles on such key issues as the debate over most-favored-nation tariff treatment, the visit of Taiwan's president to the United States in 1995, and the decision to approve China's entry into the World Trade Organization. The Chinese government endeavored to build influence with and gain access to Congress by encouraging US businesses to lobby Congress on China's behalf and by continuing to receive member and staff delegations in China.

Other entities in the Chinese official structure, including the Chinese Communist Party and the Chinese military, at times attempted to gain access to Congress. The International Department of the Chinese Communist Party engaged in growing exchanges with the major American political parties on a party-to-party basis. A Chinese united front organization, the Chinese Association for International Understanding (CAFIU), managed some of these ensuing trips. Also involved was the China Association for International Friendly Contact (CAIFC). This united front organization's link to the Chinese government was not then well known, though in recent years it has been publicly linked to the People's Liberation Army's Political Warfare Department, which has intelligence responsibilities.[6] Meanwhile, other exchanges with US congressional specialists on China were promoted by a mysterious united front operative with excellent official contacts in China named Jimmy Wong. In this troubled decade, Wong made himself known to a wide range of Americans playing a role in China policy as having the ability to set up visits to China and meetings with key officials very quickly. He occasionally even opened his spacious Beijing home to congressional staffers. His precise affiliation with the Chinese authorities remains obscure.[7]

The approaches of the Chinese government to gain influence and gather information abroad differ from the tradecraft of Russia and the former Soviet Union.[8] Notably, the Chinese focus more on individuals rather than effects, and on shaping the personal context rather than operational tricks. It is person-to-person relationships that carry the weight of Chinese information operations. Working on these personal ties, the Chinese authorities focus on facilitating meetings and contacts that may or may not result in opportunities to influence foreign targets. Still, because Chinese influence seeking is largely a governmental undertaking, it is hardly surprising that the Chinese mix influence operations with espionage. In one instance, after a visit to China supported by CAIFC, an American congressional official was asked by two employees at CAIFC who facilitated his trip to host them during a return visit to Washington.

He obliged, and they were seemingly satisfied, having shopped extensively during their stay. Subsequently, the Chinese embassy officers who had arranged the congressional official's visit to China with CAIFC were arrested and expelled for trying to steal US weapons technology, causing the US official to end all contact with CAIFC.

Current Era

Tensions in US-China relations subsided after the terrorist attack on America in September 2001 and subsequent wars in Afghanistan and Iraq preoccupied the Bush administration and Congress. Chinese and American leaders also proved to be sufficiently pragmatic to reach common ground on advancing relations in mutually agreeable ways and managing differences through a wide range of dialogues. Such exchanges only catalyzed visits by more congressional members and staff delegations to China. At this time, members often traveled to China in US government-funded trips as guests of the US embassy. Some member trips and very frequent staff delegation visits were authorized under provisions of the Mutual Education and Cultural Exchange Act (MECEA) that were in line with the guidance of congressional ethics committees.[9] In addition to the work of the US-Asia Institute, those organizing and facilitating staff delegations grew to include the Aspen Institute, the National Committee on US-China Relations, and the US-China Policy Foundation.[10]

China also increased its own capacity to engage Congress beyond trips. Having moved into a new embassy in Washington in 2009, the Chinese embassy increased its congressional affairs staff to twelve (as of 2011), while also retaining the lobbying services of the firm Patton Boggs.[11] During his time as ambassador, Zhou Wenzhong boasted that he had visited some one hundred members of Congress in their home districts. When certain measures, such as a bill that would have penalized China for being a "currency manipulator," came before Congress, the embassy's in-house team's efforts reflected what some US officials called a much more "nuanced" and "sophisticated" understanding of the body. Whether or not Chinese officials or lobbyists interacting with congressional offices endeavored to exert influence by means beyond persuasion—such as by offering material benefits or threatening to withdraw Chinese investments or other tangible benefits to the congressional district—remained hard to discern given the very limited public reporting on such matters.[12]

Congress, for its part, had already formalized efforts to better understand China through a variety of working groups. By 2006, both the House and the Senate had formed a US-China Inter-Parliamentary Exchange Group, which conducted periodic exchanges with China's National People's Congress. Also showing stronger American interest in China at that time were the Congressional China Caucus (led by members tending to be critical of China); the China Working Group (led by members supportive of closer engagement with China); and the Senate China Working Group (led by members supportive of closer relations). Earlier legislation had established the Congressional-Executive Commission on China, focused on human rights conditions in China (a perennial negative aspect in US-China relations), and the US-China Economic and Security Review Commission, which was known for its annual report listing a variety of developments in China seen as adverse to US interests and values. While the latter two commissions continue to be active, are robust, and have growing impact, many of the other exchange mechanisms have proven less than durable. Once the leading members who founded such groups leave Congress, interest usually wanes. The National People's Congress became even more active in supporting the growing number of congressional staff delegations to China during this period. In 2018, the House China Working Group remained active, but the House Congressional China Caucus and the Senate China Working Group were inactive.

Most recently, the 115th Congress has actively embraced the Trump administration's view that China has benefited more from the bilateral relationship than has the United States. In fact, amidst all the partisan warfare currently dividing Republicans and Democrats in Washington, a skepticism about China's intentions and reliability and a willingness to push back in a bipartisan manner against its un-reciprocal, and sometimes even predatory, policies, is one of the most surprising phenomena.

In 2018, for example, Congress unanimously passed the Taiwan Travel Act, which encourages the Trump administration to host more high-ranking officials from Taiwan, a move that angered Beijing. Still, Congress is hardly united, even on trade. Some members have objected to the adverse impacts punitive tariffs are having on their constituencies, or they have opposed imposing tariffs on allies at the same time tariffs are imposed on China. And some members criticized President Trump's decision in May 2018 to ease harsh sanctions against the prominent Chinese high-technology firm ZTE, in response to a personal plea from the Chinese president. Nevertheless, President Trump's dominance in the Republican Party means that few in the Republican ranks controlling Congress are inclined to oppose him, especially on China. Indeed, Congress is generally endorsing the most significant reevaluation of American-China policy since the start of normalization fifty years ago. As such, it can be said that Chinese influence on Capitol Hill has reached a low point.

Conclusion and Recommendations

Congress is in the midst of a major reevaluation of the very assumptions underlying the decades-old American policy of "engagement" with China. Because of this increasingly competitive, even adversarial, new climate, Chinese influence and information operations are widely coming to be seen as expressions of a political system whose values are antithetical to those of the United States and as a threat to the integrity of Congress and our democracy. Arguing, as many have done as far back as Majority Leader Mike Mansfield, that Congress should move forward with positive engagement with China while seeking to pragmatically manage our differences now seems, in the current environment, both naïve and quixotic.

Promote Transparency

Follow-on congressional oversight will go far toward educating Congress, the media, and the public about these important topics. The issues are complicated and have no simple solutions. Various specialists within and outside the US government should be consulted in determining the full scope of the problem and what should be done.

Promote Integrity

Congress needs also to distinguish between issues that present a real threat to the United States, such as Chinese espionage and Chinese-directed monitoring of Chinese students on US campuses, and institutions such as Confucius Institutes, which, as we have noted elsewhere in this report, can be better regulated by universities themselves.

Promote Reciprocity

In coming up with remedial steps, Congress must consider the broader bilateral relationship. It is asked to weigh carefully the continued important positive elements in the US-China relationship, the negative consequences that might arise from a confrontational approach to China, and America's need to protect and foster its strengths and interests.

CHAPTER TWO

State and Local Governments

In late 2017, an American city in the mid-Atlantic region was invited to form a sister-city relationship with a town in southern China. The American partner city was home to a large number of national-security professionals and university and government scientists, including many of PRC origin. The partnership was proposed and shepherded by the manager of a for-profit Chinese "exchange" company—a woman of PRC origin. She was assisted by an American citizen of PRC origin who was running for a position on the local school board.

In a briefing, an American China expert told the local sister-city committee that there was no reason not to explore a partnership, provided the American side had defined goals and was aware of Beijing's increasingly repressive domestic policies, its growing suspicions of US influence, and its well-funded efforts to increase its influence overseas. The man running for the local school board objected to this characterization and pointed out that China's constitution gives the CCP paramount authority in China.

After a long debate, the new sister-city agreement was signed in the fall of 2018. Some Americans involved objected to China's insistence that all sister-city activities be carried out "in accordance with the principles on the establishment of diplomatic relations between the United States of America and the People's Republic of China" (根据中美两国建交原则), because this seemed to be a reference to the One China Principle, which might be invoked to preclude exchanges with Taiwan. Despite these objections, the phrase appeared in the signed agreement because the Chinese side said that the Chinese People's Association for Friendship with Foreign Countries required that all sister-city agreements include such language, and the US side did not want to derail the agreement by insisting otherwise.

The story of this sister-city agreement illustrates the challenges and opportunities that "subnational entities" (local governments, cities, and states) face in the United States when dealing with a China intent on maximizing its influence in America and across the globe. As this report details in other chapters, the age of innocent engagement is over, and this is now true for American local officials as well as for representatives of the US federal government. Because most PRC attempts to influence American opinion and practices occur at the local level, and because local media, universities, companies, and advocacy agencies are often involved in these efforts, both knowingly and unknowingly, local leaders, just as much as national leaders, need an understanding of PRC goals and strategies.

"We Have Friends All Over the World"

China pursues sister-city relationships under an organization called the Chinese People's Association for Friendship with Foreign Countries, which is part of China's united front bureaucratic structure (see Appendix 1: China's Influence Operations Bureaucracy) that aims to strengthen the rule of the Chinese Communist Party and increase China's influence overseas. With its long-standing Maoist slogan "We Have Friends All Over the World," the association had its heyday in the 1950s, when China was isolated and the group became a bridge between China and overseas supporters. It was marginalized in the 1980s, as China opened to the West and established diplomatic relations with hundreds of countries. However, under the administration of Communist Party leader Xi Jinping, the association has been revitalized as China seeks to groom local business, political, and media leaders in countries around the world. Its new standing is exemplified by the splendor of its headquarters located in the elegant old Italian embassy compound near Tiananmen Square.

The way the association and other Chinese organizations cultivate relationships with local officials follows a general pattern. First, in the United States, China demands that sister-city relationships and state-to-province sister relations be carried out under the "principles" on which Sino-US relations were established in the 1970s (as interpreted by the Chinese side). This means that China's representatives will likely protest should local officials seek to maintain ties with representatives of Taiwan or with other individuals, such as the Dalai Lama, whom China regard as hostile forces. Second, it is important to understand why China seeks a relationship with localities, especially during times of tension with the federal government: China seeks to build alternative networks of interaction and support, while using these new relationships to help gain new traction back in Washington. Local American expertise, information, and opinion are also of more than passing political interest to Beijing, even if on paper an exchange relationship is only to "enhance people's friendship, further international cooperation, safeguard world peace and promote common development,"[1] for Beijing understands clearly that local leaders today become the national leaders of tomorrow. For China, all exchanges have a political character and hopefully a political harvest.

Third, it is important for local officials to understand that local American "exchange" companies that bring Chinese delegations to the United States and promote professional interactions between the United States and China all depend on official PRC sanction and have received approval to receive Chinese delegations. The business model of such companies is, of necessity, as much political as financial. Even if they conduct high-quality programs, they should not be viewed as disinterested actors. They, too, are subject to rules made by the Chinese Communist Party, its united front bureaucracy, and united front strategic imperatives.

Finally, American citizens of PRC origin have played a key role in promoting mutually beneficial engagement over the past forty years. As US-China relations grow more contentious, however, and as Beijing calls more aggressively for diaspora Chinese to serve the "Motherland," it will be necessary for citizen diplomats (including those who are not of PRC origin) to better educate themselves about American national interests in the US-China competition and the areas in which the nation's values,

institutional practices, and strategic goals are incompatible. Such awareness is even more vital for Chinese Americans who seek political office
and whose abilities to navigate these shoals will depend on their knowledge of this complex system of interaction.

American Communities as Engines of Engagement

The American federal system allows subnational governments considerable leeway to pursue local interests generally regardless of Washington's
security concerns. Free from geostrategic worries, state, county, and
municipal leaders who have formed commercial and people-to-people
relationships with the PRC have been a bulwark of better US-China relations since the early 1970s, and their efforts to build mutual understanding and solve joint problems have formed the bedrock of bilateral
relations over four decades. However, as China becomes more reliant on
its old Leninist system and "united front" tactics (统战战), Sino-US relations become more contentious, and the CCP seeks to more forcefully
build influence in American communities through channels detailed in
this study, local leaders will be called upon to give greater weight to
national interests when forming exchange relationships with PRC actors.
Conversely, as Beijing's relations with Washington worsen, China will
likely seek to use tried-and-true "divide and conquer" tactics by cultivating new relations with more state and local-level officials.

Beginning in the early 1970s, China and the United States built trust
and common prosperity through cooperation at the local level. The work
of two hundred sister-city pairs and more than forty sister state/prov-
ince partnerships was reinforced by state and city trade and investment
promotion offices, chambers of commerce, Chinese American and traditional clan associations, Chinatown cultural centers, and various and
sundry activities at US colleges and universities, secondary schools,
church groups, and museums. Following the establishment of the pioneering Washington State China Relations Council in 1979,[2] centers for
joint innovation and entrepreneurship, such as the Michigan China
Innovation Center[3] and the Maryland China Business Council,[4] were set

up in nearly every state. Twenty-seven states now maintain trade offices in China—more than in any other nation.[5] Americans of mainland, Taiwanese, and Hong Kong ancestry have founded cultural centers like the Asia Institute–Crane House in Louisville, Kentucky,[6] and the China Institute in New York.[7] After forty years of engagement, the US-China-focused foundations, educational and exchange programs, research institutes, and arts and entertainment initiatives throughout the country are too many and various to be cataloged. American mayors, county executives, and governors—many of whom travel to China often and host an unending stream of Chinese visitors—have leveraged the work of these groups to enrich local coffers and local culture.

American Communities as Targets

While American local governments value such "exchanges" for financial and cultural reasons, "exchange" (交流) has always been viewed as a practical political tool by Beijing, and *all* of China's "exchange" organizations have been assigned political missions.[8] The US-China People's Friendship Association (USCPFA), for example, has more than thirty sections across the United States that promote "positive ties." While its activities are not usually overtly political, the USCPFA Statement of Principles includes the following: "We recognize that friendship between our two peoples must be based on the knowledge of and respect for the sovereignty of each country; therefore, we respect the declaration by the United States of America and the People's Republic of China that the resolution of the status of Taiwan is the internal affair of the Chinese on both sides of the Taiwan Straits."[9] More than 150 Chinese Students and Scholars Associations (CSSAs) at American colleges and universities (see the chapter on "Universities") also promote local exchanges and, in some cases, political activities,[10] as do the 110 Confucius Institutes in America. The China General Chamber of Commerce–USA was founded in 2005 to build stronger investment environments for Chinese companies through local corporate citizenship programs planned by its six regional offices and municipal affiliates.[11] These and other organizations maintain close ties to China's diplomatic missions in the United States and are often in contact with training or "cultural exchange" companies that bring delegations of PRC experts and Communist Party members to US cities and states for so-called study tours.

US and Chinese groups promoting exchanges and investment have often been a valuable resource for American local leaders—see, for example, the Virginia Museum of Fine Arts's annual China Fest[12] or the Chinese investment program in Greenville, South Carolina[13]—but there have been other instances in which American politicians working with Chinese organizations have been drawn into schemes that cost them their jobs.

Perhaps the most telling case is that of four officials in Ypsilanti, Michigan, who, in 2017, accepted a trip to China that they had been told was paid for by the Wayne State CSSA. The trip was eventually revealed as a boondoggle funded by a developer, Amy Xue Foster, who hoped to build a $300 million "Chinatown" in the area.[14] The four officials, including the mayor, were fired.

This is not to suggest that shady Chinese nationals are always plotting to corrupt otherwise innocent American leaders; US politicians have a long history of willingly accepting free trips, gifts, and other favors from the PRC or its fronts. As other chapters of this study make clear, however, Beijing-directed activities such as the secret purchase of American Chinese-language newspapers and radio stations, harassment of local Chinese American dissidents, and the operation of CCP cells in local American businesses and universities do require heightened vigilance by US subnational authorities, regardless of how much investment, how many tuition-paying students, or how many tourists China is able to produce.

China Exchanges and Chinese Leverage

Engagement with China for over forty years has created for American cities and states, as it has for American corporations and universities, deep interests and traditions with regard to China. However, the local policies that have guided these relationships are sometimes at odds with Washington's policies, even our larger national interest. Although the

United States has pulled out of the Paris Agreement, the seventeen governors who have joined the United States Climate Alliance,[15] for example, continue to work with Beijing, which many would agree is a very salutary thing. But sometimes subnational solidarity with China can become overexuberant, as it did on a July 2018 trip to Hong Kong by Los Angeles Mayor Eric Garcetti, who declared his city's independence from the looming Sino-US trade war. Garcetti stated that Los Angeles and China "have closely integrated economies, closely integrated cultures and closely integrated geography. . . . We hope to be the leading Chinese city in America for investment, tourism and students."[16]

Sometimes federalism, in the form of local leaders' independent China policies, is a good thing and may, during times of upheaval in Washington, DC, help to offset unwise national policies. But if US-China relations continue on their current downward trajectory, there will be an increased danger that independent state and municipal China policies will sometimes conflict with national interest and hinder the United States in its competition with China to shape global norms and practices. As China's wealth and ambition grow and as Beijing is becoming more adept at turning local American "China interests" into Chinese leverage, subnational American governmental entities that formed their China policies in the era of engagement must become mindful that they will be required to develop new strategies for a new era of competition.

Conclusion and Recommendations

The following practices can foster the kind of constructive vigilance that local governments will need to exercise in their continued cooperation with China.

Promote Transparency

- Not have secret agreements with Chinese entities, including foundations, corporations, and individuals. All Memoranda of Understanding and contracts should be transparent and public. All cooperative proposals should be subject to public hearings. All potential projects should receive the same due diligence that partnerships with American entities would demand. No exceptions to American laws or best practices should be made to placate allegedly "Chinese" customs. And in no way should China be allowed to have a veto over potential exchanges with other countries, entities, or individuals such as Taiwan or the Dalai Lama.

- Share experiences and concerns with peers through the National Conference of Mayors, the National Governors Association, the National Council of County Association Executives, and the National Conference of State Legislatures. Best practices for cooperating with China in ways that do not undermine national interests should be a regular topic at annual meetings.

- Meet with stakeholders across sectors—local leaders of industry, academia, the arts, religious groups, Chinese American organizations, and professional associations—to discuss issues emerging from cooperation with China, because a community-wide approach is required.

- Celebrate successes and share best practices. In the era of US-China competition, there is more reason than ever to publicize cooperative projects that enrich local communities, build understanding, and solve common problems, while always being mindful of the larger framework of China's goals and American interests.

Promote Integrity

- Educate themselves and other stakeholders on the goals and methods of Chinese influence operations. While Americans are quick to label any wariness of communist parties as McCarthyism, and while the potential for racial stereotyping is real, the Chinese Communist Party's United Front Work Department and International Liaison Department—two of the main bodies overseeing such exchanges—are in fact active, well-resourced, and determined. No mainland Chinese organization in the United States— corporate, academic, or people-to-people—is free of Beijing's control, even if it is not formally part of the united front.

- Keep abreast of Washington's China policies and improve political risk analysis capabilities. American China policy is evolving rapidly and cannot be incorporated into local practice without expert counsel and advice. China's responses to US actions are also fast moving, as are Chinese domestic events that have an impact on local American interests. The 2018 sell-off of Chinese-owned properties in the United States was instructive in this regard.[17] State and municipal governments should therefore improve their political-risk-analysis capabilities and continually reassess their cooperative relationships with China. In effect, to successfully play in the China arena, subnationals need to develop their own sources of expertise.
- Communicate regularly with federal agencies like the FBI whenever doubts arise about a cooperative proposal or the Chinese institutions promoting it. Pay attention to who is on Chinese delegations. Get name lists beforehand and do due diligence on them.

Promote Reciprocity

- Follow the money and the power. In any cooperative venture, US local governments should determine exactly where Chinese investments originate and know which Beijing ministry has final decision-making authority related to the project. They should also check lists of funders and organizations against lists of known united front agencies and registered foreign agents.
- Not treat other stakeholders—other countries, Taiwan, or companies—in a prejudiced manner to win favor in Beijing.

CHAPTER THREE

The Chinese American Community

Chinese Americans have made essential contributions to almost every aspect of American life for over a century. They form a vital strand in the social fabric of the United States. At the same time, however, Beijing views Chinese Americans as members of a worldwide Chinese diaspora that, whatever the actual citizenship of individuals may be, presumes them to retain not only an interest in the welfare of China but also a loosely defined cultural, and even political, allegiance to the so-called Motherland (祖国). Under Xi Jinping's leadership, diaspora Chinese have been called on to help achieve the rejuvenation of the Chinese Nation—a summons that places growing pressure on ethnic Chinese around the world to serve the "China Dream" (中国梦). While many overseas Chinese do feel pride in China as a country, Beijing's demands that they actually serve China can put them in a difficult position.

Under both the Nationalist and Communist parties, overseas Chinese have played an important role in modern Chinese politics as well as in China's relations with the outside world. Diaspora communities worldwide have been key sources of legitimacy and support for whatever government held power in Beijing, but just as often they have been centers of antigovernment agitation. With PRC influence-seeking activities now expanding, China's long-standing focus on diaspora communities has also intensified to become an important element in overall US-China relations. Such trends demand not only greater societal attention and understanding but also an appropriate response from the US government as well as nongovernmental institutions.

As the Chinese Communist Party seeks to encourage, even entice, ethnic-Chinese communities and individuals overseas to more fully support its interests, Chinese Americans in the United States and ethnic Chinese in other free societies need to better inform themselves as to the nature of this dynamic, and our governmental institutions may need to do more to defend their freedoms against harmfully intrusive and coercive activities. At the same time, it is essential that we not allow overseas Chinese as an ethnic group to fall under any kind of indiscriminate cloud of suspicion. Above all, it is important to bear in mind that while ethnic Chinese can be quite naturally expected to take an interest in things Chinese, it is the Chinese Communist Party that puts a target on their backs through its presumption that they are all somehow the "sons and daughters of the Yellow Emperor" (炎黄子孙) and thus owe some measure of loyalty to the Chinese Communist Party.

Origins and Structure

From the 1950s to the 1970s, when the United States maintained an alliance with the regime of Chiang Kai-shek on Taiwan, pro-PRC organizations faced challenges gaining traction in the United States. During the 1950s, the FBI, aided by pro-Kuomintang security organizations, closely monitored their activities and participants. This antagonistic state of affairs began to change after President Nixon's historic trip to China in 1972.[1] On February 24, 1973, more than forty Chinese on the East Coast, most of them immigrants from Taiwan, established the Washington Association to Promote China Unification to help advocate for Beijing's official positions. One of the founders was a professor at the University of Maryland who was actively involved in organizations that already supported China's position on Taiwan and Tibet.[2] However, a more beneficial contribution came in the form of advancing US-China scientific, educational, and cultural exchanges that began to be promoted by a growing number of preeminent Chinese American scientists, engineers, and academics who were also advising the Chinese government to launch reforms in science and education. These Chinese Americans were also personally helping them establish various programs to bring thousands of talented Chinese students to American institutions of learning.

Recognizing the achievements, influence, and growth of the Chinese diaspora, Beijing undertook a systematic program designed to target and exploit overseas Chinese communities as a means of furthering its own political, economic, and security interests. The Beijing government used specialized bureaucracies to manage what it called "united front" activities abroad. Organizations such as the Overseas Chinese Affairs Office (OCAO), the Communist Party Central Committee's United Front Work Department,[3] and the State Council's Taiwan Affairs Office led the charge. Almost all of these agencies have established nongovernmental fronts overseas, including the China Council for the Promotion of Peaceful National Reunification, the China Overseas Exchange Association, and the China Overseas Friendship Association (COFA).[4] Other united front organizations, such as the Chinese Enterprise Association and other Chinese chambers of commerce, are almost always linked both to the United Front Work Department and to the Ministry of Commerce.

Following the violent crackdown on the prodemocracy movement in Beijing on June 4, 1989, the Chinese Communist Party redoubled its efforts to reach out to overseas Chinese. Many members of these communities had supported the student democracy movement, providing funds and safe havens for fleeing dissidents. But senior Chinese leader Deng Xiaoping was not dissuaded. In 1989, and again in 1993, he spoke of the "unique opportunity" overseas Chinese offered the PRC. Deng insisted that by drawing on their help, China could break out of international isolation and improve its international political standing. Gaining influence over overseas Chinese groups in order to "turn them into propaganda bases for China" became an important task of overseas Chinese united front work.[5]

In China, all of the organizations involved in outreach to the overseas Chinese community are led by senior members of the Chinese Communist Party. Party officials run the China Overseas Friendship Association and the China Council to Promote Peaceful Reunification.

The head of the Overseas Chinese Affairs Office, Qiu Yuanping, also leads the China Overseas Exchange Association. Qiu has a career background with the Party's International Liaison Department. The president of the China Council for the Promotion of Peaceful Reunification is none other than Yu Zhengsheng, the former chairman of the Chinese People's Political Consultative Conference and a former member of the Standing Committee of the Political Bureau of the Communist Party's Central Committee.[6]

Goals and Methods

The key goal of the party's united front work with overseas Chinese is to gain support for the Communist Party's efforts to modernize the country by convincing members of overseas Chinese communities that the party is the sole representative of China. A second goal is to isolate competing forces that the party perceives to be adversarial, or even hostile. For example, as part of a massive campaign to monitor, control, and even intimidate China's ethnic minorities (no matter where in the world they are), Chinese authorities are creating a global registry of Uighurs who live outside of China. Chinese authorities threaten to detain Uighur relatives who remain in China if they do not provide personal information about their relatives living abroad to the Chinese police. This campaign has particularly targeted Uighurs living in Germany but is now reaching Uighurs in the United States as well.[7] Uighurs are not alone; Tibetan exiles living in the United States have long reported similar campaigns against members of their families and community. Chinese security officials have even been known to travel to America on tourist visas to exert pressure on Chinese dissidents living here.[8] FBI agents have contacted prominent Chinese exiles in the United States offering them protection from Chinese agents who might travel to the United States to menace them.[9]

For most Chinese Americans, however, China's efforts to influence them are far more anodyne. The official description of the Overseas Chinese Affairs Office states its purpose as: "to enhance unity and friendship in overseas Chinese communities; to maintain contact with and support overseas Chinese media and Chinese language schools; [and] to increase cooperation and exchanges between overseas Chinese and China related to the economy, science, culture and education." Over the past three decades, the OCAO has dispatched former reporters and editors from the OCAO-run China News Service to establish pro-Beijing Chinese media organizations in the West. (Chinese officials have described such Chinese-language media outlets, schools, and other kinds of organizations as the "three treasures" [三宝] of united front work overseas.)[10]

Officials from Beijing have stated clearly that they do not view overseas Chinese as simply citizens of foreign countries, but rather as "overseas compatriots" (华侨同胞们) who have both historical connections and responsibilities as "sons and daughters of the Yellow Emperor" to support the PRC's goals and the "China Dream." As Xi Jinping[11] described it in a 2014 speech to the Seventh Conference of Overseas Chinese Associations, "The Rejuvenation of the Chinese Nation is a Dream shared by *all Chinese*" [emphasis added]. In January 2018, Politburo member and former state counselor and foreign minister Yang Jiechi made this presumption even clearer when he called upon the government to expand and strengthen "Overseas Chinese Patriotic Friendly Forces" in the service of the "Great Rejuvenation" of the Chinese nation.

In addition to appealing to the cultural affinities of Chinese Americans, the Chinese government has also implemented a wide range of programs to strengthen ties with elite members of this community. China has appointed hundreds of Chinese Americans to positions in its united front organizations and provided thousands with free trips to China, during which they have been feted by senior united front officials. In some cases, Chinese Americans are offered senior positions in united front organizations. For example, in 2013, one Chinese American, a native of Guangdong Province, became the first and only foreigner to become a vice president of the COFA.[12]

China has used this tactic of handing out what one senior Chinese American called "honors" to Chinese Americans as a way for united front departments, and even espionage agencies, to cultivate contacts in the United States, often to the detriment of other groups—such as Tibetans, supporters of Taiwanese independence, supporters of the Republic of China, Uighurs, prodemocracy activists, and other independent Chinese voices with which the party does not agree. Chinese Americans appointed to such positions in organizations established by the Communist Party have led protests against Taiwan and Tibet and participated in campaigns to silence Chinese dissidents, such as the exiled billionaire Guo Wengui. For example, the Chinese American who is a vice president of COFA spearheaded a campaign against Guo that was encouraged by officials from the PRC. On a video posted to YouTube, this individual is seen railing against Guo, vowing that he will "not rest" until Guo is returned to China to answer charges against him.[13]

United front organizations in China have been surprisingly aggressive and transparent in their public tasking of Chinese Americans to carry out activities that support the PRC policies. One example occurred after the 19th National Congress of the Communist Party in October 2017. The state-owned *Fujian Daily* reported on November 24, 2017, that representatives of local Chinese community associations based in the United States, Australia, the Philippines, and Europe had gathered in Fujian and received letters of appointment from local provincial and city united front agencies in China to serve officially as "overseas propaganda agents" on their return to their home countries. These commissions obliged them to accept responsibility for promoting the decisions of the party's national congress in their home countries. The article noted that this practice of offering party commissions to overseas Chinese to work on united front tasks in their home countries was not new. The president of the United Fujianese American Association (美国福建公所) told reporters: "I have received quite a few letters of appointment on previous occasions, but none for which I have felt such deep significance as the one today. It's a heavy responsibility."[14]

Peaceful Reunification Councils

A key goal of PRC overseas activities is to convince, and sometimes pressure, Chinese in the United States to accept that the PRC government in Beijing is the sole representative of China and all things Chinese, and that the Republic of China on Taiwan is an illegitimate government. To this end, in 1988, the party's United Front Work Department founded the China Council for the Promotion of Peaceful National Reunification, and the Washington, DC–based Association to Promote China Unification was folded into the council. The DC chapter's assignment was to organize concerts, demonstrations, and other gatherings to support the PRC.[15] Other chapters soon opened, so that by 2018, the council had established thirty-three in the United States and more than two hundred branches overseas. In America, these organizations are generally registered as domestic nonprofit community organizations, even though their leadership in Beijing includes senior members of the Chinese Communist Party. An article in the *People's Daily*, the mouthpiece of the Chinese Communist Party, spoke in glowing terms about how useful the Peaceful Reunification Councils were in furthering China's goals of taking over Taiwan, noting that while chapters of the Peaceful Reunification Council complied with US law by registering as nonprofits, they were established to support Chinese government policies and coordinate activities with PRC consulates in the United States.[16] "Over the years, the China Peaceful Reunification Council in Northern California has actively cooperated with the local Chinese consulate to work against 'Taiwan independence' and promote national reunification activities, and has some influence in San Francisco's overseas Chinese community," the Northern California Council notes on its website.[17]

Around the United States, the councils count numerous prominent Chinese Americans as members. For example, one successful California businesswoman was for years the honorary chairwoman of the council in Northern California.[18] While helping promote US-China educational exchanges, this individual has also consistently advocated on behalf of PRC policies in the United States, including China's claims on Taiwan, and has helped to organize demonstrations against "Taiwan independence." She is listed as an adviser to the China Overseas Exchange Association, which is part of the United Front Work Department.[19]

The Chinese government has also sought to co-opt local Chinese American community associations to serve its goals.[20] In the past, organizations such as regional associations had generally been close to the Nationalist government of Taiwan. In San Francisco, however, that began to change as early as the 1980s when Suey Sing, one of San Francisco's six major community organizations (Tongs) representing Chinese immigrants, became the first major Chinese group to fly the flag of the PRC on its building. Then a second Tong flew Beijing's flag, and a competition broke out between the PRC and Taiwan in San Francisco's Chinatown to see which side could fly the most flags. This competition can be vividly seen from the seventeenth floor of a public housing project overlooking Chinatown, where PRC and Republic of China flags sit atop adjacent buildings stretching into the horizon. The flying of the PRC's flag reflects two things: increasing PRC influence in America's traditional Chinatown, as well as a recognition of reality by these associations that Beijing had been recognized, even by the United States, as the legitimate capital of China.

The value of these associations to Beijing can be seen in this example: When China's president Xi Jinping visited the United States in September 2015, one of the leaders of San Francisco's local Chinese American community associations was listed as first among twenty prominent Chinese Americans honored by the Chinese president.[21]

Chinese Americans and the Chinese People's Political Consultative Conference

Several Chinese Americans have been given membership on China's most prominent national united front body, the Chinese People's Political Consultative Conference (CPPCC). The preamble of China's constitution defines the Chinese People's Political Consultative Conference as "a broadly based representative organization of the united front which . . . will play a still more important role in the country's political and social life, in promoting friendship with other countries and in the struggle for socialist modernization and for the reunification and unity of the country." In practice, the CPPCC has served as an important advisory committee to help legitimize the Chinese Communist Party's rule to audiences both domestic and abroad.

Beijing has been appointing Chinese Americans to the CPPCC for years. In some cases, authorities in Beijing seem to have had problems finding willing Americans to take seats on the committee, such as in 2017, when a Chinese property developer and educator (who appears to still be a Chinese citizen) was one of seven "Americans" listed as CPPCC members.[22]

In doling out prestigious positions on the CPPCC, China seeks to show overseas Chinese that prominent members of their community want to be connected with China's government. The American contingent to the thirteenth CPPCC (announced in March 2018) was perhaps the most remarkable in years, comprising four highly successful Chinese American academics, scientists, and businessmen.[23]

The appointment of Chinese Americans to positions on this advisory body to the Chinese Communist Party raises difficult questions of divided national loyalty. Americans should, of course, be free to participate in whatever organizations they see fit, since freedom of association is hardwired into the constitutional DNA of the United States. However, the CPPCC is not an independent civil-society NGO but an organization controlled, managed, and dominated by the Chinese Communist Party. Members of these organizations are expected to adhere to the disciplines and goals of the party and work to strengthen China and the party's rule of China. Members of the CPPCC are expected to write reports about how their activities have aligned with China's interests and to detail their work on China's behalf.[24] The potential exploitation of Chinese American members in this body by the Chinese government not only risks harming the interests of the United States but also has the potential to harm the security, reputation, and welfare of these Chinese Americans.

A similar quandary could present itself to those Chinese Americans who have chosen to accept positions as consultants for another united front organization, the All-China Federation of Returned Overseas Chinese, which also serves the party's interests. In 2018, twelve representatives from the United States, including wealthy businessmen and civic leaders, were listed as advisors of the federation's 10th National Congress. The Chinese government picked them in recognition of their prominence and efforts in advocating positions friendly to Beijing.[25]

To engender a sense of close support, state-owned Chinese media outlets routinely report about contacts made between prominent Chinese Americans and senior Chinese officials. There are literally hundreds of such reports in the Chinese-language press about prominent Chinese Americans escorting leading figures from China's united front bureaucracy in the United States or being hosted by them in China.[26] In May 2017, Li Kexin, the deputy chief of mission at the Chinese embassy in Washington, praised the Peaceful Reunification Council's DC chapter for holding a "peaceful reunification forum" in Washington and for opposing Taiwan's independence.[27] Officials from China have also traveled freely to the United States to take part in conferences and activities designed to further China's influence operations in the United States. For example, united front officials traveled to the United States in November 2016 for the annual executive meeting of the Peaceful Reunification Council, during which the council pledged to renew its efforts to "oppose Taiwan's independence."[28]

Conclusion and Recommendations

As US citizens, Chinese Americans enjoy the same constitutional rights of freedom of speech, association, and political participation as everyone else, and their exercise of these rights is fully legitimate and protected by the Constitution and law. What's more, it is incumbent on the US government and American society as a whole not to demonize Chinese Americans for their feelings for and pride in China.

At the same time, it is also important that all American citizens be aware that feelings of pride can sometimes be exploited by an authoritarian regime to advance its goals and interests. Here it is not Chinese Americans who are at fault for having an attachment to their "Motherland" but the Chinese Communist Party for cynically attempting to use Chinese Americans to further its own interests, in the process making overseas Chinese communities vulnerable to distrust.

While the US government needs to adopt a no-tolerance policy toward attempts by Chinese security forces to travel to the United States to secretly harass, manipulate, intimidate, and monitor China's perceived enemies in the United States, the best antidote to such intrusion is for federal and local governments to do more to strengthen ties to Chinese American communities and to give greater visibility into the various inducements and pressures Beijing exerts on these communities. That the FBI has begun to reach out to prominent Chinese in the United States, offering protection, is a good beginning. But the FBI and the rest of the US government must approach this problem with great sensitivity and be mindful of the sad history of political repression in the Chinese American community and the legacy of the McCarthyite purges of the 1950s.

This is particularly important, as such demonization can lead to the unwarranted targeting of Chinese Americans or long-term Chinese residents of the United States for alleged crimes involving illegal cooperation with China. Over the past decade, there has been a significant number of examples of prosecutorial overreach, such as the case against the hydrologist Sherry Chen, who was exonerated in 2015 of all espionage charges.

A sustained education campaign is also urgently needed to inform the members of the Chinese American community of the potential adverse consequences of involvement with China's united front activities. Chinese American organizations also need to do a better job of informing themselves about the underlying goals of PRC's united front organizations as there are potential reputational costs of allying with them and losing independence. It can be taken as a positive sign that, for example, the Committee of 100, an organization founded by many illustrious Chinese Americans, has begun to debate the possibility of encouraging its leading members from accepting positions with PRC united front organizations officially aligned with the Chinese Communist Party.[29]

China's activities in the United States can also be made more transparent by requiring spin-off groups from united front organizations in Beijing to register under the Foreign Agent Registration Act as agents of a foreign power. This would include all of the bureaus of the Peaceful Reunification Council, the China Overseas Exchange Association, and the China Overseas Friendship Association, among others that are, in fact, influence-seeking organizations with political implications run by a foreign state. In addition, Chinese Americans who accept positions in united front structures—such as the Chinese People's Political Consultative Conference—should also be required to register as agents of a foreign power seeking influence in the United States. China has tried to sell these "honors" to the Chinese American community as a cost-free way of expressing their sincere feelings of pride in China. However, the reality is that once a person accepts such "honors," along with free travel to China and other emoluments, the Chinese Communist Party will always seek to exact a further price. And where that price creates divided loyalties and results in actions harmful to American interests and values, the US government must respond with appropriate legal and regulatory measures.

CHAPTER FOUR

Universities

American universities have long played a leading role in relations between the United States and China. Ever since the Carter administration first explored the possibility with Deng Xiaoping and other Chinese counterparts of sending Chinese students to the United States in 1977–78,[1] PRC government authorities (like their Republican-era predecessors) have seen American universities as integral to China's economic and scientific development. For the first two decades after normalization, the Chinese government placed a priority on sending students in STEM subjects (science, technology, engineering, mathematics). Over time, however, fields of study broadened into the humanities, social sciences, and the arts, a change that has mirrored the shift in educational exchange from primarily a state-directed to a private consumer–driven phenomenon that saw an increasing number of middle-class Chinese parents opting to send their children to the United States for a liberal arts undergraduate education, and even a secondary school education. The net result has been that several million Chinese students have now successfully matriculated through the US higher education system. During the 2017–18 academic year, for instance, a record 350,755 Chinese students were enrolled in American universities (with an additional 80,000 in high schools),[2] out of a total of 1.5 million Chinese students studying worldwide in the same year.[3] (Altogether, since the late 1970s, an estimated 5.2 million Chinese have attended foreign universities.)[4] Unlike the early years of this epic exchange, the majority of Chinese students are now able to pay full tuition, creating an extremely significant source of revenue for financially stressed American universities and colleges. (Chinese pay tuition worth an estimated $12 billion per year, according to the US Department of Commerce.)[5]

US universities and American society have benefited significantly from this exchange, and from the presence of international students generally. Chinese students have helped to diversify the makeup of US student bodies; they often contribute positively in the classroom, and they have made a real contribution in joint research projects with university faculties. Many have remained in the United States postgraduation to pursue professional careers, build their lives, and become American citizens—a sizable contribution to American society, to the US economy, and to technological innovation and the knowledge base in numerous fields. The engineering, medical, and hard sciences have benefited particularly, but so have the humanities and social sciences. Indeed, those who negotiated the initial educational and scientific exchange accords back in 1978–79 could never have envisioned how much of a success story US-China higher educational exchanges would become over the next four decades.

For their part, American universities and US scholars have also engaged in China during this period, although in far fewer—but not insignificant—numbers. (For example, in 2015–16, 11,688 American students and scholars were studying in China.)[6] For those in the field of Chinese studies, it is *de rigueur* to study and do research in Chinese universities. Professional collaboration among faculty—mainly in the sciences and medicine—has also flourished. Some US universities—notably Johns Hopkins School of Advanced International Studies (Hopkins-Nanjing Center), New York University (NYU-Shanghai), and Duke University (Duke-Kunshan)—have gone so far as to establish campuses in China, while others have opened centers (e.g., Stanford, Virginia, Chicago, Yale, Harvard, Columbia). Many more American universities have forged collaborative exchange programs with Chinese counterparts.

While US-China exchanges in higher education have primarily been a success story, as in many other dimensions of the Sino-American relationship, clouds have appeared on the horizon.[7] American students have become less keen than in the past to study in China due to concerns about pollution, lack of open internet access, and expanding political controls. American scholars trying to conduct research in China have run into an increasing number of restrictions and impediments since 2010, due to a broad campaign against "foreign hostile forces" and an increasingly draconian political atmosphere that has cast a shadow across Chinese society, especially over higher education. Whole subject areas and regions of the country are now off-limits to American and other foreign scholars for fieldwork; previously normal interactions with Chinese scholars are now often heavily circumscribed; many Chinese scholars have become reluctant to meet with American counterparts; a growing number of libraries are off-limits; central- and provincial-level archives have been closed; municipal archives are increasingly restricted; interviews with government officials (at all levels) are more difficult to arrange; public opinion surveys must be carried out with Chinese partners, if they can be conducted at all; simple eyewitness social research in rural and even some urban areas is considerably more limited than previously. In short, normal scholarly research practices permitted elsewhere in the world are regularly proscribed in China. These restrictions also include the inability to hold open and uncensored public scholarly discussions, conferences, and other kinds of events. Meanwhile, Chinese students and scholars enjoy unimpeded access to all of these activities in the United States, resulting in a severe asymmetry in Sino-American scholarly exchange. This contravenes the spirit of the bilateral US-China educational exchange accords.

At the same time, storm clouds are also gathering on American campuses with respect to another aspect of this important relationship, namely, growing concerns about unfair Chinese "influence-seeking activities" in the United States.

Confucius Institutes

One of the most controversial aspects of the whole US-China educational exchange is the Confucius Institutes (CIs), of which there are now 110 (plus 501 Confucius Classrooms in secondary schools) across the United

States.[8] For secondary schools and colleges that have no or little other coverage of China on campus, CIs are an important resource. Sponsored by the Hanban, an organization directly under the purview of the Ministry of Education in Beijing, but also with ties to the External Propaganda Leading Group of the CCP Central Committee, the primary mission of CIs is to teach Chinese language and culture abroad. However, faculty and other watchdogs have warned that they may present risks to intellectual freedom by using American universities as vehicles through which to advance Chinese Communist Party propaganda. Accusations leveled at CIs revolve mainly around the exclusive use of PRC materials that promote PRC Chinese viewpoints, terminology, and simplified characters; the avoidance of discussion in American classrooms and programs on controversial topics such as Tibet, Tiananmen, Xinjiang, the Falun Gong, and human rights; and potential infringement on theoretically independent studies curricula on American campuses.

Although proponents of CIs like to compare them with branches of France's L'Alliance Francaise, Germany's Goethe Instituts, and Spain's Cervantes Institute, they are different in important ways. Unlike these other institutions, CIs are joint operations located inside—and cofunded by—a host university or secondary school for which the Hanban arranges a Chinese university to supply teachers, textbooks, and other materials. The teachers are paid by the Chinese university (and hence do not hold green cards or pay US taxes). Typically, the Hanban provides a $150,000 start-up grant with $100,000–$200,000 per year follow-on funding (depending on the institution) directly to the American university. Secondary schools normally receive $50,000 in initial funding and $15,000 subsequently per annum. Most troublesome are two provisions in the Hanban contracts with US host institutions: One forbids the CIs from conducting any activities that contravene Chinese law while the other requires that the enabling contract remain confidential, making oversight by the academic community difficult.

Some participating American institutions have belatedly had second thoughts about their partnerships. In 2014, the University of Chicago terminated its CI contract with the Hanban after months of controversy among faculty, spurred by a high-profile critical article by an emeritus member.[9] Since that time, at least two additional American universities have also closed their branches (Pennsylvania State University and University of West Florida),[10] and Senator Marco Rubio (R-FL), a leading critic of alleged Chinese "influence activities," has written letters to a number of other Florida institutions hosting CIs requesting that they also be closed.[11] Representatives Michael McCaul (R-TX) and Henry Cuellar (D-TX) called for the same termination in their own state, stating in a letter addressed to their state's universities that these organizations "are a threat to our nation's security by serving as a platform for China's intelligence collection and political agenda." They added that "we have a responsibility to uphold our American values of free expression, and to do whatever is necessary to counter any behavior that poses a threat to our democracy." The Texas A&M system complied with this request by ordering the closure of all CIs.[12] Then, in August 2018, the University of North Florida announced the closure of its CI.[13]

Similar calls have been made in other states, and the 2019 National Defense Authorization Act restricts Department of Defense language study funding if a university hosts a Confucius Institute.[14] Several other universities (including Dickinson State University in Pennsylvania, the University of Pennsylvania, and Princeton University) that had contemplated opening CIs have now decided not to do so. At the same time, Columbia University (and elsewhere) has come under criticism, more for lack of transparency than for its specific violative activities.[15] That said, the majority of CIs have so far carried out their mission of language and cultural education without controversy.

In 2014, both the Canadian Association of University Teachers (CAUT) and the American Association of University Professors (AAUP) called on universities to terminate CIs unless their agreements with Hanban were renegotiated to provide for total transparency and compliance with norms of academic freedom.[16] In 2017, the National Association of Scholars (NAS), a politically conservative nonprofit advocacy group,[17] undertook an exhaustive study of CIs in the United States and produced a 183-page report.[18] Echoing the AAUP's recommendations, the NAS urged closing all CIs on the basis of four areas of concern: a restriction of intellectual freedom; lack of transparency; "entanglement" (with

Chinese party–controlled institutions); and worries about them being used for Chinese "soft power" or pro-PRC propaganda.

In addition to the above concerns, some have argued that the fact that CI language programs exclusively use PRC textbooks with "simplified" (or mainland-style) Chinese characters biases the contribution CIs make to Chinese language instruction on American campuses. In our view, this is not a serious problem, since students should learn this vocabulary and this form of written characters, so long as the university also provides the opportunity for students to learn traditional "complex" characters (used in Hong Kong, Taiwan, Singapore, and many diaspora communities) and to learn non-mainland vocabulary. A review of the entire set of Hanban textbooks used by CIs undertaken for this report finds they contain no overt political content. Only in one of six levels of textbooks was there a single lesson on US-China relations, and it was a speech by former president Barack Obama in which he asserted that the United States does not seek to "contain" China. Nor have we found *any* evidence of interference by CIs in the mainstream Chinese studies curricula on US campuses to date. (See below for our recommendations concerning CIs.)

Chinese Students and Scholars Associations

Chinese Students and Scholars Associations (CSSA) on American campuses maintain regular contact with China's diplomatic missions in the United States. Even when these contacts are purely for cultural purposes, the CSSA provides a ready channel or entry point for the political departments of China's embassy and consulates in the United States to gather information and coordinate action, which in some cases includes pressuring the behavior of Chinese students. Sometimes pressure is even applied by China's security services on the family members, back in China, of those students it finds speaking out in unacceptable ways. What is more, Chinese scholars and diplomats have sought to influence on-campus debates in China's favor and have even protested when American universities have exercised their right to invite speakers whom China identifies as unfriendly. Finally, some Chinese students and scholars have exploited the collaborative research environment on US campuses to obtain sensitive American technologies.

Chinese Students and Scholars Associations now exist on more than 150 US campuses.[19] A second type of on-campus association has also recently started up, the China Development Student Think Tank (CDSTT), with chapters at Syracuse University, Boston University, and George Washington University. As voluntary associations of Chinese citizens on campus, these groups perform many appropriate social functions, such as orienting new students to life in the United States and arranging networking get-togethers. Nonetheless, their links with Chinese diplomatic missions and some of their activities, because of their attempts to interfere with other campus activities and broader political discourse and debate, present cause for concern. CSSAs at Washington, DC, universities make no secret of their ties to the Chinese embassy and receive small amounts of operating funds directly from it. CSSAs elsewhere have similar ties to nearby Chinese consulates, which also provide them with funding, other kinds of support, and surveillance. It has also been reported that Chinese Communist Party cells have been established on several US campuses.[20]

CSSAs often alert PRC diplomatic missions about events on campus that offend official PRC political sensitivities, e.g., speeches or discussions on Tibet, Taiwan, Xinjiang, human rights, and Chinese elite politics. Once notified, the local PRC mission has sometimes contacted university faculty or staff members to prevent such events from proceeding. In some instances, it is difficult to know whether opposition to events originates with a CSSA or the local PRC mission. In 2017, the CSSA at the University of California–San Diego (UCSD) mobilized opposition to the chancellor's invitation to the Dalai Lama to be the commencement speaker, which at least some CSSA members ultimately coordinated with the PRC consulate in Los Angeles.[21] After the event finally took place anyway as planned, the Chinese government retaliated by banning students and scholars with funding from the Chinese government's China Scholarship Council from attending UCSD. Other US universities have come under similar pressure when they have contemplated inviting the Dalai Lama or his associates to campus. Academic authorities at one Washington, DC, university were even warned by the Chinese embassy that if an event concerning Xinjiang went ahead, they risked losing their Confucius Institute.

CSSAs also serve as a channel of political "peer monitoring" of Chinese students, constraining the academic freedom of Chinese students on campus—and thereby also undermining core principles of free speech and academic freedom. This issue has become more serious over the past several years, as the political environment in China has tightened and Chinese students widely fear that things they say on campus (even in class, at other campus activities, or in private conversations) that contradict official PRC policies are liable to be reported to the Chinese authorities and risk putting their families into jeopardy back home.

A very public example of this kind took place during the commencement ceremonies at the University of Maryland in May 2017, after a Chinese student was selected as the commencement speaker. When Yang Shuping praised the "fresh air of free speech" and contrasted what she had found in the United States with China—and her comments went viral on the internet and social media in China—she received an avalanche of email threats, and her family in China was harassed.[22] Another well-reported incident occurred at Duke University in 2008 when a twenty-year-old female undergraduate student became caught up in a pro–Tibetan independence demonstration. She was vilified online, and her parents were harassed back in China.[23] In other cases, Chinese government authorities have visited students' families in China and warned them about their children's allegedly subversive statements abroad.

In Australia, another kind of disturbing phenomenon has occurred: Several instances have occurred in which Chinese students have recorded professors' lectures that were deemed critical of the PRC and then uploaded them onto the internet, thereby prompting harassment of the lecturers on social media.[24] There is no evidence that this has occurred on American campuses to date. But the presence on campus of a student organization linked to the Chinese government creates an understandable concern that faculty lecturing on politically sensitive topics might fear that their lectures are being monitored and thus self-censor themselves. This prospect is especially concerning when it involves a faculty member who, because he or she needs to travel to China for research or other professional purposes, feels under duress.

Gifts and Grants

Thanks to growing wealth accumulation in China, prosperous Chinese are beginning to develop the practice of philanthropy and to exercise giving both at home and abroad.[25] This is potentially a good thing for American universities. Indeed, since 2011, Chinese sources have participated in at least 1,186 donations or contracts worth more than $426 million to seventy-seven American universities, according to disclosures made to the US Department of Education, making China the fifth most active country by number of gifts, and fourth, behind Qatar, the United Kingdom, and Saudi Arabia, in total monetary value of gifts. (These disclosures are only required of universities that accept federal aid, and the figures also include funds from Taiwanese sources.)[26]

All US institutions of higher education cultivate lifetime giving from both graduates and their families. Given the numbers of Chinese students matriculating from American universities and the wealth of many of their families back in China as well as their own potential career earnings, Chinese students have become a growing priority for university development officers. Indeed, some Chinese families also seem to believe that they can ensure, or at least enhance, their children's chances of acceptance into top colleges through charitable gifts.[27]

Given the government's extensive role in China's economy, acceptance of all Chinese gifts and grants requires due diligence that should be above and beyond the standard practices currently employed by universities for other charitable giving. This is obviously the case when funding comes from the Chinese government itself, for example via the Hanban (the oversight body of the Confucius Institutes), which doles out research grants via its Confucius China Studies Program,[28] the "Young Sinologists" program of the Chinese Ministry of Culture and Chinese Academy of Social Sciences,[29] and, in one instance, the endowing of a faculty position at Stanford University.

Chinese corporate and private donors are now also starting to pour millions of dollars into the US educational system, think tanks, and non-profit organizations. Given that privately owned companies in China exist and prosper at the sufferance of political authorities there, even

seemingly independent actors are often likely to act at government direction or in ways that they believe will please the government. Major
mainland Chinese and Hong Kong companies and individuals with active
business ventures in China have now pledged or donated substantial
funds to US universities.

This is also the case with some Hong Kong-based or US-based foundations that are linked directly or indirectly to the Chinese government
or to enterprises and families that have prospered with the help of the
Beijing government. The most notable case is the China-United States
Exchange Foundation.[30] CUSEF was established in 2008 on the initiative of former Hong Kong chief executive and shipping magnate Tung
Chee Hwa (C. H. Tung) who continues to be the chairman of the foundation. Tung is also the vice chairman of the Chinese People's Political
Consultative Conference (CPPCC), China's highest-level united front
organization,[31] and he attended the Communist Party's 19th National
Congress in October 2017. Moreover, the number of mainland-based
members of the foundation's official advisors and the foundation's easy
connections with Chinese government organs belie the foundation's
assertion that it is independent of the Chinese Communist Party and the
PRC government.

CUSEF undertakes a range of programs aimed at Americans that can
accurately be described as influence-seeking activities; as such, it has registered in the United States under the Foreign Agent Registration Act
(FARA). Its lobbying activities include sponsoring all-expenses-paid
tours of China for delegations composed of what the foundation's website refers to as "thought leaders," including journalists and editors, think-
tank specialists, and city and state officials.[32] CUSEF has not often
collaborated with American universities and think tanks, but it recently
offered funding to the University of Texas at Austin for its China Public
Policy Center. However, after receiving criticism from Senator Ted Cruz
(R-TX) and others, the university declined the grant.[33] CUSEF grants
have generally gone to leading US think tanks, such as the Brookings
Institution, the Carnegie Endowment for International Peace, and the
Asia Society.

There have not yet been many offers by Chinese donors—private, corporate, or government—to fund faculty positions or centers for Chinese studies on US campuses, although many universities are believed to be seeking such gifts. In one instance in 2014, a leading Washington, DC, university was approached by a chinese university with a proposal for a $500,000 *annual* grant to establish a center for Chinese studies in partnership with the Chinese university.[34] The Chinese side had three main conditions for the grant: (1) that a series of Chinese officials and other visitors would be given public platforms for frequent speeches; (2) that faculty from the Chinese partner university could teach China courses on the US university campus; and (3) that new Chinese studies courses would be added to the university curriculum. The Washington-based university turned down the lucrative offer, on the advice of its Chinese studies faculty.

In August 2017, the Johns Hopkins University School of Advanced International Studies (SAIS) announced that it had received a substantial gift from CUSEF for an endowed junior faculty position, as well as program funding for a Pacific Community Initiative. SAIS administrators stated that there were no political or other strings attached to these grants, despite media insinuations to the contrary.[35] At Yale Law School, the China Law Center founded in 1999 was renamed the Paul Tsai China Center after receiving a $30 million endowment from Joseph C. Tsai, a Taiwanese Canadian billionaire who is a cofounder and executive vice chairman of the China-based Alibaba Group.[36] Tsai, an alumnus of Yale College and Yale Law School, made the gift in honor of his father, also an alumnus of Yale Law School.

China is not the only authoritarian government that has given or facilitated gifts to American academic institutions or think tanks, but it is the wealthiest. There is no evidence so far that any of these gifts has compromised the independence of the recipient institution. But the trend toward large gifts from Chinese sources, many with some kind of government linkage, underscores the need for vigilance in enforcing a stricter code of due diligence and transparency on the part of university administrations and faculties.

Pressure on University Administrations

There is a large number of successful exchange programs between American and Chinese universities. Three US universities have developed campuses in China (Johns Hopkins, Duke, NYU); more than one hundred universities participate in cooperative-education programs in China; and countless US faculty members participate in collaborative projects with Chinese colleagues (principally in the sciences). These relationships have not been easy to establish or maintain, but they have generally been successful. A 2016 report by the Government Accounting Office, which reviewed the cooperative programs of twelve American universities, found that the universities "generally indicated that they experienced academic freedom," while noting that self- and internet censorship remain a problem.

In recent years, the outlook for these collaborations has deteriorated in line with broader restrictions on academic freedom on Chinese campuses. In 2013, commensurate with CCP Central Committee Document No. 9, universities were reportedly instructed to avoid discussing topics including "universal values" and civil rights,[37] and admonitions against the teaching of Western values have continued. Since 2017, foreign university collaborative institutions have been required to institute Communist Party committees and place a party secretary on their management boards.[38] In July 2018, the Ministry of Education ended 234, or one-fifth, of its international university partnerships. More than twenty-five programs with American universities were among them.[39]

The Chinese government has demonstrated a penchant for turning to these collaborations as points of leverage when US universities have hosted the Dalai Lama or held other events deemed politically sensitive or offensive to the Chinese government. In such instances, existing collaborative exchange programs have been suspended or put on hold, planned visits of university administrators have been canceled, programs between university institutes and centers have been suspended, and Chinese students wishing to study at these US institutions have been counseled to go elsewhere. Such punitive actions resulting from campus visits by the Dalai Lama have been taken against Emory University, the University of Maryland, the University of California–San Diego, and others. In the case of the University of Maryland, which hosted the Dalai Lama in 2013, there was temporary fallout, and then following the 2017 graduation incident the Chinese government again halted cooperation, seriously damaging one of the most extensive exchange programs with China.

Such cases establish a worrying precedent of Chinese intrusion into American academic life. The message from China to US universities is clear: do not transgress the political no-go zones of the Chinese Communist Party or government, or you will pay a price. Sometimes the pressure is overt; other times it is more subtle and indirect, but no less alarming. Some American faculty members report troubling conversations with university administrators who continue to view Chinese students as such a lucrative revenue stream that it should not be endangered by "needlessly irritating Chinese authorities."

Censorship and Self-Censorship

The final category of troubling Chinese influence on American campuses involves the vexing issue of self-censorship among faculty and students in Chinese studies.[40] In a much-quoted essay, Perry Link described censorship within China as the use of vague threats to induce academics, writers, and others to self-limit what they say; he called this "the anaconda in the chandelier" syndrome.[41] More recently, the phenomenon has begun to loom over scholars working outside China, and the Chinese government has started deploying a variety of techniques to also encourage self-censorship beyond China's borders, including in the United States. In some cases, this syndrome has led to outright self-censorship of academic work. Here are some of the most egregious examples:

- Denial of visas to qualified scholars and students seeking access to China for research or training purposes. The State Department estimates that fifteen to twenty individuals are on an outright "blacklist," while scores of others appear to be on a "gray" list, where denials are less absolute and sometimes temporary or limited only to certain categories of visa. But being cast into the "gray" status helps create exactly the kind of uncertainty about what behavior might lead to visa denial, thus inducing self-censorship in the hopes of not offending anyone further, much less turning one's status from "gray" to "black." In other words, the power to withhold or deny access through the issuance of visas affords the Chinese government a full spectrum of powerful control mechanisms over scholars.

- Denial of access to interviewees, archives, libraries, and research institutes, even when visas are granted.
- Restriction of visiting scholar status for American researchers to a few institutes under the Chinese Academy of Social Sciences, Chinese Academy of Sciences, and some universities. Other think tanks and research institutes do not permit foreign resident researchers. At the same time, it should be noted, Chinese researchers from a wide variety of institutes are free to regularly come to US universities and think tanks for short- and long-term stays.
- Attempts to control the agendas, participant name lists, what is written, and what is said at joint scholarly conferences held in China, and now sometimes even in the United States. (A recent technique is to require that a talk or paper by an American participant in a Chinese-organized event be handed over to the organizing group for vetting well before the event itself, so that a participant can be disinvited, if necessary.)
- Restriction of internet and email communications when in China.
- Monitoring, even following, some American scholars by security services while in China.
- Demands for censorship by foreign publishers of their digital content as a condition for allowing it to be made available online in China.
- Insistence on censorship of Chinese-language editions of foreign books by the State Press and Publishing Administration. This places foreign authors in the difficult position of having to acquiesce to such censorship in order to have translations of their books published in China.
- Censorship of online archives of PRC journals and publications, such as the China National Knowledge Infrastructure (CNKI) database. American universities each pay tens of thousands of dol-

lars annually for access to these electronic databases. However, recent research has shown that CNKI in particular is now "curating" its catalogs and holdings by deleting articles the current government appears not to wish to see remaining in the historical record.[42] Since American universities have started to dispose of paper copies of many of the journals carried in CNKI periodical index, this amounts to PRC distorting the historical record, not just for China but for the entire world.

In addition to these specific restrictions affecting American scholars, the PRC government also influences the field of Chinese studies in the United States (and elsewhere) via controls over key regions of their country (especially minority areas such as Tibet and Xinjiang) and by creating no-go zones around a wide variety of research subjects within the broader areas of politics, religion, ethnography, and civil society that cannot be researched in-country. As a result, American professors cannot themselves work in these areas, nor can they in good conscience advise their graduate students to work on these subjects either because of risk to the researcher's career, as well as to the human subjects whom researchers would be observing or interviewing. Such restrictions have real consequences for the open future of Chinese studies around the world.

Conclusion and Recommendations

US-China academic exchanges are valuable to both China and the United States and should be maintained and developed. However, in doing so, universities must be alert to the risks of engaging with the Chinese government, institutions, and funders and be proactive in applying a higher level of due diligence and vigilance as a defense of the core principle of academic freedom, especially when conflicts take place at home in their own universities.

Promote Transparency

- Manage agreements with Confucius Institutes: We do not endorse calls for Confucius Institutes to be closed, as long as several conditions are met. US institutions should make their CI agreements public to facilitate oversight by members of the university community and other concerned parties. Those agreements, in turn, must grant full managerial authority to the host institution (not on a shared basis with the Hanban), so the university has full control over what a CI teaches, the activities it undertakes, the research grants it makes, and whom it employs. The clause in all Hanban contracts that CIs must operate "according to China's laws" must be deleted.

If these standards cannot be attained, then the CI agreements should be terminated. Furthermore, universities should prevent any intervention by CIs in curricular requirements and course content in their overall Chinese studies curricula or other areas of study by maintaining a clear administrative separation between academic centers and departments on the one hand, and CIs on the other. Finally, universities must ensure that all public programming offered by their CIs conforms to academic standards of balance and diversity and does not cross the line to become a platform for PRC propaganda, or even a circumscribed view of a controversial issue. In fact, this report would suggest that universities should not permit Confucius Institutes to become involved in public programming that goes beyond the CI core mission of education about Chinese language and culture. To go beyond these two categories invites opportunities for politicized propaganda.

- Apply due diligence: To minimize the risks just identified, universities must rigorously apply far stricter due-diligence procedures to scrutinize the sources and purposes of gifts and contracts from China to ensure that they do not interfere with academic freedom. Universities accepting gifts from Chinese nationals, corporations, or foundations must insist that there be no restrictions on academic freedom. Foreign donations should continue to be welcomed, but universities must ensure that the conditions of acceptance are reasonable, consonant with their principles, and subject to oversight, and do not allow the program to become a beachhead for inappropriate influence. It is important that all universities exercise high standards of due diligence and not only scrutinize the source of the gift but consider the implications of such things as naming rights. Above all, they must insist that the terms of each gift impose no restrictions on academic freedom. The activities of all chairs, centers, and projects funded by Chinese support need to be fully transparent and supervised by independent faculty committees and university administrators, who must bear in mind that even when a joint project, research grant, or gift has undergone due diligence and has no explicit or evident strings attached, it can still produce a natural sense of obligation because no institution wants to offend a generous donor. This is a problem not restricted to grants from China, but one that is deeply entrenched in the fund-raising structure on which American institutions of higher education depend for their well-being.

- Defend the academic freedom of faculty: Governance is the core technique for protecting academic freedom in American universities and is the key to their leading role in research and teaching. It takes various forms in various institutions, but its key principles must be applied consistently to interactions involving China. Transparency must be maintained in the terms of a university's contracts with all outside actors, whether individuals, foundations, donors, or collaborating institutions such as the Hanban, which funds Confucius Institutes. Such actors must be subject to regular oversight by faculty bodies and by administrators answerable to faculty bodies so that faculty, students, visiting scholars, and others associated with the university in an academic capacity will have uncompromised freedom of speech, research, teaching, and programmatic activities.

Universities and their associated institutions—such as university presses—must refuse all forms of censorship of—or interference in—their publications, conferences, curricula, participants in events, and other academic activities. Some universities have formal rules barring such censorship, but they need to increase awareness, training, and enforcement. Other universities may need to enact or update such rules. While maintaining the openness of US universities to Chinese students, scholars, and researchers, universities should push for reciprocity from Chinese partner institutions with respect to various forms of research access.

In short, universities should enhance protection for faculty and students—especially international students—from interference in their academic freedom, and campuses with large numbers of international students from authoritarian countries should introduce training for students on their academic rights in the American educational system, and on the proper distance that independent student organizations should maintain from government actors. Finally, universities should provide a confidential complaint procedure for students who feel they have come under pressure that threatens their academic freedom, and university advisors should stand prepared to counsel and assist these students to deal appropriately with such pressures.

Promote Integrity

- Be alert to risks: The primary risk is of inappropriate influence over admissions, course content, and program activities stemming from the influence of Chinese government–linked donors, diplomatic missions, student groups, and institutions. This is not a new challenge for US university administrators and development officers. They have dealt with political quid pro quos from donors from South Korea, Taiwan, Japan, Israel, Russia, Kuwait, Qatar, Saudi Arabia, and other countries in the past and currently, and American universities have long learned how to refuse donations with strings attached. This historical experience and the existing safeguards should also help inform and guide US universities when it comes to dealing with this new wave of Chinese money. Faculty and administrators must continue to protect the open debate, diversity of opinion, freedom of expression, faculty autonomy, and transparency on which the health and reputation of their institutions are based. Funding from Chinese sources should be as welcome as funding from other sources, but only to the extent that fundamental academic values can be maintained and protected.

  A second risk is of a loss of sensitive or proprietary technology through academic instruction or cooperation. There are indications that the US government is now strengthening measures to prevent the theft of sensitive technology and intellectual property that is being developed on US campuses. These measures may require heightened screening and, in some cases, outright denials of visas to individuals from certain state-run institutions or even from certain sensitive research fields. Such calls have understandably prompted concern from the academic community fearing that this will undermine the principles of academic freedom, hinder collaboration, and deny American universities access to a rich talent pool. These reservations are merited and require that any tightening of visa categories be as narrow as possible. For their part, universities will of course have to comply with whatever regulations are imposed. They should, additionally, proactively review and update their procedures for protecting both proprietary and classified research. They should also enter into far closer collegial discussions with one another, relevant professional associations, and government agencies to collectively refine solutions to the difficult problem of balancing the pursuit of innovation and academic freedom with preventing the theft of technology and other intellectual property.

To meet these challenges, American universities may need to update their rules and intensify faculty and researcher training and institutional oversight for protection of proprietary research information. Some US universities refuse to accept contracts for classified research. Those that do accept such contracts must comply with government regulations for the protection of research findings. But all research universities conduct research that produces valuable intellectual property, which is proprietary in various proportions to the funder. And so, it is necessary for the university and researchers to intensify efforts to protect their proprietary intellectual property from loss.

Promote Reciprocity

- The academic community nationwide should work toward a common set of principles and practices for protecting academic freedom and promoting greater reciprocity. To prevent influencers from using divide-and-conquer strategies (by rewarding some institutions while punishing others), it is important for the national academic community as a whole to come together to formulate and implement these principles. US universities should not only work together, but they should also work with other universities around the world to develop a code of conduct for acceptable and unacceptable practices in academic exchanges with Chinese institutions and funders. (The chapter on think tanks in this volume recommends similar measures.) The academic community and government should also monitor instances where Chinese entities may acquire financially challenged American colleges outright. This would ensure that their academic integrity is not compromised.[43]

Universities can and must continue to play a positive role in the US-China relationship. Indeed, by introducing international students to American life and values, and connecting them to new personal and professional relationships, universities are arguably the important means by which the United States exercises its soft power. Generally—but not always—individuals undergoing such an experience take a more positive view of the country. Unfortunately, as Chinese students contribute much, not least monetarily, to American universities, universities have been too slow to help them integrate themselves more organically into campus life. As a result, Chinese students report unacceptably high levels of depression and isolation, or of simply clubbing up with one another.[44] While acting to mitigate the risks of improper interference, universities must not forget their obligations to these students nor lose sight of the far greater opportunity to advance cooperation and understanding.

CHAPTER FIVE

Think Tanks

Think tanks play an unparalleled role in shaping American public opinion, media narratives, and US government policy. For this reason, they are high-value targets for lobbying and influence activities by foreign governments and nongovernmental actors, including those from the People's Republic of China.

Think tanks in the United States date to the early twentieth century, when industrial capital and private philanthropy (led by the likes of Andrew Carnegie, John D. Rockefeller, Andrew W. Mellon, and Henry Ford) began to endow private nonprofit research institutions at a time when there was increasing government demand for expertise on a growing range of public-policy issues. Over the past century, think tanks have come to play ever more vital roles in the American public-policy process, and they contribute both directly and indirectly to public education, a richer public dialogue via the media, greater civic engagement, and better-informed government policy formulation.

Of the approximately 1,800 think tanks in the United States today, about half are research institutions located within US universities. For the purpose of this chapter, however, only those think tanks located in non-university private-sector settings are considered. Most of these think tanks and research institutions enjoy tax-exempt status under section 501(c)(3) of the Internal Revenue Code, which stipulates that they are restricted from legislative lobbying as "action organizations." Institutions that receive this tax-exempt status must either be charitable philanthropic organizations or research organizations (think tanks) that

operate in a supposedly nonpartisan way and in the general public interest. Because they are largely privately funded through donor contributions, US think tanks compete tenaciously for support, professional
expertise, and public impact.

Roles of Think Tanks in American Society

The universe of think tanks in the United States is very diverse, and each
think tank performs a different mission for different audiences and clients through different means of output. Four roles are especially relevant to discussions of Chinese interest and potential influence seeking.

The first and most important role of think tanks is in educating the
public and better informing the "policy community." The majority of
mainstream think tanks consciously perform these functions through a
variety of mechanisms: publishing books, articles in journals, shorter
"policy briefs," or "op-eds," and by contributing to policy "task force"
reports on specific issues; holding public seminars, briefings, and conferences; speaking to the print, television, radio, and electronic media;
and maintaining informational websites that disseminate think-tank vid-
eos of events on a worldwide basis.

The second role is to influence government policy. This is done
through meeting face to face with government officials; providing testimony before congressional committees; engaging in track-two discussions, emails, and other communications aimed at targeted audiences; and
issuing a wide variety of publications.

The third role, undertaken by some but not all US policy think tanks, is
to provide specific research on a contractual basis for government agencies that is generally not for public consumption.

The fourth role is to provide personnel to go into government service for fixed periods of time through the famous American "revolving
door," whereby think tanks become "governments in waiting" for ex- and
would-be officials until just after an election, when there is usually a
large-scale turnover of personnel in Washington as each new administration is formed.

In American think tanks, selection of general research topics can be
influenced by outside sources (management, external funding agencies,

or government policy shifts). But the final selection is usually subject to mutual agreement, and the findings of research are not supposed to be dictated by outside pressures. At the same time, both US think tanks and university research institutes are expected to maintain analytical independence from their funders. If the funding body does seek to interfere with a research project or promote its own agenda, there is an established expectation that its funding should be rejected. More often than not, there is a process of mutual consultation between researcher, think tank, and potential external funding bodies—through which interests are de-conflicted and grants are negotiated to the mutual satisfaction of all parties. While this is the optimal scenario, there have been cases revealed in the US media in recent years in which such principles were abridged.

The Role of China in American Think Tanks

It is against this general backdrop that the role of expanding Chinese influence on American think tanks needs to be considered. What follows are the findings gleaned through interviews with seventeen think-tank analysts from eleven Washington- and New York–based think tanks[1] that explore the nature of interactions that US think-tank specialists have recently been having with Chinese counterparts. The analysts are all recognized China experts (with the exception of one, who is more broadly an Asia expert but has extensive experience with China-related projects) who have served as directors of programs or centers in their respective institutions. About half have served in the US government. One directs a think tank that is partially supported by Chinese government funds. The interviews were all conducted in 2018.

China has become a priority field for US think tanks concerned with international relations, and most now have staff members (often several) devoted to researching and publishing on China. Many possess PhD degrees and Chinese language skills, and have lived in or visited China over many years, with some being originally from the PRC. Some stay on staff for many years, while others work on short-term (two- or three-year) contracts. Most think tanks also employ student research assistants and interns (including those from China).

There is significant interaction between American and Chinese think tanks—as think-tank researchers need to visit China as well as host and receive visitors in the United States to be well informed and to perform their own research work. Most interviewees reported hosting or participating in ad hoc meetings in their home institutions with visiting Chinese officials or scholars on a regular basis; although two do not host any meetings with Chinese, they will attend such events if hosted by others. All but one of the interviewees travel to China for their work: to deliver lectures, to participate in conferences or Track 1.5 or Track 2 dialogues, and to do research for articles, books, and reports.

A number of scholars noted a marked shift in the nature of their interactions with Chinese colleagues and research projects over the past few years. While long-standing Track 2 dialogues continue on issues such as cyber policy, nuclear policy, and US-China interactions in third-world countries and regions, overall they seem not as open, robust, and productive as in the past. Indeed, several long-standing Track 2 dialogues have been curtailed or stopped altogether—with scholars reporting that it is increasingly difficult to establish sustained dialogues that are meaningful with Chinese think tanks because of new rules, restrictions, and uncertainties. For instance, Chinese institutions (both think tanks and universities) must now obtain central-level government approval, such as vetting dialogue topics and foreign participants, before being able to host foreign participants in China. New Chinese government regulations generally limit Chinese think-tank scholars and university professors to one foreign trip per year, and even go so far as to withhold passports to make even personal travel more difficult.

When dialogues do occur, another noticeable recent trend has been a decline in candor and greater uniformity in what Chinese interlocutors say. One US think tanker noted, "The conversations have declined in productivity," while another commented that he had "moved away from Track 2 because China does not have much to say beyond the Xi catechism. Even in private conversations, we are not getting anything interesting." And yet another indicated that he no longer participates in many joint events because they need to be "framed in a way to fit the Chinese narrative, including the speakers, agenda, topics, and writing." Achieving true candor in such dialogues with the Chinese side has long been difficult, as Chinese interlocutors routinely stick to "talking points" and stock slogans, stay strictly "on message," and are afraid to say anything in front of their peers that might subsequently get them in political trouble back home.

One US analyst commented that at a recent conference in Beijing, Chinese scholars demonstrated little interest in putting forth ideas for cooperation, a marked change from earlier meetings. This individual believes that tensions in the US-China relationship are at least partially responsible. And it is not only the Americans who see less utility in such dialogues. One Track 2 initiated by the Chinese side concerning global norm cooperation ended abruptly when the Chinese said they did not see any productive benefits, despite the willingness of the US side to move forward with the project.

While these are long-standing problems, they have gotten demonstratively worse during the Xi Jinping era. As one think-tank scholar commented, "Collaboration has become much more difficult, more authoritarian, and finding a common definition of a program is more difficult. We could usually find areas on which to work collaboratively, but there is a gap in worldview." One US think-tank analyst who directs an innovative program to foster dialogue among rising American and Chinese strategic thinkers, which used to be hosted alternately in both China and the United States, has moved the program entirely out of China because of the repressive political atmosphere. Another institution has transitioned away from cooperative projects with China to emphasize bolstering the capacity of other countries in their dealings with China.

Many US think-tank scholars have also become concerned that the relationship between Chinese and American scholars has regressed into a one-way street—with Americans providing intelligence to Chinese interlocutors, whose main purpose is to take the information back to their government. Indeed, some Chinese interlocutors arrive in the offices of American think tanks with barely disguised "shopping lists" of questions, which are presumably set by government "taskers" in Beijing. This is a regular occurrence, but it tends to spike when a high-level governmental visit or summit meeting is pending. A related Chinese goal is to transmit Chinese government policy perspectives to American think-tank counterparts.

Since 2010, American (and other foreign) researchers have encountered a progressively more restrictive research environment in China.
One American scholar noted that a previous research project that
involved on-the-ground interviews across many provinces was no longer possible. The registration and information requirements of the
2017 Law on the Management of Foreign NGOs is part of the problem,
she believes, by severely constraining opportunities to conduct joint
projects and research in China. It has also become exceedingly difficult to
arrange interviews with Chinese think-tank scholars and government
officials; many institutional libraries are now off-limits; central-level
archives are inaccessible with provincial and local ones also increasingly
circumscribed; survey research is impossible (unless in partnership
with an approved Chinese counterpart, which is increasingly hard to
find); and other bureaucratic impediments make it increasingly difficult for foreign think-tank researchers to undertake their basic jobs
of researching China. At the same time, Chinese researchers working in the US are able to schedule appointments easily with their
American counterparts and government officials, enjoy open access to
American libraries and government archives, are able to conduct surveys
anywhere, and may travel freely around the United States to do field
work.

US Think-Tank Centers in China

Only two American think tanks operate real satellite centers in Beijing,
and one does so in Hong Kong. Both Beijing centers are cohosted by,
and located on, the campus of Tsinghua University. One has a robust
program of research by Chinese fellows, brings in people from the think
tank's other centers, has a young ambassador program for Americans and
Chinese, and boasts a "wide open internet." One center uses its facilities
primarily for presentations from the resident fellows and other visitors.
Some talks are open to the public, but most are restricted to faculty
and graduate students. The center's ambitions were originally greater;
for example, to host a set of annual conferences with senior experts and
officials on both sides. However, the Chinese side could not live up to

its end of the bargain, demanding that senior US officials attend while not delivering Chinese officials of equivalent rank.

These two centers have also become caught up within the increasingly strained US-China relationship as well as the tightening political atmosphere inside China. According to one affiliated research fellow, "Connections with the center are a liability because institutions and people can cause you problems if you don't say the right things." At least one of the centers in Greater China has occasionally limited its public programming from addressing sensitive political issues, because it did not want to jeopardize the institution's presence in China and Asia. Yet that think tank's other staffers and fellows have also proved adept at circumventing political restrictions by, in one instance, inviting a well-known Hong Kong activist denied access at one center event to participate in an event at the US headquarters later.

Chinese Outreach to US Think Tanks

Chinese outreach to American think tanks takes several forms, including via embassy and consular officials, via Chinese think-tank scholars, and via representatives of China's state-run media.

Embassy and Consular Officials

Chinese embassy and consular officials meet frequently with many (but not all) of the interviewees. Sometimes their aim is to assess Americans' views on particular issues or offer feedback on particular articles (generally those that are critical of China). In one case, for example, a Chinese official stated that a particular analyst's understanding was "too gloomy," and in another that a scholar "didn't have the correct data." One think-tank scholar noted that Chinese officials use both threats and praise to try to influence her. On the one hand, they took her to lunch and expressed "concern with her mind set" indicating that she "just do[es] not understand the situation." But embassy and Chinese government officials can also be effusive in their praise and offers of assistance, suggesting that she "knows too much about Chinese policy."

Oftentimes officials ask for meetings with think-tank members to transmit messages after important Communist Party or government events. After the annual meeting of China's legislature (the National People's Congress) in 2018, for example, one think-tank analyst was invited to lunch, only to endure an hour-and-a-half lecture on how US media and analysts misunderstood the new change in presidential term limits and Xi's reform efforts. Another was visited by military attachés from the Chinese embassy in an effort to convey China's opposition to the Taiwan Travel Act, US Defense Authorization Act, possible prospects for US Navy ship visits, and submarine sales to Taiwan. In concluding his stern warnings, one attaché warned: "We are no longer weak and can inflict pain on Taiwan if the United States is not careful and does not abide by the Three Communiques."

On other occasions, Chinese embassy officials ask for meetings to warn think tanks against hosting speakers on topics often related to Taiwan, Hong Kong, or Tibet. Several think-tank analysts reported that they or others in their institutions had received calls from senior Chinese embassy officials regarding projects related to the Dalai Lama, in one case stating, "This is very troubling—it will have consequences." As far as the analysts were concerned, however, there turned out to be no consequences. Another received a complaint from the Chinese embassy after the think tank hosted a delegation from Taiwan's Democratic Progressive Party (DPP)—but again there were no discernible consequences. In a separate case, a senior Chinese Ministry of Foreign Affairs official warned that a particular interactive website focusing on Chinese security issues was "anti-China." In response, the think tank invited contributions by a prominent Chinese think-tank scholar: "The content of the website didn't change, but the official didn't complain again." In another instance, the Chinese government withdrew an offer to a US think tank to host foreign minister Wang Yi after that think tank refused to disinvite a Taiwanese speaker for a separate event.

Chinese officials have also requested that US think tanks bar certain scholars or NGO activists from participating in discussions with senior Chinese officials. When Wang Yi spoke at one high-profile Washington think tank, the embassy requested the guest list in advance and then demanded that several individuals—including at least one senior China scholar—be disinvited. The think tank refused. In yet another case involving the director of the National People's Congress Foreign Affairs Committee, Fu Ying, a US think tank was strongly advised to exclude a well-known China specialist as a condition for a meeting going forward. Think-tank analysts report that in most cases, but not all, such requests have been rejected and events continue as planned.

Generally speaking, PRC visitors either steer clear of or limit their contact with think tanks that have strong relations with, or extensive funding from, Taiwan. One analyst who writes extensively on Taiwan and PRC-Taiwan relations finds that Chinese officials typically do not engage with him. At one time, there was a conflict between an event that he was hosting for a Taiwanese official with a significant event that same afternoon hosted by a colleague that featured very prominent Chinese and American officials. The Chinese embassy instructed them to move the Taiwan event, but they refused. Both events took place with no apparent negative repercussions.

Think Tank to Think Tank

As noted above, Chinese officials and think-tank counterparts reach out to American think-tank China specialists for the purposes of collecting information/intelligence and influencing US policy debates. One Chinese scholar reported to an American think-tank analyst that every time an American expert meets with a Chinese interlocutor, a report is written afterward. Another Chinese visitor indicated to a leading Washington think-tank expert that China's foreign ministry has staff dedicated to tracking the activities and publications of about twenty leading American China specialists.

Any number of Chinese think tanks sponsor meetings and conferences in China and the United States with American counterparts. In some instances, the Chinese partners are well-known government entities. The China Institutes of Contemporary International Relations (CICIR) and the University of International Relations, both of which have links to the Ministry of State Security (MSS), host conferences on US-China relations and Track 2 dialogues. So do the foreign ministry–affiliated China Institute of International Studies, Chinese People's Institute for Foreign Affairs, and China Foreign Affairs University. The Charhar Institute is also involved in such activities, although its institutional linkages are unclear.

More recently, Chinese think tanks professing to be independent from direct government control (despite being required to register formally with a government entity) have begun to actively engage US counterparts. The think tank Intellisia is one such organization that has sponsored dialogues with US scholars. The Center for China and Globalization (CCG), with more than a hundred researchers and staff, is another. According to several US think-tank analysts, CCG's founder and head actively solicits invitations to speak in US think-tank settings. In May 2018, however, Senator Marco Rubio publicly questioned why the CCG head's CCP affiliation—most particularly his work with the CCP's United Front Work Department as a standing director of the China Overseas Friendship Association—was not publicized. A subsequent article in *Foreign Policy* about the Rubio letter—which did not include the fact that the US think tank had planned to mention the CCG head's CCP affiliation at the event itself—was published and deterred the Chinese scholar from speaking at the event. He later appeared, however, at another US think tank event without his government affiliation noted and without provoking attention from any member of Congress.[2] For such Chinese think tanks, organizing conferences can give them a significant boost in prestige at home. One Chinese think-tank director informed an American think-tank analyst that he received several hundred thousand dollars from the hosting university's party secretary as a bonus for bringing such a prestigious delegation of Western China watchers to China.

Finally, a group of several senior Chinese government officials and think-tank scholars from different institutions has emerged as an important generator of China-US think-tank cooperation. This group includes such well-known figures as Fu Ying (director of the NPC's Foreign Affairs Committee), Wang Jisi (director of Peking University's Institute of International and Strategic Studies), Yuan Peng (president of CICIR), and Wang Wen (executive dean of the Chongyang Institute for Financial Studies at Renmin University), who are all well funded and able to pay for the activities of the Chinese side, as well as travel and hotel stays for Americans who participate in their projects in China.

Fu Ying emerges as the senior figure in a growing number of US-China interactions. According to several think-tank analysts, she works hard to structure projects in ways that ensure the best possible outcome from the Chinese perspective. This includes, for example, partnering primarily—although not solely—with scholars who are considered to be more favorably disposed to the Chinese government perspective and ensuring that those with challenging views are excluded. One analyst noted that former Hong Kong chief executive C. H. Tung's and Fu's relationships with US think-tank scholars and presidents provide them with frequent opportunities to speak before large public audiences at prestigious American venues and to advance an official Chinese narrative while gaining a certain added legitimacy at home.

Fu is also explicit in her desire to cultivate relations with think-tank experts she believes may enter government. Following the election of Donald Trump, she "rushed in to see" one think-tank analyst with ties to the new administration, and a flurry of embassy officials followed. However, when it became evident that said analyst would not be going into the administration, there was no more interest. In addition, at a meeting around a project on US-China relations advanced by Fu, she noted that she hoped some of the people would be entering the government; otherwise it would not prove to have been worth much to have done the project.

Chinese president Xi Jinping has also encouraged Chinese think tanks to "go global"—establishing a presence within the United States and other countries as a way "to advance the Chinese narrative." In 2015, the Institute for China-America Studies (ICAS) set up shop in Washington, DC, as a 501(c)(3) nonprofit organization. ICAS is funded by the Hainan-Nanhai Research Foundation, which receives its seed funding from the National Institute for South China Sea Studies, a Chinese government–supported entity, as well as from the China Institute of the University of Alberta, Nanjing University, and Wuhan University.

The head of ICAS, Hong Nong, retains ties to these institutions. ICAS maintains a small staff of researchers as well as a diverse board of international experts from China, the United States, Canada, Australia, and Indonesia. ICAS projects focus on the central issues of the US-China relationship, including US-China cooperation, maritime security, North Korea, and trade relations. Hong herself focuses on the South China Sea and the Arctic policies of non–Arctic Council member countries, of which China is the largest and most significant. The institute also holds an annual conference.

While President Xi's call to establish think tanks was contemporaneous with the establishment of ICAS, Hong has made it clear that the decision to set up ICAS in Washington came as a result of an effort by her and some of her colleagues both in China and in Canada to understand better how American think tanks operate. She was asked to lead ICAS, and she then selected a board of directors, as well as advisory members. She views the mission of the think tank as being to serve as a bridge in perception between the United States and China. Hong does not want people to view the institute as advancing a Chinese government perspective or as wearing a "Chinese hat," but she believes that in Washington there are too few voices that reflect a Chinese (not necessarily government) perspective. While she acknowledges that there is not much diversity in the nature of the views represented by ICAS—there is no overt criticism of Chinese government policies—she is hopeful that once ICAS gains greater standing, it will be able to attract senior scholars from other institutions with a greater range of views to write for its website.

More recently, Chinese publishing entrepreneur Zhou Zhixing has established the US-China New Perspectives Foundation, with offices in both Los Angeles and Washington, DC. As of yet, these offices have no track record of activities or publications. It is likely that more such think tanks initiated with or without formal Chinese government support will follow in the United States.

Think-Tank Funding

Different US think tanks have different funding models. At least one type (federally funded research and development centers) is funded entirely by the US government, while several others accept some US government funding, as well as money from other governments on a contracted work basis. Three think tanks interviewed accept no US or other government funding: One is funded entirely by central operating funds from an endowment, while two others rely on a mix of foundation and private support. One think tank's work is funded entirely by foundations. Most interviewees allow Chinese funders to pay for travel and meeting costs to Beijing for conferences, while a few categorically do not—either because of regulations or on the principle of conflict of interest.

At least one think tank differentiates between funding that is dedicated to its work in Washington and that which supports its center in China. For the center in China, a US-based scholar has raised funds from the China Development Bank, Huawei Corporation, and private entrepreneurs from Hong Kong. This same think tank has a "China Council" of donors (including Chinese Americans, but no Chinese nationals) that supports the think tank's activities. Some US institutions refuse to accept funds from China-based commercial entities, although they are occasionally willing to accept donations from these entities' US-based subsidiaries. Other think tanks, however, accept funds from Chinese corporations and individual businesspeople. One has taken money from Alibaba America for a particular event celebrating the fifteenth anniversary of accession to the World Trade Organization; another has taken money from the Chinese real estate firm Vanke for a project on the environment. A Chinese businessman, Fu Chen, supports work at one China center that also has several prominent Chinese businesspersons on its board. One has an advisory council with Chinese Americans, and yet another think tank is building an advisory council that will include Chinese, but only those who have become American citizens. (This analyst is also considering accepting private Chinese money but not money from Chinese state-owned enterprises.)

C. H. Tung and his China-US Exchange Foundation (CUSEF) have emerged as a leading funding source for several think tanks, providing financial assistance for a variety of projects ranging from supporting book research and writing to funding collaborative projects and promoting exchanges. CUSEF's work in this area extends back to the mid-1990s. (For more on CUSEF, see the chapter on universities in this volume.) The interviewees differ, however, in their assessments of whether CUSEF funding reflects direct linkages with Beijing. As one analyst noted, "C. H. is a special figure because he is half Hong Kong and half PRC." Another commented that he currently has the potential to undertake a joint project with C. H. Tung and will "probably do it for the money and the contact." Another has accepted funds for work on cultural exchange and climate change, while yet another is far more circumspect, describing Tung as an "open united front agent" in his capacity as vice chair of the Chinese People's Political Consultative Congress. Many of the partnerships CUSEF establishes in conjunction with US think tanks represent efforts to find common ground, particularly in line with PRC initiatives and policies, for example: the New Model of Major Power Relationship Research Project 2014, the Taiwan Arms Sales Research Project 2014, and the Pacific Community Initiative.

CUSEF also funds a number of annual exchange programs, including for members of Congress; state and local officials; and historically black colleges and universities; as well as several journalist delegations, including one for students of journalism. CUSEF often partners with the Center for American Progress, the American Foreign Policy Council, and the East-West Institute. However, each partnership is different. The Center for American Progress, for example, pays its own way in its work with CUSEF. CUSEF also funds projects with think-tank analysts who are not China scholars, such as a project on US-China relations in the Arctic. One think-tank analyst who was involved in the CUSEF-funded Creating a Pacific Community project became uncomfortable with the overall orientation of the project and dropped out.

C. H. Tung is personally proactive, often visiting the United States and meeting with think-tank experts. On one occasion, he encouraged an American scholar to write an article together with a noted Chinese scholar on the South China Sea. He also offered to establish a massive program with one institute in which the think tank would train Chinese Party School officials on free-market economics (the idea was eventually rejected by the think tank). In addition, CUSEF has funded the publication of at least two books in which US analysts were involved. In both cases, the analysts state that Tung was "hands-off" in the process. Yet, in another instance, when a US scholar approached the CUSEF for possible funding of a major book on US-China relations, the foundation insisted on two conditions: that half of the contributors be Chinese scholars, and that the foundation have the right to review the manuscript prior to publication. The American scholar in question refused these conditions and looked elsewhere for support.

The Taipei Economic and Cultural Representation Office (TECRO), Taiwan's diplomatic mission in Washington, DC, also supports work at several think tanks. In rare cases—because one usually excludes the other—US think tanks end up accepting funds from both Taiwanese and mainland Chinese sources.

Visa Access

Most American scholars consider travel to China an important element of their ability to do their job—attending conferences, participating in delegations, and undertaking independent research. Given this imperative, the issue of visa access is a central one. While most analysts receive single-entry professional exchange (F) visas, a few routinely receive one-year multiple-entry F visas, while some have ten-year tourist (L) visas. Others receive double-entry visas, if proof of specific invitations is produced. One US think-tank scholar, a Chinese national, travels to China on a Chinese passport. While ten-year multiple-entry tourist visas are, of course, optimal, there is also a serious potential downside; namely, that they are for "tourism," and, according to Chinese law, professional activities are not permitted. One senior scholar who holds a ten-year tourist visa was recently visited and interrogated at his hotel in Beijing after several days of meetings with Chinese think tanks and universities.

Several think-tank analysts expressed the opinion that Chinese officials are now paying more attention to the writings of American think-tank analysts—not only through books, articles, and op-eds, but also social media. They do this not only to become familiar with changing views but also to catalog who is supportive and who is critical of China's policies. One scholar believes that, as a result of a comment posted on

Twitter, he was required to go to the Chinese embassy for an interview before being granted a visa. This had never happened in his previous decades of China-related travel. In another instance, Beijing attempted to enforce its sovereignty claims through the visa process. A visa was initially denied because an American scholar had stated that "Hong Kong" and "Taiwan" were places he had previously visited, instead of "Hong Kong SAR," and "Taiwan, China." Most of the scholars interviewed believe that the process of gaining a visa has become much more politicized and difficult in the past year or two, with much more scrutiny given to an applicant's political views. Among those interviewed, only one think-tank scholar reported actually being denied a visa. (However, there have been reports of other think-tank analysts being rejected who are reluctant to go public about their denials.) In addition, most of those interviewed observed that the Chinese embassy now often issues visas the day before or even the morning of departure, making the visa process laborious and nerve-racking.

Two interviewees reported that companies that specialize in expediting visa applications have indicated that their respective think tanks are on a blacklist that makes obtaining visas problematic. In one case, an interviewee related a case in which a junior researcher was told not to list the think tank as her place of employment on her visa application or it might be rejected. (To avoid this scenario, the senior researcher reached out to a Chinese official to pave the way, and the visa was issued.) In another instance, a visa expediter was banned from doing business with the Chinese embassy after it informed a think tank that it had landed on a list making it difficult to get visas.

A senior Chinese official told one think-tank analyst that responsibility for reviewing visa requests has shifted from the Ministry of Foreign Affairs to the Ministry of Public Security, thus creating many delays and difficulties. One US think-tank scholar reported that he not only has been advised on a number of occasions not to even apply for a visa but also has had a planned invitation to a conference hosted by an American company revoked because the foreign ministry told the company not to invite him. Others have been granted visas only for "personal" trips, with the proviso that they do no public speaking nor meet with anyone out-side of family members or cultural figures.

Think-tank scholars report that on several occasions, when one member of a delegation has been in danger of not receiving a visa (or not receiving it in time), reaching out to the Chinese embassy or consular officials (in one case threatening to cancel the delegation) has resulted in a favorable disposition. Two think tanks now routinely reach out to Chinese officials before submitting applications in order to pave the way. Nonetheless, a few think-tank analysts are concerned about being beholden to the embassy or the consulate and the shadow such dependency casts on their ability to continue their work. One analyst indicated that although he is asked to help other members of the think tank with their visa issues, he does not want to be in debt to the embassy and therefore does not offer to help proactively.

Chinese Media and Think Tanks

The Chinese media offer both opportunities and pitfalls to American think-tank analysts. A significant part of a think-tank analyst's job is to influence official and public opinion—and the media, whether Chinese or Western, is an essential part of that process. Think-tank analysts are under no illusion, however, that the Chinese media can be trusted to present their ideas as they are delivered. As one interviewee underscored, "The desire of Chinese media is to make Americans see things the Chinese way—in a positive and beneficial light—and to present positive American views to the Chinese public. You have to be prepared that the Chinese media will have leading questions and know that they will not include critical things." One senior US scholar has had multiple experiences of censorship, and one case of fabricated quotations, by Chinese newspapers. It is also apparent that Chinese journalists increasingly flood public events put on by US think tanks in Washington, using the events as press conferences and to pose leading questions. While Western reporters are not immune to this type of behavior, the Chinese media undertake such distortions in a far more systematic manner, with a pointed political agenda that is usually determined by the government's current political "line."

With this in mind, US think-tank analysts have developed a varied set of approaches to their interactions with the Chinese media. Some see the Chinese media as an opportunity to get their views across to the Chinese public, even though, as one think-tank member acknowledges, he knows he may be censored in "inappropriate ways." Another stated that despite the obvious biases, he still gives a lot of interviews—to CCTV, CGTN, Xinhua, *People's Daily*, and the Shanghai Media Group, among them. At least one claims that while he does frequent CGTN interviews, he has never been censored.

Several US think-tank scholars indicate that they keep track of their interviews, and if they are misquoted, they stop speaking to that journalist. One notes that he refuses to do interviews on sensitive political issues, such as party congresses. Another indicates he will only do live television as a hedge against being censored, while another indicates he will only be interviewed in written email form. Two analysts refuse to give interviews to Chinese media at all, with the exception of those that occur in the immediate aftermath of a public talk when an analyst is approached by Chinese journalists. In one case, an analyst reported that Xinhua conducted an in-person background interview after she refused to write an op-ed, but she was willing to share her views (which were negative). Xinhua then drafted a full, positive-sounding op-ed in her name, which they planned to publish without her approval. She successfully blocked it, and her institute now has a blanket ban on interviews with the Chinese press unless there is a special reason. This is intended to send a message that they do not believe the Chinese media can be trusted.

The opportunity to earn money through interviews was mentioned by one scholar. She noted that CGTN pays $150 per interview. The network warned her, however, that if she was too critical of the Chinese government, she would not be invited back. CGTN also indicated that she should be "more like" another think-tank analyst who had become a regular on CGTN.

Writing and Publishing in China

The majority of the think-tank analysts who have been interviewed for this chapter have refused to write op-eds for Chinese newspapers, with several stating that they have had bad experiences in which content has been censored. One scholar reports several instances of pieces being commissioned by the *Global Times*, only to have his piece spiked after submission because of its controversial content. Others, however, have written for Chinese publications and have not experienced any such issues. Several analysts noted that they have heard that their articles and reports have been translated into Chinese in *neibu* (internal circulation) channels for consumption by think tanks and government officials. One interviewee commented that if what she writes is positive, it is published openly; if it is critical, it is only published internally.

A number of interviewees also reported that their work had been improperly published on Chinese websites. Sohu has taken think-tank reports and put them online without permission; one analyst forced the company to take them down from the web. Another scholar reported that a Chinese think tank at one point claimed she was one of its fellows and posted bogus content on its website that it alleged she had written.

While some of the think-tank scholars interviewed have had their books translated into Chinese by mainland presses, most have not. A growing number do not try, recognizing that significant parts of their books would never make it past the censors. When informed privately by the translator of her book that large portions were being excised, one scholar halted the Chinese publication process. Another scholar battled for two years with the Chinese publisher after the contract had been signed between the Western and Chinese publishers. The State Press and Publishing Administration demanded more than seventy deletions, finally settling on five with the agreement of the scholar. In the end, however, the Chinese publisher informed the scholar's publisher that the book could not proceed to publication because of "unfriendly remarks" the scholar had been making in the media. Most US scholars simply do not bother with mainland publishers and look for publication opportunities in Taiwan or Hong Kong. Several US scholars believe that there are pirated copies of their books or at least partially translated copies available within China. At least one scholar found that a search on Baidu yielded half of her most recent book online.

Not all scholars are willing to sacrifice the opportunity to be published in China. One analyst reported that a senior non-China expert at their think tank permitted his book to be published in China, even though several pages had been mistranslated and the editors had actually created some new passages that did not exist anywhere in the original text. Even the title and subtitle of the book, as well as the author's own professional title, were incorrectly identified.

Public Voice

The issue of censorship also arises in the context of how think-tank analysts present their own views publicly, especially when in China. On the whole, think-tank scholars show determination to raise sensitive topics and be forthright in presenting their views. But it is an understandable human instinct to want to be polite and diplomatic while still conveying one's own views honestly. As one scholar, who also does a lot of consulting, noted, "Access to China is my livelihood." At the same time, he argues, "I never say anything contrary to my views, but I write in a way that is less shrill."

Another scholar noted, "I don't self-censor, but there is no need to launch a polemic every day of the week. . . . Polemics get your visa cut off. China's greatest power is the power of visa control." A third commented, "I don't censor the substance, but I may modulate what I say." He argued that he sometimes indulges the sensibilities of the PRC in order to get his deeper point across. As another analyst noted, "I avoid sensationalizing. I am willing to be critical, but I try not to make attacks on Xi." And different interviewees distinguish between writing and speaking: "I do not compromise on writing, but I am cautious in interviews: I will say the same message but indirectly, not confrontationally." One analyst said, "I make sure that if I go into battle, I do so thoughtfully, not accidentally." She tries to be very strategic about the messages that she sends and tries not to weigh in on every small issue or bluntly charge, "You are wrong!" In a similar vein, one other scholar says he often uses an interrogatory, rather than accusatory, approach when raising challenging issues, such as human rights.

The knowledge that what an analyst says publicly reflects not only on the individual but also on the analyst's institution also shapes at least one scholar's thinking: "There is a conflict between protecting your institute and speaking truthfully. Whether it is over access or money. Sometimes I put the positive first—and then say . . . 'but some people say.' I might not start right off with Xi Jinping—I might be more indirect. In public meetings, there is a tacit understanding that you will not be super critical of China." Another suggests that it is "very hard not to subconsciously self-censor." This person indicated that when their institute does projects on counterterrorism in the Middle East or Southeast Asia, they are very careful about discussing China's restive region of Xinjiang, where up to one million Uighurs are presently believed to be in reeducation camps. In general, they do not take on projects concerning Taiwan or Xinjiang.

Interviewees expressed a deep sensitivity around the issue of Taiwan and how to refer to the island and its officials. One analyst observed that in an invitation, his institute would not identify Taiwan's representative to the United States as an "ambassador," but that during the event, he would indeed orally introduce the official as the "ambassador." Or as another scholar noted, "I am tactful but keep to my original point of view. I don't change the substance. On Taiwan, in private conversations, I use President Tsai—but I also maintain neutrality in public to ensure that is acceptable to Taiwan and the PRC."

Two analysts stated that they do not self-censor "at all." They understand the temptation, but they try to write and say in public exactly what they would in private.

Pressure from Think-Tank Boards or Outside Influencers

Interaction between think-tank analysts and the members of their institutions' boards of trustees varies significantly. Some engage frequently,

socialize, and consult on China-related issues, while others have virtually no contact. Only three interviewees reported incidents of attempted
interference. In one case, a prominent former board member complained
to the head of the think tank about an article that was "too tough" on
China. However, no pressure, besides the obviously intimidating impact
of having a piece of writing singled out by an overseer, was brought to
bear on the scholar. In another case, a board member tried to pressure a
think-tank president to avoid hosting the Dalai Lama but failed. A third
instance involved the Hong Kong political activist discussed earlier (in
the chapter on US think-tank centers in China). The tendency can also
work in the other direction. One scholar indicated that his board is very
involved and has lately become tougher on China in recent years, focusing on "how do we still counter China, yet still engage."

Chinese Nationals in US Think Tanks

American think-tank analysts differ in their assessment of the risks and
rewards for hosting Chinese scholars as visiting fellows or employing
Chinese nationals on staff, with most suggesting that it is better to have
them inside the think tanks to understand how they are thinking and
working. One analyst said he "assumed some or all would be interrogated" when they returned to China. "RAND," he said, "should be worried." One researcher noted that she is "careful to keep Chinese nationals
from attending sensitive meetings featuring US officials or military officers" but otherwise welcomes them to events.

Only one Washington think tank hosts Chinese scholars on a regular and continuous basis (although Washington-based universities do so
more often), including them in programming and most meetings, even
when funded by a Chinese host institution. Scholars at this institution
view them as valuable for gaining insights and for training purposes.
Another think-tank analyst who has hosted visiting fellows from China
pointed out that two prominent Chinese scholars who spent time at
their institution went back and wrote "important papers." Still, some
expressed concern over all the "bright young Chinese showing up on
Mass [Massachusetts] Ave." and the potential that they might have for

reporting back to Beijing. The scholar noted that think tanks want young people to "plow through the Chinese literature," and this means hiring Chinese nationals, Chinese Americans, or Taiwanese because of their language abilities. Some analysts expressed concerns that think-tank analysts who are of Chinese ethnicity (either nationals or American citizens) may face special pressures from the imputation that as ethnic Chinese, they are susceptible to Chinese influence and control.

Broader Concerns

Think-tank analysts voiced a range of concerns around the issue of Chinese influence–seeking activities in the United States. One is the deliberate effort to manage US perceptions and to frame issues in ways that are favorable to the Chinese Communist Party. As one analyst noted, "This requires pushback, which is tough work." While many believed that they could adequately defend themselves against efforts to influence them, noting as one did that "the general capacity of US society to push back is not bad," they worried about their colleagues who were not knowledgeable China experts and might therefore be more easily deceived. For example, one scholar pointed out that with US-China cooperation, the incentive is to come up with shared values and ideas. He noted that in the case of the Sanya Initiative (the US-China dialogue featuring retired military officers from both sides), he has had to "talk them [the American participants] off the ledge; they think they are being tough, but they are mistaken." This same analyst sees the American media as complicit in echoing Chinese perspectives, noting that when Xi Jinping delivered his speech in Davos in January 2017, few reporters understood that the Chinese were in the midst of a major propaganda campaign to promote Globalization 2.0. He also suggests that there is "de facto self-censorship" of entire areas of scholarship: human rights for one. Another analyst noted that outside of the National Endowment for Democracy, she does not see much foundation interest in normal discourse in this issue either.

One scholar worried about growing Chinese control over all areas of US-Chinese interaction: "The Chinese are following people, bugging our hotel rooms. There is imbalanced control that serves CCP interests, not ours. There is lack of serious training by the US side on how to deal with Chinese influence." The potential for Chinese money to give China leverage over American think tanks also provoked a degree of anxiety. Several scholars expressed concern over funding issues, noting that reliance on a single funder with an agenda makes scholars vulnerable. In addition, one scholar worried that the amount of money China is spending to promote its views, whether through think-tank cooperation or the Chinese media (such as CGTN paying for its interviews) means that China will ultimately be able to "buy its way in."

A number of analysts believed that the involvement of the US government in these issues will only make things more contentious. There is concern that Washington will overreact. As one analyst noted, there is a type of "binarism in Washington, in which you must be 'for or against' China; you are either friendly to China or producing stuff that says China is evil." This scholar, along with several others, raised the issue of the rise of anti-China sentiments, such as the "yellow peril" and McCarthyism, and expressed concern about Chinese Americans and anyone who has interests with China coming under attack. One analyst mentioned the Committee of 100, a collection of prominent Chinese Americans, as being particularly vulnerable to unfair attack.

Another analyst noted that we need "a granular view on issues of sharp power." He pointed in particular to Confucius Institutes, arguing that he would not accept Confucius Institute–sponsored research, but was fine with language training, although it would be better to get them off campuses. He laughed at the idea that they were "effective instruments of Chinese propaganda." Along these lines, a few individuals indicated that they were less concerned about Chinese influence in the social sciences and more concerned about reports that Chinese students and postdocs in scientific research labs bring restricted technologies back to China.

Finally, there were calls from some analysts for far more reciprocity than currently exists. These analysts felt that the playing field between the two countries was out of balance and argued that there should be a much stronger dose of reciprocity and "hardball" in US-China exchanges, arguing that the American side should curtail or cut off contacts until Chinese institutions were willing to operate at a level of openness similar to that found in their American counterparts.

Conclusion and Recommendations

American think-tank scholars working on China face an increasingly challenging research environment. But in this challenge, they are hardly unique. Members of the media and the civil society/NGO world also share similar, even more daunting, challenges. The process for obtaining visas has become more onerous; the quality of engagement with Chinese counterparts has declined and become more difficult; and opportunities to do field-based research, as well as archival work, have diminished. Track 2 dialogues are viewed with increasing skepticism as to their value by more and more US scholars and policy specialists, who find their Chinese colleagues ever more unable or unwilling to share their perspectives in an open and meaningful manner. Many think-tank analysts are responding by limiting their Track 2 efforts and changing the way they conduct their research.

At the same time, a small but growing group of well-funded Chinese scholars and officials are proactively seeking to shape the American narrative and American views of China. They are doing so by supporting and funding joint projects with US partners in ways that reflect Chinese government priorities, but they give them the opportunity to choose and work with only those American scholars viewed by China as sympathetic to China's goals. To date, these efforts do not appear to have influenced the US debate over China in a significant manner, but it is important to be aware of the money and effort being thrown at the endeavor.

Chinese funding of American think tanks remains limited. C. H. Tung, through his China-US Exchange Foundation, is to date the most common source of financial support, although most report his funding as "hands-off." A few Chinese companies have also bankrolled a limited number of American think-tank activities. However, American think tanks with centers in China have actively engaged in fund-raising from mainland Chinese sources. With only a few exceptions, American think-tank analysts do not foresee that Chinese money will become a significant factor in their work at home any time soon, although because of endemic funding shortages at most nonprofits, worries about reliance on Chinese money are not unfounded.

Chinese media relentlessly solicit American think-tank scholars' opinions for consumption within both the United States and China. At least one outlet pays participants for their time and makes it clear that criticism of China is unwelcome. Censorship of written work is common, even expected, so that few interviewees expect to have their books published in China. American think-tank analysts appear most annoyed when their work is illegally or incorrectly published on Chinese websites. In most instances, they seek to have the work taken down from the web.

American think-tank analysts have a highly developed understanding of Chinese efforts to influence their views—whether in the form of heavy-handed criticism from the Chinese embassy for an article or for a proposed meeting with someone like the Dalai Lama or a Hong Kong dissident; or via more subtle efforts that arise through joint projects funded by Chinese partners. To the latter point, all interviewees for this study indicated that they refuse to be pressured into changing their practices. Some think-tank scholars acknowledge that they try to be diplomatic in their public discourse on China—but insist that they do not change their overall message, only their tone or choice of wording. Some argue that they save their tough language to deliver the most important messages. But some also admit to acceding to Chinese demands on how to present Taiwanese officials in public settings—such as in the announcements of a meeting on the think tank's website—but then adopting the Taiwanese preference during the meeting itself. The general view—although not shared by all—was that seeking to avoid unnecessarily insulting or upsetting the Chinese is the better strategy. But most agreed that the arena of acceptable parlance was shrinking and that pressures were growing.

As an antidote, the American think-tank community should understand that its position is one with significant leverage. Chinese officials and scholars seek to use think tanks as venues for visiting Chinese officials, as legitimating partners for Chinese-supported research projects that will influence the American narrative, and as important sources of information concerning the changing US political landscape. The American scholars should celebrate their principles of independence, use the leverage their institutional frameworks provide to resist incursion, and constructively push for greater reciprocity. Some specific recommendations follow.

Promote Transparency

- Think tanks should—in partnership with universities—jointly and regularly produce summaries of difficulties in China-related research (access to regions, agencies, persons, visas, etc.) and make these available to each other and to US officials. The latter, in turn, should be mindful of the reciprocal nature of think-tank work and how the inability of American scholars to secure meetings with Chinese officials and scholars when Chinese scholars are afforded such privileges is harmful to the stability of the overall relationship.
- Think tanks should publicly disclose the source of funding for events, publications, and other activities. If think-tank leaders elect to solicit funds from Hong Kong or mainland Chinese sources, they should be transparent about from where the money came and how it is being used, to ensure that there is no opportunity for the Chinese funder to harmfully affect the research agenda or outcome.

Promote Integrity

- A code of conduct should be worked out among US think tanks—perhaps in conjunction with American universities' China studies centers—to establish "dos and don'ts" in their exchanges with Chinese institutions. Once this is worked out among American institutions, then counterparts in other democratic countries should also be approached with an eye toward establishing multilateral codes of conduct.

Promote Reciprocity

- US think-tank representatives—the presidents and senior China scholars—should arrange a meeting with the Chinese ambassador to express their collective perspectives on these issues and call for changes. Such a meeting could be usefully coupled with a jointly signed letter of concern by directors of all major US think tanks.

- If any member of any think-tank delegation is denied a visa, the delegation should cancel the trip. It sends a profoundly wrong signal to proceed, if China is able to control the composition of a delegation. The think tank should also consider a moratorium on Chinese officials visiting or speaking at the think tank until the visa issues are resolved. The same principle may be applied to Chinese think tanks that refuse to receive American scholars for visits. In such cases, US think tanks should seriously consider not hosting residential stays for Chinese visiting scholars from institutions that do not offer parallel opportunities for American scholars in China. (At present, only the Chinese Academy of Social Sciences and the Shanghai Institute of International Studies permit foreign scholars in residence.)

- The US government should not unilaterally grant Chinese think-tank or university scholars ten-year visas, as it has been doing, without exacting across-the-board reciprocal treatment for US think-tank and university scholars. At the same time, the US government should also advocate consistently on behalf of US think-tank and university scholars who have been barred from visiting China.

Two core values cut across all of our concerns: *freedom of speech* and *reciprocity*. As a democratic society, we should tolerate *no* infringements—overt or covert—on our freedom of speech and freedom of analysis concerning China. A "leveling of the playing field" in terms of upholding the principles and practicalities of reciprocity in our exchanges with Chinese counterparts is needed, because it is an essential part of making the relationship both more equitable and reciprocal, and more stable and thus durable.

CHAPTER SIX

Media

When the Xinhua News Agency leased a massive sign in Times Square in 2011 and then agreed to a twenty-year lease for a new US headquarters on the top floor of a Broadway skyscraper, it was clear that, as analyst He Qinglian put it, "The Chinese have arrived."[1] Xinhua's foray into Manhattan was followed by a website of the *People's Daily*, the mouthpiece of the Communist Party, which set up shop in the Empire State Building.[2]

At a time when Western media outlets are challenged by the internet and weakened by uncertain business models, China's rise as a major player in the media landscape around the globe has become all the more worthy of attention. The Chinese government's campaign to "grab the right to speak" from Western media outlets and independent Chinese voices, which it accuses of distorting news about China and sullying China's image, has come with a rapid expansion of China's English-language media operations, a concerted campaign to control overseas Chinese-language media, and ongoing efforts to block attempts by Western media to contend inside China. Xinhua News Agency journalist Xiong Min summed up the motivation for China's new campaign in 2010. "The right to speak in the world is not distributed equally," she wrote. "Eighty percent of the information is monopolized by Western media."[3] It was time, she said, to end that monopoly by means of what China has called the Grand Overseas Propaganda Campaign (大外宣).

China refers to its attempt to control the narrative about China as a war, a *huayuzhan* (话语站) or a discourse war.

Since coming to power, President Xi Jinping has overseen the intensification of this external propaganda blitz, which was launched in 2007 by former party general secretary Hu Jintao. As Xi told the November 2014 Foreign Affairs Work Conference in Beijing: "We should increase China's soft power, give a good Chinese narrative, and better communicate China's messages to the world."[4] This is the task CCP propagandists have now undertaken in an increasingly fulsome way. On February 19, 2016, Xi visited the headquarters of the *People's Daily*, Xinhua News Agency, and China Central Television (CCTV), where he again stressed the importance of external propaganda work.[5] At the August 2018 National Meeting on Ideology and Propaganda, Xi stated: "To present good images, we should improve our international communication capability, tell China's stories well, disseminate China's voice, show an authentic and comprehensive China to the world, and raise the country's soft power and the influence of Chinese culture."[6] External propaganda work has long been an important foreign policy instrument for the Chinese Communist Party and the People's Republic of China, but under Xi it has become a top priority of China's party-state.

State Media

China's Communist Party and government have a long history of trying to influence international opinion. Over the years, the themes of its external propaganda have varied substantially—usually in parallel with dramatic fluctuations in its own domestic political campaigns (运动) and related slogans (口号), shifts in ideology (意识形态), meta propaganda narratives (提法), and substantive elements in China's diplomacy (外交). The shifts in Beijing's propaganda lines (宣传路线) throughout PRC history have been dizzying, but they are always important to follow as indicators of the country's direction.

During the 1950s, Communist China used organizations such as the China News Service (CNS), a successor to the party's International News Agency (founded in 1938), to appeal to overseas Chinese for support of the new revolution. The party placed this news service under the State Council's Overseas Chinese Affairs Office. Other propaganda campaigns targeted allies in the Western world, such as black nationalist figures from the United States like Robert Williams, who were given airtime on shortwave broadcasts from Beijing, and a few Western writers and journalists, like Edgar Snow, Felix Greene, and William Hinton, who were offered rare, and sometimes lucrative, peeks behind the Bamboo Curtain.

During the Cultural Revolution, from 1966 to 1976, Beijing's propaganda outreach to overseas Chinese slowed, as the party persecuted those in China with foreign ties. But following the arrest of the Gang of Four in 1976 and the economic reform program led by Deng Xiaoping in the early 1980s, the party once again directly engaged with the overseas Chinese community as well as with mainstream Western society and media, appealing to all comers to help China modernize. In 1980, the party formed the External Propaganda Group (对外宣传小组) and placed it under the Propaganda Department of the CCP Central Committee. Zhu Muzhi, the former chief of the Xinhua News Agency and a vice minister of propaganda, was its first head. In 1991, the group was transferred to the State Council, where it was still internally referred to as the External Propaganda Group. For foreign consumption, however, it was called the State Council Information Office.

As the reform period began and the Cultural Revolution ended, Beijing added to its stable of foreign-facing propaganda publications—such as *Beijing Review*, *China Reconstructs*, and *China Pictorial*—by starting or reopening more than twenty periodicals, including the English-language *China Daily*, the overseas edition of the *People's Daily*, the overseas edition of *Outlook* (望), and the *Voice of China* (华声报). The party also resumed publishing material for overseas Chinese. During the Cultural Revolution, the number of magazines targeting overseas Chinese had shrunk to ten, whereas by the end of the 1980s it surpassed 130. Before 1982, the state-run Xinhua News Agency had focused almost solely on providing news to domestic Chinese clients. In 1983, however, it also began sending news to international clients. The China News Service, which had suspended operations during the Cultural Revolution, also resumed work, sending hundreds of stories a day to overseas Chinese-language media. Today the CNS employs more than two thousand people worldwide, working out of forty-six bureaus. The party directed its media outlets in their overseas work to support socialism with Chinese characteristics, push the policies of reform and opening up, and oppose hegemonism—or, in other words, fight against Western ideological control.

In the run-up to the 2008 Beijing Olympics, China's propaganda agencies redoubled their efforts to "grab the right to speak," or gain "discourse power" (话语权). The worldwide torch-lighting ceremony touched off free-Tibet rallies and other human-rights protests that angered Chinese authorities and some Chinese as well. An anti-CNN movement began in China, alleging that Western media outlets were distorting "China's story." This was the genesis for what has come to be known as the Grand Overseas Propaganda Campaign, first promoted by the administration of party chief Hu Jintao and Premier Wen Jiabao. The *International Herald Leader*, a publication of the Xinhua News Agency, reported in 2009 that foreign propaganda work had been elevated by the party to a "systematic, strategic position," the goal of which was to "grab back the right to speak, and improve China's international image."[7] Reports that had first surfaced in Hong Kong's *South China Morning Post* in 2009 that China had earmarked $7 billion for the campaign were reprinted in the Chinese media, most notably in the March 14 edition of *Phoenix Weekly*.[8]

The Grand Overseas Propaganda Campaign has been grand. Chinese sources report hundreds of millions of dollars being spent on a multitude of projects designed to bolster China's image. The expansion of the Xinhua News Agency is but one example. From 120, the number of Xinhua bureaus around the world has now grown to more than 200, and its client base has expanded to more than 1,450.[9] What is more, it now reports in seven languages and competes directly with all the major wire services of the world. In the United States, Xinhua doubled the number of bureaus, adding Chicago, Houston, and San Francisco to its original footprint in Washington, New York, and Los Angeles. Xinhua, like other state-owned Chinese media outlets, also began hiring local talent, and in 2009 it began a TV broadcast in English.

As part of this vigorous propaganda campaign, the party has sought to turn China Central Television into a global competitor to CNN. CCTV was already airing in America as of 2004, when it cooperated with EchoStar, America's second-largest satellite TV company, to launch the Chinese "Great Wall Platform" package, including twelve Mandarin channels, two Cantonese channels, one Hokkien channel, and one English channel. That same year, Rupert Murdoch's News Group helped CCTV place programming on Time Warner and NewsCorp's US television network. CCTV also expanded its offerings in the United States, expanding its bureau in Washington and hiring American reporters too. By 2012, CCTV, recently renamed the China Global Television Network (CGTN), was broadcasting in seven languages. Its programs for American audiences regularly feature personalities from Russia's state-funded propaganda outlet, RT, which, like CGTN, was recently required to register as a foreign agent; RT, in turn, regularly features CGTN personalities.

China Radio International (CRI) was also given a foreign platform. Decades ago, the Beijing-based propaganda outlet relied solely on short-wave broadcasts to beam China's message to the world, but in the late 2000s it began leasing local stations around the globe and across the United States that it supplied with content made in Beijing. CRI has used a US-based company through which it leases stations. That firm is EDI Media Inc. (鷹龍傳媒有限公司), which also owns other media properties that toe Beijing's line: G&E TV, G&E Studio Network, and EDI City Newsweek (城市新聞週刊).[10] A CRI subsidiary in China, Guoguang Century Media, holds a majority stake in G&E Studio.[11] When it comes to reporting on mainland China, the content of all of EDI's outlets mirrors that of China's state-owned media.

China's state-run media have proved to be nimble in accomplishing Beijing's goal of penetrating US markets. In 2013, the Hong Kong–based Phoenix Satellite TV group, which has close ties to the Chinese state and broadcasts in China, attempted to purchase two major FM stations in Los Angeles that shared the same frequency. One of them, KDAY, covers West LA, while KDEY stretches into Riverside and San Bernardino counties to the east of the city. Greater Los Angeles is home to more than a half million Chinese, the second-biggest concentration next to New York City. But none of the region's Chinese-language radio stations are particularly loyal to Beijing, representing either independent Chinese voices or those supporting the banned religious sect Falun Gong. According to sources close to the deal, Phoenix structured the offer to avoid a US law that limits foreign ownership of US radio stations to 25 percent. In filings with the Federal Communications Commission (FCC), Phoenix was listed as owning 20 percent of the US-based investor RBC, while the remaining 80 percent was owned by an editor at Phoenix who is also a US citizen.[12] Under such a setup, no FCC regulations would have been broken. To be extra sure that the deal would go through, however, advisors to Phoenix convinced the Hong Kong company to seek approval from the Committee on Foreign Investment in the United States (CFIUS), a Treasury Department bureau that monitors foreign investments in the United States on national-security grounds. In a ruling that surprised the potential investors, CFIUS declined to approve the deal, referring it to then president Obama. Sources close to the deal noted that the fact that a Phoenix employee in the United States had pleaded guilty to espionage-related charges did not help Phoenix's case.[13] RBC pulled out of the deal on September 25, 2013.

But the efforts to break into the LA radio market did not end there. In the summer of 2018, a New York firm, H&H Capital Partners, announced that it was buying a Mexican radio station, XEWW, whose signal covers much of Southern California.[14] Sources involved in that deal said that H&H sought to buy a Mexican station in order to avoid scrutiny in the United States. H&H is a New York–based firm led by several individuals who worked as reporters for *Global Times* (环球时报), a state-run newspaper in China. Filings from H&H to the FCC about the deal suggest that Phoenix Satellite TV remains a player in the purchase, as the address that H&H gave for its Los Angeles–based holding company was the same as Phoenix's offices in LA.[15] H&H's attempt to buy XEWW to broadcast into the United States has been challenged at the FCC by a Chinese-language radio station linked to Falun Gong.[16]

China's main English-language newspaper, *China Daily*, has also expanded operations in America, starting a North American edition in

2009. In addition, through its marketing arm, China Watch, the paper began distributing English-language content directly as advertising inserts in the *Wall Street Journal*, the *Des Moines Register*, and the *Washington Post*, among other leading US newspapers. Often, it's hard to tell that China Watch's material is an advertisement, as was the case highlighted by President Donald Trump with a China Watch insert in the Sunday *Des Moines Register*—an insert that the president suggested was aimed at undermining political support both for the president and the Republican party.[17] Rough estimates from newspaper executives indicate that *China Daily* pays $250,000 for each insert in major US dailies. In 2009, the *Global Times*, part of the *People's Daily* group, started an English-language newspaper as well.

Chinese investment in the US media market is not limited to the central government. Chinese provincial media firms also have a footprint in the United States. Sky Link TV (天下衛視) is one example. It is fully owned by Guangzhou Media American Co. Ltd. (美國廣視傳媒有限公司), which, in turn, is owned by GZ Television Media (广州影视传媒有限公司), a Chinese state-owned media outlet. Sky Link's story also illustrates the switch from Taiwan money to mainland money in the US Chinese-language media world. Sky Link was established in 1989 by a Taiwanese corporation. In 2009, it was purchased by a private Chinese company; three years later, the Chinese state-owned GZ Television Media bought Sky Link TV, a takeover that was hailed by the PRC's Ministry of Commerce as a key "cultural export" in 2014.[18] When Sky Link TV reports on China, the Sino-US relationship, Taiwan, Hong Kong, and other important issues concerning China, it follows and quite often repeats verbatim the official line from PRC media. Its major business partners include CCTV and Xinhua.

Xi Jinping clearly has an abiding interest in the success of the Grand Overseas Propaganda Campaign. In March 2018, the party announced plans to unite its various individual efforts into a mammoth overseas-facing propaganda organ, known as the Voice of China, by merging the foreign operations of China Global Television Network, China National Radio, and China Radio International.[19] (It is not clear whether the parallel with the Voice of America was intentional.)

Despite all of these efforts, President Xi still appears to be unsatis-fied with the results of the party's "discourse war." In August 2018, the Chinese government announced a shake-up in its propaganda organs, reflecting significant concern at the heart of the party that China was not winning its ideological battle with the West.[20]

Diaspora Media

In the early 1990s, the state-owned China News Service and the Over-seas Chinese Office of the State Council dispatched editorial personnel to the United States to found the Chinese-language TV broadcaster SinoVision and the newspaper *Qiaobao* (侨报). Shanghai's *Xinmin Wanbao* sent staff to the United States to start up an American edition as well. Chinese officials backed this push as part of an effort to fight back against the negative publicity generated by the party's crackdown on protests around Tiananmen Square on June 4, 1989.

The SinoVision/*Qiaobao* story is illustrative of Beijing's push to dom-inate Chinese-language media in the United States. SinoVision, *Qiao-bao*, and the *Sino American Times* (美洲时报) all belong to the Asian Culture and Media Group (美國亞洲文化傳媒集团). Sources in these firms say that the Overseas Chinese Affairs Office of the State Council of PRC (OCAO, 中国国务院侨务办公室) set up the firm in the early 1990s but hid its financial role in these companies.

Most of the major executives and editors in these businesses served either as editors and reporters for the state-run China News Service or as officials for the Overseas Chinese Affairs Office of the State Council.[21] The chairman of the board of the group served as a deputy director of the OCAO. The president of *Qiaobao's* Western edition worked for years as a CNS reporter.[22] In 2015, CNS described the work of the top exec-utives of *Qiaobao's* Eastern edition (美东侨报) as part of the PRC's broader push to strengthen its "soft power" and fight back against "West-ern media hegemony."[23] *Qiaobao* is the sole major newspaper to use sim-plified Chinese characters in an effort to appeal to immigrants from mainland China living abroad. Almost all the news stories in *Qiaobao* about China, the Sino-US relationship, Taiwan, Hong Kong, and other important issues important to China are taken directly from official Chinese media outlets or websites, including CCTV, Xinhua, and the *People's Daily.* Its current editor is I-Der Jeng. In an email communication with *Foreign Policy* magazine, Jeng stated that the paper receives no editorial direction from Beijing.[24] However, like its parent company, numerous reporters and editors on the paper come from China's state-owned press outlets.[25]

The group's main TV outlet is SinoVision. It operates two twenty-four-hour channels (one Chinese and one English language), and it is on the program lineups of cable systems covering about thirty million people in the United States. Like its sister newspapers, SinoVision was established in 1990 as part of the PRC's first push to establish propaganda outlets in the United States. It is headquartered in New York City, with branches in Boston, Washington, Chicago, Los Angeles, San Francisco, and Seattle. According to Wang Aibing (王艾冰), a former executive of SinoVision, starting in 1990, the State Council's Overseas Chinese Affairs Office gave $800,000 a year to SinoVision, ultimately increasing its subsidy to between $2 million and $3 million a year. Wang made this charge in a 2011 letter to the Overseas Chinese Affairs Office alleging widespread corruption at the station.[26] Allegations of corruption and governmental subsidies have not been corroborated.

What is clear, however, is that, like *Qiaobao,* SinoVision's content echoes China's official media. The vast majority of its stories about China, Sino-American relations, Taiwan, Hong Kong, and other important issues for the PRC government are taken directly from official Chinese media outlets or websites, including CCTV, Xinhua, and the *People's Daily.* In an essay, *Qiaobao's* Eastern Group president, You Jiang, defended his paper's support of the PRC's agenda by saying that it stemmed not from Beijing's direction but from demands from pro-PRC immigrants in the United States.[27]

Forays such as these by PRC organizations to assert direct control over Chinese-language media in the United States sparked a battle with publications owned by private interests from Taiwan and Hong Kong that did not share the PRC's ideological bent. PRC officials openly acknowledged the political nature of this battle, and in a 2007 interview,

Guo Zhaojin, the president of the state-owned China News Service, noted that if China could gain control of Chinese-language publications in the United States, China would be better able to influence the overseas Chinese community, have a say in American politics, and "protect the national image." Guo further observed that more than one-quarter of America's minorities relied on foreign-language media to obtain their news. Foreign-language media, said Guo, was a "giant hiding in plain sight."[28]

Beijing seems to be winning the battle against Chinese-language outlets expressing dissenting views. Over the course of the last twenty years, a series of once-independent Chinese-language media have fallen under Beijing's control. The Sing Tao Newspaper Group was established in Hong Kong in 1938. In the mid-1990s, its original owner[29] was forced to divest her interests in the paper, and it was soon taken over by a pro-PRC businessman,[30] who, starting in 1998, became a member of the Chinese People's Political Consultative Conference, which functions as part of the broader united front organization network. Sing Tao's coverage of China is now aligned with that of state-run media from Beijing. In fact, in May 2001, the year he purchased Sing Tao, the new owner established a joint venture with the Xinhua News Agency to create an information-service company known as Xinhua Online.

Another case in point is the *World Journal* (世界日报), for years the premier Chinese-language paper in the United States serving immigrants from Taiwan and only one of the six newspapers owned by the United Daily News, Taiwan's most influential newspaper company. The paper once dominated news coverage in Chinatowns across America, and it acted as the voice of the Chinese Nationalist Party of Taiwan. Unlike PRC-controlled outlets, the *World Journal* did cover events such as the death of the jailed Chinese human-rights advocate and Nobel Peace Prize laureate Liu Xiaobo. But the *Journal*'s coverage has shifted in recent years and become more pro-PRC in a variety of areas, such as China's militarization of the South China Sea and its handling of Taiwan and Hong Kong. Sources at the *Journal* observe that the paper's owners in Taiwan are interested in growing their business in China, which may help explain the paper's evolving editorial stance. For example, in March 2004, the *World Journal* published recruitment notices on the front page, announcing its intention to establish a mainland news group and recruit reporters in China. In a 2015 essay, an executive[31] at *Qiaobao*, one of the *Journal*'s main competitors, noted the *Journal*'s evolving editorial stance. "No longer do they only report negative news about the mainland," he wrote.[32] According to sources inside the newspaper, Chinese consulates in both New York and San Francisco have pressured *World Journal*'s local offices not to publish ads related to the religious sect Falun Gong, which has been outlawed in China. The New York office has already acquiesced in full for the East Coast edition. The West Coast edition now only runs Falun Gong ads in throwaway sections of the paper. The *World Journal*'s executive editor, Vincent Chang, took issue with the view that the *World Journal* has modified its position on China. "Since I took the post as *World Journal*'s chief content officer in October of 2016, I have made it my goal to make this paper as neutral and journalistic as possible," he wrote, adding that the paper's content is "independent of any government influence."

Ming Pao is another formerly independent newspaper that has fallen under Beijing's control. For years, its US edition was popular among Cantonese-speaking immigrants in the United States. In January 2007, the Hong Kong Ming Pao Group announced a $600 million merger with the two largest Chinese-language media outlets in Malaysia, the Xingzhou Media and Nanyang News. The merger was welcomed in Beijing. Guo Zhaojin, then president of the China News Service, said the new company would develop into one of the largest Chinese print media platforms in the world, with more than five newspapers in major cities in North America, Southeast Asia, and Greater China and a daily circulation of more than one million copies.

China's efforts to dominate Chinese-language media coincided with two other developments in the 1990s. The Chinese immigrant community boomed in the United States as hundreds of thousands of mainland Chinese became US citizens, transforming the complexion of a community that had previously been dominated by immigrants from Hong Kong and Taiwan. Second, Taiwan's political system transitioned from an authoritarian state to a democracy, leading to new calls from the island

and from some of its immigrants in the United States for an independent Taiwan. Seeking to capitalize on the ever-larger number of mainlanders in the United States and to battle the nascent Taiwan independence movement, PRC authorities established organizations and Chinese-language schools to bolster their propaganda work in the United States. The party's United Front Work Department founded the China Council for the Promotion of Peaceful National Reunification in 1988, and within a decade it had more than one hundred chapters in sixty countries, including more than a dozen offices in the United States. Chinese officials described Chinese-language media, Chinese-language schools, and Chinese-backed organizations as the "three treasures" (三宝) of united front work overseas.[33]

By the mid-1990s, analyst He Qinglian estimated that, of the some one hundred Chinese-language newspapers in the United States, more than one-third were funded by money from the mainland.[34] Owners of these newspapers, seeking subsidies from Beijing, cozied up to PRC authorities with statements such as "opposing Taiwan independence and fostering peaceful unification are the glorious missions and historical responsibility of overseas Chinese publications."[35]

Beijing also moved to take control of online and social media outlets. *Duowei* is an online news site that was for years an independent Chinese-language media outlet. Among its many scoops was the prediction of the composition of the sixteenth Politburo Standing Committee. But in 2009, *Duowei* was purchased by a Hong Kong businessman with substantial business interests in China,[36] including two companies listed on the Hong Kong Stock Exchange. The businessman is a founding member of the Tsinghua University Center for US-China Relations and is also fond of writing pro-Beijing essays on China's claims to the South China Sea. *Duowei* is now headquartered in Beijing. Since selling *Duowei*, the online news source's founder[37] has moved to *Mingjing* (Mirror Media), a Chinese-language web presence based in Canada, where he indicated that last year he received a large investment from the PRC. Since then, *Mingjing* has significantly modified its editorial stance, switching its focus from politics to real estate, immigration, and investing. Part of the reason for this modification appears linked to the disappearance in China of the wife of one of *Mingjing*'s reporters after *Mingjing* aired interviews with a dissident Chinese businessman.[38]

Beijing has also moved to tighten the ideological consistency for these papers. In 2001, the Overseas Chinese Affairs Office and the China News Service began a biannual conference, the Forum on the Global Chinese Language Media, hosting representatives from hundreds of Chinese-language periodicals from around the world. Kicking off the first conference in 2001, Guo Zhaojin, the president of the China News Service, said a key goal of the meeting was to persuade participating overseas Chinese media to use copy from the China News Service instead of reports from competing Chinese-language news services from Taiwan or from the West.[39] The conference also appears to serve as a platform for Beijing to convince critics to modify their tone and to ensure that overseas Chinese-language newspapers follow the party's line. Essays released during the conferences praised the censorship of views opposed by the party and stressed the necessity of, in the words of one piece in 2015, "properly telling China's story" (echoing Xi Jinping's instructions).

And Beijing's efforts have had some successes. Ranked the number-five Chinese website in the United States, BackChina was once an independent media voice like *Duowei*. But in 2017, its editors attended the ninth forum in China, and since then BackChina's reporting has become far more positive about the PRC.

In 2006, the China News Service held the first Advanced Seminar for the Overseas Chinese Language Media, for select groups of editors and reporters from overseas; a seminar in 2006, for example, focused on the correct reading of "socialism with Chinese characteristics," while a workshop in 2010 concerned China's policies in Tibet and Xinjiang. At the thirteenth seminar in 2015, He Yafei, then the assistant director of the Overseas Chinese Affairs Office, argued that overseas Chinese media needed to promote the Belt and Road Initiative and essentially embrace the role of becoming a mouthpiece of the CCP, promoting China's national strategy.[40] Beijing also dispatched Chinese officials overseas to instruct Chinese-language media on how to "correctly" report the news. As the Beijing 2008 Olympics approached, Politburo member and head of China's Olympic Committee Liu Qi met at the PRC consulate in New York with representatives of the Chinese-language press to lay out China's demands for their coverage of the event.[41]

In a further effort to shape the overseas Chinese press, the China News Service established the China News Service Overseas Center, which provides news reports, editorials, and layout for overseas Chinese media outlets around the globe. The idea behind the center was that if Beijing were to provide and package content for overseas Chinese papers, and could convince them to run it, Beijing would then mold the message.[42]

Given these efforts by Beijing, the space for truly independent Chinese-language media in the United States has shrunk to a few media outlets supported by the adherents of Falun Gong, the banned religious sect in China, and a small publication and website called *Vision Times*. According to the publisher of its New York edition, Peter Wang, *Vision Times* was formed expressly to address the issue of the shrinking space for independent Chinese voices in the United States. Since then, it has focused on two areas—human-rights reporting and traditional Chinese culture. Wang noted that while some of the staff of the paper may be Falun Gong adherents, the paper is not a Falun Gong operation. *Vision Times* began its online presence in 2001, started printing a newspaper in 2005, and claims a circulation in the United States and Canada of below 60,000.[43]

Much of the competition between pro-PRC and dissenting voices plays out within the chat rooms of Wenxue City (文学城), the most popular Chinese-language website in the United States. Launched in 1997 by a group of students from the University of Michigan, the website was sold in 2000 to a Taiwanese American businessman, Wayne Lin.[44] Lin conceives of Wenxue City as a Chinese-language version of Reddit, a platform for political, economic, educational, business, and cultural information for Chinese-speaking people. For years after Lin bought the site, China attempted to cultivate Lin and his business, inviting him to three of the biannual Chinese-language media conferences in China

(2007, 2009, and 2011) and providing him with a CNS feed. Then, starting in 2012, Chinese authorities blocked Wenxue City's website in China but would not tell Lin why. Wenxue City has also been the target of numerous denial-of-service attacks, Lin said, adding that he suspected China was the source. "Over the past few years, the Chinese government has become more aggressive in influencing Chinese-language media," he said.[45]

WeChat as a Source of News in the Diaspora Community

China's social media giant WeChat is another major source of news within the Chinese American community. But it is more than that; for many users in the United States, China, and around the world, WeChat is a digital ecosystem so ubiquitous that it constitutes a lifestyle—a drumbeat that determines the rhythms of the day. In the United States, as in China, WeChat censors news and comments in accordance with rules set by China's Communist Party. Indeed, WeChat is an example of how China is now exporting PRC media censorship overseas. Links sent via WeChat between users in the United States routinely won't open if those sites are blocked in China.

In an analysis of WeChat articles popular in the United States, researcher Zhang Chi found that the most successful pieces skewed significantly to the right of the US political spectrum.[46] Zhang noted that the right-wing view on WeChat generally embraces a social Darwinist, zero-sum conception of racial politics, with Chinese in America portrayed as beaten down by a system that favors other racial groups and illegal immigrants from Latin America. One popular WeChat channel blamed the wildfires in 2017 in Northern California on an undocumented immigrant.

Numerous other channels reported on alleged plans for mass riots and a civil war in the United States led by the leftist group Antifa. When a Chinese jogger was struck and killed in a DUI case in a suburb of Los Angeles, a popular WeChat channel reported that the motorist was undocumented and had committed the act to extend his stay in the United

States.[47] Zhang noted that another cause of concern was the fact that these WeChat channels helped foster anxiety among first-generation Chinese. As with other Chinese immigrants who rely on traditional Chinese-language media for information, the anti-American hothouse created by WeChat's "news channels" leads to a type of resentful pro-Chinese nationalism that is ripe for exploitation by the Chinese government.

WeChat may be no more slanted in its treatment of information than American media that serve domestic political extremes, but there is no precedent for the situation WeChat has created: A vast and vital community of Americans gets most of its "news" from, and does most of its communicating via, a platform known to be censored by a foreign government that opposes free speech and has been named by the US National Security Strategy as the greatest long-term security challenge the nation faces.

WeChat also appears to have different rules for different regions. In 2014, some Chinese Americans began to lobby against a law that sought to reintroduce race as an element of admissions into the University of California system. The campaign started just as WeChat was gaining popularity among the Chinese American diaspora. WeChat's owner, Tencent, tweaked its own rules and gave campaign organizers the ability to collect hundreds of people into supergroups of five hundred or more. Ten WeChat supergroups were handed out to movement organizers and then used to connect with Chinese American voters. The law died in the California legislature.

Western Media

The Chinese Communist Party has always recognized the usefulness of the overseas media (both in local languages and Chinese) as a means to get its message out. Foreign- and Chinese-language media have always served the cause of China's revolution. For example, in the 1930s, foreign journalist Edgar Snow sang the praises of the Chinese Communist Party and specifically its chairman, Mao Zedong. The party conducted a campaign in the United States in the 1940s to turn the American public against the regime of Chiang Kai-shek and to soften criticism of China's Communists. Organizations such as the Institute of Pacific Relations, which provided Americans with in-depth coverage of Asia, were staffed by Communist agents and played an important role in fashioning public opinion on America's relations with China. To be sure, these techniques were not unique to the Chinese Communist Party. The government of Chiang Kai-shek and its "China lobby" also used the overseas press to serve its purposes. In the 1950s, the KMT government conducted a campaign against pro-Communist newspapers in the United States, convincing the US government to shutter several pro-PRC outlets and expel pro-PRC journalists.

The events of 1989 sparked a significant change in China's foreign propaganda campaign. Following China's crackdown on pro-democracy demonstrators in Beijing and other cities, China's image sank to a low not seen by Chinese officials in decades.[48] China Books and Periodicals, which had been operating in the United States since the 1950s, closed its offices on Fifth Avenue in New York City. And the Foreign Languages Press (a department of the China International Publishing Group) saw its cooperative agreements dwindle.

It was then that Chinese officials revived an old tactic that the Communist Party had employed before the revolution—using friendly foreigners and pro-PRC Chinese immigrants to publicize China's story. Chinese officials called this tactic of localizing the work of foreign propaganda, the "borrowed boat" strategy.[49]

One such friendly American was a China scholar[50] who was for years associated with Random House. According to Huang Youyi, the chief editor of the Foreign Languages Press posted to the United States in the late 1980s and early 1990s, this American argued that for China to improve its image in the United States, it needed to work through American organizations, and so he collaborated with Huang on a book series, "The Culture and Civilization of China," which the Yale University Press began publishing in 1997. The American's "understanding of the US publishing industry and his friendly attitude towards China became an indispensable condition for the success of the cooperation," Huang wrote.[51] Books from the series are still given to foreign guests of the Beijing government.

In a period of deep crisis for China's reputation, Huang's success in using foreigners to publish material beneficial to China's image became a model for other Chinese operations. From the early 1990s, the Chinese Communist Party began to seek opportunities to cooperate with Westerners, Western media and publishing companies, and overseas Chinese to tell its story.

Lack of Reciprocity

It is important to compare Beijing's efforts to wage its "discourse war" and garner "discourse power" overseas with the efforts, and ability, of Western media organizations to access China's market to a similar degree. For decades, those efforts have faced roadblocks placed in their path by the Chinese government. A key roadblock has been China's ban on Western investment in media except when it involves such things as fashion, cars, and lifestyle.

Unlike Chinese reporters in the United States, who are restricted only from entering high-security military installations, Western reporters in China are subject to a panoply of regulations, many of them unwritten. A 2017 report by the Foreign Correspondents' Club of China notes that in a survey of 117 foreign journalists based in China, 40 percent felt reporting conditions had deteriorated compared to 2016; nearly half said they had experienced harassment, interference, and physical violence during their work in China; 15 percent said they encountered difficulties during their visa renewal process; and over 25 percent said they had learned that their Chinese contacts had been detained and otherwise hounded by Chinese authorities for speaking with them.[52]

China has also moved against Western media outlets on many fronts. Both Chinese- and English-language websites of the *New York Times* have been blocked in China since 2012 following a story detailing the wealth of the family of China's then premier Wen Jiabao.[53] The English- and

Chinese-language sites of the *Wall Street Journal* and Reuters are also blocked, and those belonging to the *Financial Times* and the *Economist* are blocked on an intermittent basis.

The Chinese government has also made it difficult for resident foreign reporters to obtain and renew journalist visas. Following the *New York Times* report on the Wen family's money, China did not approve a new journalist visa for a *Times* reporter for three years. While the situation has improved somewhat since 2015 for resident journalists, the Chinese government still delays visa applications for journalists and uses the threat of expulsion from China as a way to pressure Western media outlets to soften their coverage of China. This is especially true of freelance journalists or independent documentary filmmakers who are dependent on onetime visas to carry out a specific assignment. Here delays and outright refusal to process visas in a timely manner have been common.

There is some indication that China's pressure tactics have paid off. In 2013, Bloomberg News was preparing to publish a report detailing connections between one of China's richest men and members of the Politburo—the top organ in the Chinese Communist Party—when Bloomberg spiked the story. The outlet's editor in chief, Matthew Winkler, was quoted on a conference call likening the decision to censorship of foreign news bureaus that wanted to continue to report in Nazi Germany.[54] Other observers noted that the real reason Bloomberg News killed the story involved the company's substantial business interests—especially in "Bloomberg Boxes" selling access to financial information—in China.

International Service Broadcasters

Another roadblock in Western attempts to bring alternative messages to China has been Beijing's efforts to limit the influence of the Mandarin services of the Voice of America (VOA) and Radio Free Asia. Starting in the first decade of the 2000s, the Chinese embassy in Washington, DC, and the leadership of VOA's Mandarin service began an annual meeting to allow embassy officials to voice their opinions about VOA's content.

PRC embassy officials have also reached out to VOA hosts to convince them to be more supportive of the regime. VOA personalities have hosted events at the embassy. One of VOA's TV editors even publicly pledged his allegiance to China at an embassy event.[55]

It is not surprising, then, that some VOA staffers interviewed for this report believe that China's outreach campaign has succeeded in pushing the VOA Mandarin service away from programs with direct relevance to China toward programming that seeks instead to highlight American everyday life or teach American-style English to Chinese listeners. An example would be a program called *Cultural Odyssey*, a VOA TV series that focused on Americana, such as fried chicken, doughnuts, and national parks. For years, *Cultural Odyssey* ate up one-third of the Mandarin service's travel budget. Another program featured English teacher Jessica Beinecke, which launched her on a career as an English-teaching TV personality on mainland China itself. VOA officials internally praised these programs as both "non-political and non-sensitive," a current senior VOA staff member noted. What's more, VOA officials sought to scale back what were perceived to be sensitive reports. After running two years of a radio series on aspects of modern Chinese history, including the Cultural Revolution and other events post-1949, VOA cut the program in 2009 despite several of those shows garnering well over three million hits each on the web. In 2011, the Broadcasting Board of Governors sought to cut 65 percent of the workforce from the Mandarin service. However, reporters and editors in the service fought back: they lobbied Congress, and the cuts were restored. In 2012, a Chinese immigrant, who was also a former Chinese dissident and a specialist on the US political system, became the first female Chinese head of the service. She was later fired over a controversial interview that drew the official ire of the PRC, which threatened repercussions.[56]

Since her dismissal, VOA's Mandarin service has resumed a pattern of avoiding stories that could be perceived to be too tough on China, according to several staffers. For example, blogs written by dissidents such as Cao Yaxue, who runs the human rights–related site China Change, have been removed from the VOA website. Several prominent Chinese commentators are no longer on VOA's lineup of analysts. Many staffers now describe VOA's content as neither pro- nor anti-China. The emphasis, the staffers observed, is on travel, culture, and language, programming the likes of which Chinese viewers can access equally well on CGTN or China's internet. By contrast, the content of Radio Free Asia remains far more hard-hitting than its counterpart VOA.

Conclusion and Recommendations

China has used America's openness to convey its message both to English- and Chinese-speaking residents of the United States. US rules allow foreign media companies, even ones run by foreign governments, to broadcast freely via American cable and satellite networks. Unlike in China, the United States government does not block any Chinese websites, many of which are funded by the PRC government. While the Communications Act of 1934 theoretically allows foreigners to own only 20 to 25 percent of terrestrial wireless radio and TV stations, the law has been loosened considerably over the past decade, and it does not even apply to cable channels or leasing arrangements wherein a foreign entity, including one owned by a foreign government, can pay an American licensee for airtime. Chinese media outlets have used all such strategies to publicize the views of the Beijing government.[57] Perhaps more worrisome, China has also been successful in funding or convincing pro-PRC businessmen to fund pro-PRC media outlets in the United States that nominally appear independent so that the three most important traditionally independent Chinese-language newspapers now increasingly side with Beijing.

By contrast, the Chinese government severely limits the scope of US and other Western media outlets in China and has banned Western media investment in China, except in very limited innocuous areas, such as in fashion, automobiles, investing, health, and lifestyle. The idea that a Western TV news network could lease a Chinese station and broadcast news to China around the clock—as their Chinese counterparts do here in the United States—is not even thinkable. Equally, there is no chance that a Western media company would be allowed to invest in a Chinese publication that reported mainstream news.

Both the expansion of Chinese state owned English-language media in the United States and Beijing's increasing control of Chinese-language media outlets in the United States are very problematic for an open dialogue. For one, these media are under the control of a foreign government, not simply a foreign individual or firm. Second, the diminishing space within America's Chinese-language media for independent voices runs counter to the goals of a liberal society seeking a diversity of perspectives. Furthermore, the PRC's control of Chinese-language media outlets in America, and its increasingly strong position among English-language outlets, provides China with the potential for mobilizing Chinese Americans and Americans alike to espouse policies counter to US interest. The constant drumbeat of anti-American reporting in pro-Beijing media outlets headquartered in the United States creates an unhealthy environment.

Promoting Transparency

A major challenge is the fact that China has worked successfully to mask its influence operations with respect to US media. On paper, for example, the Asian Culture and Media Group controls the pro-China SinoVision and *Qiaobao* as a private company. The reality is that it is staffed by people who served the state-run China News Service and were, sources insist, dispatched to the United States by the Chinese government to establish propaganda operations in the United States. Given its nominal status as a private company, taking action to shut down its operations would be fraught with even more legal and ethical challenges than those involving media corporations directly owned by the PRC. The same holds true for publications and websites that were once independent but have now increasingly fallen under the sway of the PRC. If US law protects the rights of publishers of newspapers or websites to put their personal political imprint on their enterprises, how can the US government move to deny it to those of a pro-PRC bent?

At a minimum, what US authorities can do is work to establish the real ownership structure of Chinese (and other foreign) companies purchasing US-based media. Any foreign-owned or foreign-controlled media (including print media), and particularly those that advance a foreign government line, should be required to register under the Foreign Agents Registration Act (FARA).

Beyond FARA, there should also be a review to see whether these organizations and their employees should also register under existing lobbying laws as foreign agents. In addition, there is an argument to be made for ensuring that employees of these organizations be given a disclosure package making them aware that they are working for a foreign-agent institution.

Promoting Integrity

Figuring out how to properly counter the PRC's influence operations in both English- and Chinese-language media presents enormous challenges in a free society. The United States could consider restrictions on state-controlled media outlets, which would not include publicly funded broadcasters, such as the BBC, which maintain editorial independence. Failing that, the recent requirement that state-run publications, TV and radio broadcasters, and potentially their employees, register as agents of a foreign government is a partial solution.[58] And in late 2017, Russia's RT registered as a foreign agent[59] while in September 2018, the US Justice Department reportedly also ordered CGTN and Xinhua to register as agents of a foreign power.[60]

When it comes to independent Chinese-language media, the US government should consider doing more to help such independent outlets survive, including using grants via the Fulbright program or other vehicles, such as the State Department International Visitors or Speakers' Bureau. Domestically, the US government could also consider aiding the operations of independent Chinese-language media, including manufacturing credits for printing press operations, and nonprofit tax designations to allow journalism business models to survive the current transitional crisis. Private charitable foundations can also make a difference in helping independent Chinese-language media remain editorially independent and financially viable.

Promoting Reciprocity

The time has come for the US government to demand reciprocity for American journalists attempting to do their professional work in China. To the extent that they are prevented from doing so as a result of visa denials and restrictions of access, the US State Department should respond in kind by restricting visas and access for Chinese journalists in the United States. To the extent that American journalists experience harassment and physical violence, this should also have a bearing on the granting of visas and access to Chinese journalists.

CHAPTER SEVEN

Corporations

American corporations wield significant political influence domestically and are some of the most significant sources of American soft power abroad. Foreign leverage over American corporations can thus advance important strategic interests of the country in question. In addition, as Chinese corporations go abroad, they, too, bring with them the potential of being leveraged by the Chinese government to advance China's interests. This chapter examines improper influence in the US corporate sector, as well as the potential for future influence because of significant economic exposure to China.

The US-China economic relationship is large and multifaceted. Trade statistics illustrate just one aspect of this tangled web: in 2017, the United States exported goods worth $130 billion to China while importing goods worth $505 billion.[1] With trade also comes extensive foreign investment, as well as significant levels of employment of each country's citizens. Since 2000, the cumulative value of Chinese foreign direct investment in the United States has exceeded $140 billion, with US investment in China being more than double that amount.[2] In the United States, there is more Chinese investment in the real estate sector than any other area. But until recently more deals were being done in the information technology sector, which has attracted the growing attention of the Committee on Foreign Investment in the United States (CFIUS).

China is increasingly willing to engage in aggressive forms of economic statecraft.[3] This includes not just denial of access to, or harassment in, China's own market, but also targeting of other countries' domestic economies and companies. These actions are sometimes state-led; at other times China's state-run media will encourage "consumer-led" boycotts (as in the cases of Japan, Norway, and South Korea, among others).[4] Chinese corporations abroad are all well aware of Chinese official policy and understand the value of acting in support of their country's foreign or industrial policy objectives. China's growing commercial presence in other countries' economies strengthens its ability to potentially influence their politics.

This chapter examines corporate sector influence through three lenses: (1) the use of business-related united front organizations in the United States; (2) Chinese companies operating in America; and (3) Chinese pressuring and manipulation of American companies as vectors of influence. All three approaches are cause for concern, yet the pressuring and manipulation of American corporations has generally attracted less attention.

This chapter intends to highlight three main developments. First, China is supporting an increasing number of local chambers of commerce in the United States with direct ties to CCP officials. Second, as Chinese companies have become more global, they have also grown more sophisticated in their efforts to socialize and localize themselves in their new American communities as they also acquire political influence in the United States. Finally, China has increased its efforts to pressure, co-opt, and sometimes even coerce foreign corporations with the aim of influencing politics in their home countries.

The Use of Business-Related United Front Organizations

Consistent with the practice of other nations, major Chinese firms operating in America are represented by a chamber-of-commerce network. Analysis detailed below suggests that China also operates an extensive list of united front organizations purporting to be regional chambers of commerce. China's public-facing chamber in the United States is known as the China General Chamber of Commerce (CGCC), which was founded in 2005. It is headquartered in New York, with five regional operations in Chicago, Houston, Los Angeles, San Francisco, and Washington, DC. Its website states that it has 1,500 member companies, both Chinese and non-Chinese. The organization's chair is Bank of China USA president and CEO Xu Chen. Its website lists more than sixty individuals, many from state-owned companies, in governance roles; its website lists a staff of nine.

Consistent with business organizations of other countries, the CGCC engages in a mix of political engagement with its host and home countries (e.g., testifying at the US International Trade Commission[5] and hosting officials from the Chinese Ministry of Commerce[6]); informational activities for its members (e.g., a lunch-and-learn on labor and safety issues in the United States);[7] and promotional activities (e.g., dinner galas and charity events). The CGCC is actively engaged with senior American political and business leaders. In July 2017, it hosted a welcome luncheon at the National Governors Association meeting in Rhode Island, which the governors of Maryland, Kentucky, Alaska, Arizona, Louisiana, and Rhode Island attended. In September 2017, the group organized a visit of the governors of Alaska and Missouri to China.[8]

Inconsistent with the practice of other countries, China also oversees an extensive network of local chambers of commerce. This raises a question of their possible ties to the Chinese party-state, and whether these chambers may be misrepresenting themselves as local concerns when they are instead activated by, or in liaison with, the Chinese government. Research for this project has identified thirty-one business-focused organizations operating in the United States that are explicitly associated with, or whose profiles and activities are highly suggestive of involvement with, united front work.[9] Most of these groups are concentrated in Greater Los Angeles and New York City, two principal communities of the Chinese diaspora. They are typically organized by hometown province of origin. This count does not include many other professional diaspora groups that may be used to facilitate China's influence operations.

Such Chinese groups have increased their activity in the United States since 2015,[10] and many of these groups have had interactions with the United Front Work Department and other Chinese officials both in the United States and in China, contacts that are distinctly different from invitations to embassy or consular diplomats and bear further scrutiny.[11] At least eleven of the chambers identified in this analysis were established in 2016 or later, consistent with heightened activity observed in other sectors of society dedicated to projecting China's soft power and influence abroad. (Tellingly, China's spending on diplomacy has doubled to $9.5 billion per year under Xi Jinping.)[12] The US-Zhejiang General Chamber of Commerce's WeChat description explicitly references a 2015 provincial directive on strengthening the province's overseas Chinese connections (fig. 1). Many of these groups maintain their own presence via a website or, increasingly, the WeChat social media platform. In one instance, our researcher's antivirus software blocked an intrusion attempt while researching the US-Fujian Chamber of Commerce.

Chinese Companies Operating in America as a Vector of Influence

More than 3,200 Chinese-owned companies operate in the United States, employing 140,000 Americans.[13] Chinese establishments operate in all but ten congressional districts.[14] As Chinese companies' presence in the US economy grows, given the united front's penchant for using civil society organizations for its purposes, they bring with them several potential risks. First, their potential to be used by Beijing may result in activities that are contrary to US interests, as evidenced by intense scrutiny of their investment activities by CFIUS and reported warnings by counterintelligence officials. Second, growing access to the US political system, even if currently used to advance legitimate economic interests, creates openings for future exploitation by the Chinese government. Third, Chinese companies may effectively "export" corrupt or unethical business practices.

全美浙江总商会
WeChat ID: USZJGC

Intro　　全美浙江总商会是根据2015年《浙江省政府办公厅关于加强浙江省海外侨团建设的意见》精神，由美国浙江籍商人和中美及浙江发展做贡献的其他省籍优秀人才组成的非营利性社团组织。总商会为会员实现美国梦和中国梦创造更大平台，资源共享的机遇。

Type　　个人　　　　　　　　　　　　　›

View History　　　　　　　　　　　　›

Follow

Figure 1

Activities Contrary to US Interests

The technology sector has been the most consistent and prominent source of concern. In 2012, the Intelligence Committee of the US House of Representatives declared Chinese technology companies Huawei and ZTE a national security threat given the firms' alleged ties to the Chinese military and the potential for their technology to be exploited for espionage or cyberattacks.[15] Both companies were key providers of technology at the African Union headquarters building, where investigators have found widespread electronic infiltration traceable to China, whose state-owned firms constructed the building.[16] Both Huawei and ZTE have also been accused of bribery abroad to win contracts.[17]

For years, the federal government has actively discouraged American companies, local governments, and allied countries from partnering with Huawei. Nonetheless, the company's global presence has continued to grow, and it is playing an important role in setting standards for 5G wireless technology.[18] In April 2018, the United States announced sanctions against ZTE for violating restrictions on sales to Iran and North Korea, barring American companies from transacting with the company. This would have effectively put ZTE out of business because of its dependence on American inputs, but shortly thereafter, and against the objections of many in Congress, the Trump administration agreed to a settlement that would allow the firm to stay in business.

There are other instances of companies being used to advance objectives contrary to the US interest. For example, front companies have been used to aid in the illegal export of sensitive technologies to China. In another instance, *Newsweek* in 2016 reported that the United States was investigating the acquisition by the Chinese company Fosun of a US insurer that has sold legal liability insurance to senior American intelligence officials.[19]

Growing Access to the US Political System

Although federal campaign contributions by foreign nationals or companies are illegal in US federal elections, there are alternative avenues for foreign corporate interests to influence the US political system, as the Australians have learned. These include lobbying, indirect campaign contributions via US subsidiaries, and the hiring of former senior government officials. All these approaches, while currently legal, are discussed below to demonstrate the full spectrum of activities Chinese entities are involved with and to highlight where they may raise questions of impropriety.

Lobbying: The most direct and legal route to the American political system is lobbying. For example, within one day of President Trump tweeting his openness to a settlement with ZTE Corporation that would keep it from going out of business, the company signed a contract with lobbying firm Mercury Public Affairs. The lead on the ZTE account was Bryan Lanza, a former Trump campaign official.[20] Also in 2018, the former senior advisor to secretary of commerce Wilbur Ross was hired as chief of international corporate affairs for another Chinese firm, HNA. Both instances underscore the need for updated revolving-door policies, particularly with respect to foreign corporations that are subject to significant state control.[21]

All told, major Chinese companies publicly acknowledge spending $3.8 million on federal lobbying in 2017 and $20.2 million in total since 2000,[22] modest amounts by global standards. The Chinese e-commerce behemoth Alibaba was the largest source of expenditures in 2017, accounting for $2 million, followed by technology company ZTE ($510,000), Sinopec ($384,000),[23] and the Wanda America Group ($300,000), affiliated with Dalian Wanda.[24] More difficult to track is Chinese corporate participation in American trade associations. In early 2018, two Chinese companies joined two major lobbying groups noted for their political heft.[25]

Indirect donations: A key exception to the ban on foreign federal campaign contributions is permitted through activity conducted via a US subsidiary of a foreign company. The Federal Election Commission has written that "where permitted by state law, a US subsidiary of a foreign national corporation may donate funds for state and local elections if (1) the donations derive entirely from funds generated by the subsidiaries' US operations, and (2) all decisions concerning the donations, except those setting overall budget amounts, are made by individuals who are US citizens or permanent residents."

This exception inherently creates the potential for exploitation, particularly given the intrinsic difficulties of monitoring and enforcement. For example, the *Intercept* has reported that American Pacific International Capital, an American subsidiary of a corporation owned by a Chinese citizen, contributed $1.3 million to the super PAC of presidential candidate Jeb Bush on the advice of a prominent Republican campaign finance lawyer.[26] (Neil Bush, the brother of George W. and Jeb Bush, and former ambassador Gary Locke have served as advisors of American Pacific International.)[27]

Employees of Chinese enterprises, who are presumably American citizens, are also active donors. A review of campaign donation data finds that several individuals cited as members of the China General Chamber of Commerce or employed by member firms have made recent campaign contributions. For example, two individuals associated with HNA Group, including Tan Xiandong, the group's president, in 2017 donated $2,500 each to the congressional campaign of Greg Pence, the brother of the vice president.[28]

In May 2018, China-based companies reportedly invited Chinese to attend several Republican Party fund-raising dinners at which President Trump would appear. The invitations prominently featured the Republican Party's logo along with that of China Construction Bank, making it appear as if there was some formal connection.[29] The Republican Party and China Construction Bank both denied awareness of the solicitations in their name. Foreigners may attend fund-raisers so long as they do not pay their own entry, another instance in which the fungibility of money makes it easy to skirt this rule.

Hiring of former senior government officials: In other countries (such as Australia, the United Kingdom, France, and Germany), former senior government officials routinely take positions with Chinese companies. This pattern appears less pronounced in the United States. A prominent exception is the law firm Dentons, which merged with the Chinese law firm Dacheng in 2015[30] and employs numerous former government officials, including former ambassadors, members of Congress, mayors, and generals.[31]

Earlier in 2018, Bloomberg News reported on the Imperial Pacific casino, a Chinese-owned company operating in the American territory of Saipan. Its large transaction volumes have raised concerns about potential money laundering. It has also made millions of payments to family members of the territory's governor and, at one time, counted the former governors of three states as well as the former directors of the CIA and FBI as members of its board of advisors.[32]

State and local politics: Many states do not have prohibitions against foreign contributions in local races.[33] One of the most notable examples of an individual contributor comes from Virginia, where in 2013 and 2014, Wang Wenliang, a Chinese industrialist who was expelled from China's national legislature in 2016, contributed $120,000 to Governor Terry McAuliffe's campaign.[34]

Chinese firms are also involved in lobbying at the state and local levels, another means of acquiring legitimate influence. While the quality of data reporting and aggregation for local- and state-level lobbying is not always as robust as that at the federal level, this project was able to identify more than $1 million in state-level lobbying expenses over the past decade by Chinese firms. BYD Motors, which produces buses for public transit in the United States, Huawei, and Wanda America Group were among the biggest spenders on lobbying.

A 2017 complaint with the FEC against the California subsidiary of Dalian Wanda is illustrative of the potential for exploitation granted by the US-subsidiary exception. The FEC found that Lakeshore, a Chicago real estate company whose principals are US citizens, was the source of the money that funded a local ballot initiative in California that would have blocked a Wanda competitor from expanding. Wanda acknowledged that the money for the measure had come from Lakeshore, with which Wanda does business, in the form of a $1.2 million loan. In its conclusion, the FEC did not rule on whether foreign restrictions applied to ballot measure activity. Further, it argued that even if those restrictions did apply, because "none of the funds at issue appear to originate with a foreign national" (i.e., they came from Lakeshore); that because the Wanda deputy manager who was listed as the principal officer of the ballot measure committee was an American citizen (the general manager is a Chinese national); and that the funds originated in and would be paid back by revenues generated in the United States, the activity was not in violation of laws against foreign campaign activity.[35]

"Exporting" Corrupt or Unethical Business Practices

China scores poorly on international indices of corruption.[36] As Chinese companies expand abroad, it is possible that they could have a deleterious effect simply by exporting suspect business practices. An industry of particular importance is banking. The "big four" Chinese banks all operate in the United States, where their assets have increased sevenfold between 2010 and 2016 to $126.5 billion.[37] They are often extensively involved in real estate transactions of Chinese firms operating in the United States. In 2015, 2016, and 2018, China Construction Bank,[38] the Agricultural Bank of China,[39] and Industrial & Commercial Bank of China[40] were respectively subject to enforcement action by the Federal Reserve for not doing enough to fight money laundering.

Chinese corporations in the United States can also hinder the rule of law in other ways. When responding to lawsuits in US courts, Chinese state-owned enterprises have claimed exemption due to sovereign immunity; in other instances, Chinese firms with an American legal presence have refused to comply with US investigations by claiming that cooperation would violate Chinese law.[41] These actions inhibit the ability of the US government to regulate commerce, and they put American competitors at a disadvantage within their own country.

Chinese Manipulation of American Companies as a Vector of Influence

American companies play a significant role in American foreign and domestic politics, and their leaders regularly are selected to take positions of leadership in government.[42] As a result, corporate America's traditional role in favor of engagement with China, given the country's market potential, has had significant weight in American policy toward the country.[43] China, for its part, welcomed foreign companies' investment as part of its policy of reform and opening up in the hope of spurring economic development.

China's relationship with corporate America has become increasingly fraught. In this report and elsewhere, China's state-directed efforts to facilitate the theft of intellectual property, the lifeblood of developed economies, are well documented. China's forced transfer of technology by foreign firms, as a condition of operating in China, is one of the main complaints of both the Trump administration and the European Union.

But China's ability to pressure US companies also encompasses three other more elusive dimensions. First, recognizing the importance of American companies in American politics, China has frequently cultivated, even leveraged, American executives to lobby against policies it opposes. Where cultivation fails, it has threatened or exercised economic retaliation. For example, in June 2018, the *Wall Street Journal* reported that President Xi warned a group of global CEOs that China would retaliate with "qualitative measures" targeted at their companies if the United States did not back off from the tariff war.[44] Second, China is seeking to pressure American companies into legitimizing its geopolitical claims and interests, for example by demanding that Western firms overtly acknowledge that Taiwan is an irreversible part of China. Third, China has wooed American companies with both sticks and carrots into serving its strategic interests abroad, most notably via its interactions with Hollywood.

China's source of leverage over American companies comes from its large domestic market and its key role in international supply chains; by contrast, China holds little direct ownership in American companies. American affiliates (i.e., those at least half-owned by American multinational companies) employ 1.7 million Chinese workers and are indirectly responsible for the employment of millions more.[45] More than fifty American companies report that they generate at least 20 percent of their revenues from China.[46] Naturally, many companies (and industry associations) with large stakes in China lobby the American government on issues related to China, often seeking to exert a moderating influence on

US policy. This is not in itself evidence of improper influence, but it merits scrutiny and should be weighed in the context of other evidence in this chapter.[47]

Seeking to Influence American Politics via Corporate Interests

China does, in fact, exert influence on how at least some American companies and corporate executives interact with the American government. This influence generally takes two forms. In the first, China relies on American corporations to retard efforts by the American government to investigate and sanction Chinese behavior deemed harmful to national economic or strategic interests. For example, some American corporations have expressed reservations about cooperating with US trade investigations for fear of retaliation by China.

Chinese officials also regularly convene senior American executives at special meetings with government officials or major conferences. During these engagements, Western CEOs' positive comments on the country receive wide play in the foreign and domestic media, one of many ways in which the party continues to seek the appearance of outside legitimization for domestic purposes. In addition, China uses these meetings to attempt to coerce American executives to take China's side in disputes with the US government. As the risk of a trade war mounted in spring 2018, Chinese officials explicitly warned gathered executives to lobby the US government to back down or risk disruption to their businesses in China.[48] The US government does not strategically convene foreign business leaders, let alone instruct them to use their influence to shape policy favorable to the United States in their home countries.

Advancing Strategic Interests Abroad: A Case Study of Hollywood

As its market power mounts, China is increasingly able to leverage foreign corporations to not just influence their home governments but also to advance China's broader strategic interests around the world. The most visible manifestation of this strategy is the party-state's effort to influence Hollywood in a bid to advance China's global soft power agenda.

American popular culture has enjoyed worldwide influence for decades and is a key element of the country's soft power. However, by the end of the Hu Jintao era, China's leaders had begun calling for their country, too, to become a soft power leader, a theme Xi Jinping has continued to stress. The subsequent surge in Chinese spending on entertainment, or its "cultural industries,"[49] as it calls this sector, amid flat revenues in the United States, has made China's market a compelling one for Hollywood, despite continued quotas limiting the number of foreign films that can be shown in China. In 2017, the Chinese box office reached $7.9 billion on growth of 21 percent, whereas the US market grew just 2 percent to $11.1 billion.[50] (Foreign films account for roughly half of China's total, most of which is attributable to Hollywood.)

In the 2010s, in addition to investing in its domestic film industry and maintaining a restrictive import regime, the Chinese government encouraged the country's media companies to enter into alliances or attempt to acquire outright American entertainment companies. Collectively, these strategies have raised concerns about self-censorship, the co-opting of the American film industry to advance Chinese narratives, and, ultimately, the risk that the industry will lose its independence.

Hollywood, represented by the Motion Picture Association of America, has long cultivated close ties to the American government, which it has used to open access to China. For example, media scholar Aynne Kokas notes that in 2012, vice president Joe Biden met with then Chinese vice president Xi Jinping to discuss China's quota on foreign films.[51] During Xi's visit, Biden also helped broker an agreement between DreamWorks and a group of Chinese investors. Ultimately, in response to these efforts and WTO action, China increased its annual quota of imported films from twenty to thirty-four.

Film studios can attempt to circumvent the import quota by coproducing films with Chinese partners. This can invite censorship directly into the production process, potentially affecting what global audiences see, as opposed to censorship that affects only what the Chinese market sees.[52] Examples abound of studios that have cast Chinese actors, developed or cut scenes specific to the Chinese market, or preemptively eliminated potentially objectionable references to China from scripts even when source material has called for it.

Aware of the Chinese market's growing centrality to the film industry, major studios are also reluctant to produce any film that would upset China, even if that specific film was not intended for the Chinese market, for fear that all films by the studio would be blocked. Indeed, the last spate of movies made for general circulation that addressed topics that the Chinese government deemed sensitive were released in 1997 and included such productions as *Red Corner*, *Seven Years in Tibet*, and *Kundun*. Several prominent American entertainers have been subject to bans by China, most often for their association with the Dalai Lama. In an interview with the *Hollywood Reporter*, actor Richard Gere, an outspoken advocate of Tibetan culture, stated, "There are definitely movies that I can't be in because the Chinese will say, 'Not with him.'"[53]

Beyond self-censorship, American studios and creative personnel are at risk of being actively co-opted in advancing Chinese soft power. Chinese political and entertainment leaders are conscious that American entertainment companies have played an outsize role in defining China, from *Mulan* to *Kung Fu Panda*. By the time the third edition in the *Panda* franchise had been released, however, it was being coproduced with a Chinese partner. The list of films portraying China in a positive light grows each year, such as the space films *Gravity* and *The Martian*, a movie backed by Chinese money in which the American protagonists are saved by the Chinese. Ironically, in *Gravity*, a central plot twist involves the shooting down of a satellite by the Russians. In fact, the only nation to have shot down a satellite in real life is China. These positive portrayals, of course, are not inherently objectionable—and they may, indeed, provide a constructive countervailing force in an otherwise deteriorating relationship. The issue is: how do these portrayals come to be? In other words, has independent artistic vision been manipulated by political pressures to maintain commercial standing?

The rush of Chinese investment into the American film industry has raised legitimate concerns about the industry's outright loss of independence. In 2012, Dalian Wanda acquired the AMC cinema chain, followed in 2016 by the acquisition of the Legendary Entertainment studio. Before encountering political trouble at home, Wanda's chairman announced a desire to invest in each of the six major Hollywood studios. Since then, other announced partnerships and investments have faded, principally because of Beijing's pushback against what it deemed to be grossly excessive, and often ill-considered, foreign investment plans by Chinese companies.[54]

Conclusion and Recommendations

Through control of its companies operating abroad, growing influence over foreign companies, and the rapid activation of business-related united front groups, China is using commercial interests as an important means of exercising "sharp power" influence. As with other sectors, much of China's activity is, regardless of its intent, legal and thus should not be disparaged. The appropriate response to this commercial challenge must be temperate and multifaceted. In some areas, it will require that the political system increase its transparency regarding, or reduce its exposure to, corporate money entirely, which, given its fungibility, ultimately renders any distinction between domestic and foreign sources meaningless. Corporations should also provide greater clarity on their financial and supply-chain exposure to China and disclose the presence of CCP members in joint- or wholly owned ventures. In certain instances, new limitations on corporate activity that is harmful to the national interest may be required.

American business leaders should become better versed in the evolving nature of China's global ambitions, especially in the use of united front tactics for influencing almost all aspects of China's interaction with the United States. American corporations should raise their voices through chambers of commerce or other collective commercial entities that can collectively represent their interests when a company confronts pressures or coercion. To more effectively resist growing Chinese pressures, American corporations will most certainly need to find new ways to cooperate more closely with each other, and at times even in coordination with the US government. Like think tanks, universities, other civil society organizations, and media outlets, American companies will be most vulnerable to Chinese pressure when they are atomized and isolated. In this sense, the challenges with which US corporations are confronted by a rising authoritarian China with a far more ambitious global agenda are not so dissimilar to those confronted by those other sectors of American society highlighted in this report. Each confronts an un-level playing field that lacks reciprocity.

To help rectify these imbalances, in certain instances, the US government should be the one to coordinate collective action, as it recently sought to do with the US airline industry. It may also need to be more prepared to impose reciprocal penalties on Chinese companies or even compensate American companies for losses when they stand up to punitive action from China as an additional incentive to maintain resolve.

Most important, corporate executives, their boards, and their shareholders must double their efforts to exercise the kind of principled leadership and restraint that will help them resist the loss of corporate control in pursuit of short-term profit. This includes not only individual companies but also their representative organizations, notably the US Chamber of Commerce, the US-China Business Council, and other specific trade associations. These bodies not only need to promote American business interests by pushing back against Chinese restrictions where necessary, but they also need to adopt a heightened awareness of the role that corporations must play in protecting both their own interests and the national economic security of the United States itself.

In the corporate sector, China is not just taking advantage of the openness of American markets, which are rightfully a point of pride for the United States and a pillar of our economic vitality, but it is also exploiting American capitalism's short-termism. This latter predilection could end up being as much of a threat to the ability of American corporations to maintain healthy economic relations with China as Beijing's very strategic and targeted united front tactics.

CHAPTER EIGHT

Technology and Research

Technology transfers between nations exist on a spectrum of legitimacy. In many developing economies, multinational corporations willingly agree to skills and technology transfer arrangements in exchange for the right to operate. Governments support these measures in the hopes of furthering economic development. Transfers cross the threshold into illegitimacy when coercion, misappropriation, theft, or espionage are deployed with the effect of undermining a company's, and ultimately its home country's, economic competitiveness. China's expropriation of American technology is an example of how it leverages its influence among universities, corporations, and diaspora communities to further strategic objectives. This chapter reviews the targets of China's expropriation efforts, describes the state and nontraditional collectors involved, and concludes with recommendations for how the United States can better defend against this phenomenon. It is important to note that not all expropriation of intellectual property (IP) occurs at the explicit direction of the government and that China is not the sole country targeting the United States. Nonetheless, China—whether at the level of the state or individual—is considered the most serious offender.

While Chinese cyberthreats and clandestine spying against the United States dominate the public discourse, a far more serious threat is posed by China's informal or "extralegal" transfers of US technology and IP theft.[1] Operating under the radar, these quiet diversions of US technical know-how are carried out by groups and individuals in the United

States, whose support for China erodes America's technological edge and ability to compete in international markets. These groups are managed by a professional cadre of Chinese government and government-associated science and technology transfer specialists who facilitate intellectual property "exchanges" through a maze of venues. They target specific advanced technologies drawn from China's industrial planning priorities (e.g., Made in China 2025[2]) such as semiconductors, robotics, next-generation information technologies (e.g., big data, smart grid, internet of things), aviation, artificial intelligence, and electric vehicles. As a result of their efforts, a commission convened by the National Bureau of Asian Research concluded that IP theft, primarily from China, costs the American economy hundreds of billions of dollars each year, with significant impact on employment and innovation.[3] Former commander of United States Cyber Command and director of the National Security Agency General Keith Alexander was even more grave when he asserted the ongoing theft of IP by China represents "the greatest transfer of wealth in human history."[4]

The Dynamics of Chinese IP Theft

Chinese nontraditional collection and IP theft is not done randomly by individuals acting on their own. Rather, China has enacted some two dozen laws that have created a state-run foreign technology transfer apparatus that sponsors, for example, labs in China that rely wholly on information provided by compatriots working abroad. The apparatus also maintains databases of foreign co-optees and distributes stipends, sinecures, and cash to foreign donors of high-tech innovations. In addition, the apparatus is responsible for the care and feeding of agents willing to "serve China while in place" abroad.

Targets

China targets all sources of American innovation, including universities, corporations, and government labs, exploiting both their openness and naïveté. The methods and tradecraft are custom tailored to each target. For universities, China takes advantage of the commitment to intellectual freedom on campus, which strongly resists government scrutiny of the activities of foreign students in hard-science programs and international academic cooperation. For corporations, the lure of the Chinese market gives Beijing tremendous leverage in exacting tech transfer from American firms, combined with financial incentives for employees to purloin intellectual property for personal gain. Finally, US government labs have a historical commitment to international scientific cooperation, and an uneven record of monitoring that cooperation for unsanctioned transfers of information.

These efforts complement China's legitimate efforts to invest in its own indigenous innovative capacity. China has for several decades made science and technology development a priority and appears to have the political will to see it through. This is demonstrated by the research and development funding programs it has put into place, the investment in core scientific infrastructure that is in some cases unparalleled anywhere else in the world, and a national scientifically oriented industrial policy. Yet the continuing intense engagement in IP theft is, in many ways, an indication of the gaps in China's indigenous innovation efforts.

Once acquired, foreign technology is converted in China into products and weapons at 180 "Pioneering Parks for Overseas Chinese Scholars," 160 "Innovation Service Centers," 276 "National Technology Model Transfer Organizations," and an unknown number of "technology business incubators." These facilities are strategically located to ensure wide distribution of the foreign technologies.

Nontraditional Collectors

Nontraditional collectors include Chinese citizens, Chinese Americans whom the Chinese government is better able to cultivate or coerce, and other Americans. They range from students to researchers. Many are willing participants, such as students from Chinese defense universities explicitly tasked with acquiring foreign technology; others are not and are targeted for access to research they have pursued by their own passion and intellect. Indeed, some nontraditional collectors may even be unwitting in their support.

Collectors do not appear to be chosen by Beijing for their race or nationality; rather they are targeted for their access to the desired intellectual property and their willingness to violate their employee agreements or national laws. Indeed, more recent scholarship has shattered the shibboleth that the Chinese government only recruits ethnic Chinese. While Chinese intelligence does have a historically strong track record of attempting to recruit ethnic Chinese, primarily because of cultural and language affinity, more recent cases of espionage and technology transfer suggest that the Chinese government has broadened its tradecraft to recruit nonethnic Chinese assets and collectors as well, perhaps as a way of complicating US counterintelligence efforts.

China's most systematic channel for identifying foreign-based nontraditional collectors is its Recruitment Program of Global Experts (海外高层次人才引进计划), commonly known as the Thousand Talents Plan (千人计划) or the Thousand Talents Program (TTP).[5] The TTP is a massive and sustained talent recruitment campaign designed to recruit leading experts from overseas to assist in the country's modernization drive.

Initiated in 2008, the TTP aims to recruit leading overseas scientists and experts who work in areas that are deemed high priority for achieving China's modernization goals.[6] The program originally aimed to recruit one thousand "overseas talents" (海外人才) over a period of five to ten years. Official Chinese TTP websites list more than three hundred US government researchers and more than six hundred US corporate personnel who have accepted TTP money.[7] In many cases, these individuals do not disclose receiving the TTP money to their employer, which for US government employees is illegal and for corporate personnel likely represents a conflict of interest that violates their employee agreement.

State Collection Apparatus

China's nontraditional collection relies on a web of activities, including open-source research, exchanges, cooperation and professional organizations, direct funding of research, strategic acquisition, and cyberespionage.

Open-Source Research

China's efforts to exploit foreign innovation is further seen in its open-source acquisition infrastructure, which surpasses that of any other country. China employs a cadre of thousands to locate, study, and disseminate foreign journals, patents, proceedings, dissertations, and technical standards without regard to ownership or copyright restrictions. The documents are indexed, archived, and supplied to Chinese commercial and military "customers."

Exchanges

The Chinese government organizes and pays for exchanges in which participants travel from the United States, divulge technical knowledge through scripted venues, are briefed on China's technology interests, return to their US base to collect more information, and repeat the process. China has a program for what it euphemistically calls "short-term visits" by co-opted foreigners, which, stripped of its rhetoric, is indistinguishable from state-run espionage.

Cooperation Organizations and Advocacy Groups

Many Sino-US science and technology (S&T) "cooperation" organizations in the United States facilitate these transfers and have individual memberships of hundreds to thousands. The figure scales to some ninety such groups worldwide. Members usually are expatriate Chinese, although China is expanding its recruitment of non–ethnic Chinese. One significant example of a Sino-US S&T cooperation organization is Triway Enterprise Inc. (三立国际有限公司), an "external training institute" set up under the auspices of the State Administration of Foreign Experts Affairs in Falls Church, Virginia, with branches in Beijing and Nanjing.

According to the Chinese version of the website, the company "since 1993 has been putting its energy into promoting bilateral exchange and cooperation between China and the US in the fields of S&T, culture, education and management with great success."[8]

China S&T advocacy groups in the United States declare loyalty to China and acknowledge a "duty" to support China's development. Members visit China to lecture, guide Chinese technical projects, transfer technologies, receive shopping lists from Chinese entities, and engage in other kinds of "technical exchanges." Many of them sit on Chinese government boards that decide the future of China's national technology investment. Another example of a China S&T advocacy group is the Silicon Valley Chinese Engineers Association (硅谷中国工程师协会), which describes itself as "a non-profit professional organization formed mainly by the professionals in the Bay Area from mainland China with a mission to promote professionalism and entrepreneurship among members," which is achieved by "organizing a variety of professional activities and *establishing channels to allow members to engage in China's rapid economic development*" [emphasis added].[9]

Chinese government tech-transfer offices, facilitation companies, and career-transfer personnel, some of whom are posted to China's diplomatic offices, support and direct the US-based groups. In China, hundreds of government offices are devoted entirely to facilitating foreign transfers of technology "by diverse means."

Joint Research

The preferred method of establishing a research beachhead in the United States is through the formation of a joint research center with a prominent US university. One example is the China-US Joint Research Center for Ecosystem and Environmental Change at the University of Tennessee, Knoxville.[10] Launched in 2006, researchers from the University of Tennessee and the Department of Energy–funded Oak Ridge National Laboratory partnered with the Chinese Academy of Sciences to address "the combined effects of climate change and human activities on regional and global ecosystems and explore technologies for restoration of degraded environments." The center's research focuses on science at the heart of the "green technology" revolution, which is one of Beijing's major national industrial policy objectives.

The center's website lays out three goals that match nicely with a tech-transfer agenda: (1) organize and implement international scientific and engineering research; (2) serve as a center for scientific information exchange; and (3) provide international education and technical training.[11] The website goes on to outline cooperative mechanisms to achieve these goals, including joint research projects, academic exchange, student education, and *"technical transfer and training"*[12] [emphasis added]. This dynamic differs fundamentally from the mission of Western research facilities abroad, which is to adapt technology already in their portfolios to sell in foreign markets. A PRC study on the benefits of overseas "research" to obtain foreign technology put it this way: "How can you get the tiger cub if you don't go into the tiger's den?" (不入虎穴,焉得虎子).[13]

Cyberespionage

Perhaps the most damaging channel for stealing US intellectual property is cyberespionage. As noted above, NSA director Keith Alexander has called cyberespionage by Chinese state actors the "greatest transfer of wealth in human history." Cyberespionage is both a means for pilfering US science and technology and a method of intelligence collection for potential attacks against American military, government, and commercial technical systems. As a result, these cyber intrusions represent a fundamental threat to American economic competitiveness and national security.

Other Means of Misappropriation

While not technology transfer per se, counterfeiting is so common in China that it has the same practical effect. Schemes range from the subtle to blatant: benchmarking against ISO standards;[14] patent research where a design is modified slightly, if at all, re-patented in China, and "legally" produced with government protection;[15] reverse engineering;[16]

"imitative innovation" (模仿创新),[17] with or without the innovation (also called "imitative remanufacturing" 模仿改造);[18] and marketing the pirated product without or with its original logo.[19] Other reporting has detailed how the Chinese government exploits regulatory panels (often with members who have direct conflicts of interest by working for local competitors) and antitrust investigations to acquire trade secrets from foreign companies, aiding domestic industries.[20]

Conclusion and Recommendations

China's aggressive policy is threatening the advantages the United States has long enjoyed as a scientifically creative nation. This is occurring as a declining number of US students are getting advanced degrees in science and technology, R&D funds are dropping off, and the nation's manufacturing base is shrinking.[21] When combined with a more scientifically competent China that is also using the discoveries of others, the future of US competitiveness comes into question.

The best source of resiliency in the face of rampant IP theft from China is continued and expanded reinvestment in American innovation. The United States can recover its competitiveness by manufacturing what it invents and rebuilding the scientific foundation on which its competitive edge depends. But unless active efforts are made to prevent countries from inappropriately exploiting American technologies developed at great cost, efforts at national reconstruction will be wasted. The United States' current defense of intellectual property has not been effective in refuting appropriation by China, by all accounts the world's worst offender.

A key source of American creativity—the country's individualism and openness—makes it difficult to implement collective efforts to protect the products of American innovation. Nonetheless, policies and processes can be improved to reduce the risk of misappropriation without compromising the United States' innovative capacity. These require improved transparency with better information and screening, enhanced export controls, and stronger investment reviews.

Transparency, Better Information, and Screening

One of the most glaring factors that facilitates IP theft is the fact that recipients of Chinese funding programs, such as the Thousand Talents Program described above, routinely do not declare their work in China. At a minimum, recipients should be required to register as foreign agents under the Foreign Agents Registration Act (FARA).[22] Recipients who are active government employees may be breaking the law, as 18 US Code § 209 prohibits accepting supplemental income for performing the same role that falls under the scope of their government employment.[23]

The US government and universities should also make an evidence- and risk-based assessment when determining whether to admit students into major research programs. The current system, known as the Student and Exchange Visitor Information System (SEVIS),[24] is designed "to track and monitor schools and programs, students, exchange visitors and their dependents while approved to participate in the US education system." SEVIS collects data on surnames and first names, addresses, date and country of birth, dependents' information, nationality/citizenship, funding, school, program name, date of study commencement, education degree level, and authorization for on-campus employment. As of March 2011, China had the largest number of students in SEVIS, at 158,698.[25]

The FBI has access to all of the student data contained in SEVIS and no longer needs the permission of the Department of Homeland Security to initiate investigations of foreign students.[26] However, the laws, regulations, and directives governing SEVIS do not require some additional critical pieces of information, which are perceived by the Government Accounting Office to be important to managing the program:

- The nonimmigrant visa number, expiration date, and issuing post are optional and only captured if entered into the system by the school or exchange visitor program.
- The nonimmigrant driver's license number and issuing state were imposed by the interagency working group and support investigative efforts.

- The nonimmigrant passport number, passport expiration date, and passport issuing country are optional and only captured if entered into the system by the school or exchange visitor program.[27]

It is difficult to ascertain from open sources whether these problems have been fixed, but the nonmandatory data are key investigative details that would be critical for federal law enforcement seeking to assess possible illicit technology transfers by students.

Improved Export Controls

The second major policy problem involves PRC student access to controlled technology under the deemed export system. According to the Commerce Department, a restricted product or technology is "deemed," or considered exported, when it is used by a foreign national in the United States.[28] However, under these rules, a university or research lab does not need a deemed export license if a foreign graduate student is merely present in a lab. It only needs a license if it intends to export that technology to the foreign national's country.

From 2004 to 2006, the US Commerce Department attempted to change these rules[29] but was stymied by opposition from universities and research labs.[30] Yet the continued flow of controlled technology to the PRC and the findings of Government Accounting Office studies on the problems of university oversight[31] strongly suggest that Commerce's recommendations should be reexamined.

In 2009, then president Obama "directed a broad-based interagency reform of the US export control system with the goal of strengthening national security and the competitiveness of key US manufacturing and technology sectors by focusing on current threats and adapting to the changing economic and technological landscape."[32] Specifically, the initiative aimed to "build higher fences" around a core set of items, the misuse of which can pose a national security threat to the United States.[33]

The reform initiative is synchronizing the two existing control lists, the Munitions List and the Commerce Control List, so that (1) they are "tiered" to distinguish the types of items that should be subject to stricter or more permissive levels of control for different destinations, end uses, and end users; (2) they create a "bright line" between the two current control lists to clarify which controls any given item, and reduce government and industry uncertainty about whether particular items are subject to the control of the State Department or the Commerce Department; and (3) they are structurally aligned so that they potentially can be combined into a single list of controlled items.[34]

Moreover, the lists will be transformed into a "positive list" that describes controlled items using objective criteria (e.g., technical parameters such as horsepower or microns) rather than broad, open-ended, subjective, generic, or design-intent-based criteria.[35] After applying these criteria, the list will be divided into three tiers based on their military importance and availability.[36]

On the one hand, these reforms could greatly improve the efficiency of the export control bureaucracy, preventing fewer technologies from slipping between the cracks and finding their way to China. They could also make the system and its control lists better able to keep pace with technological change, which had been a major problem with the old system, particularly with regard to fast-moving information technologies. On the other hand, the reforms appear to loosen controls over dual-use technologies, which China has a long and successful track record of integrating into advanced systems, and which can form the core of new innovations. The future of these reforms is unclear as the Trump administration appears to focus on more aggressive trade strategies and policies designed to protect US industries and punish offending Chinese companies.

Strong Investment Reviews

The Committee on Foreign Investment in the United States (CFIUS) is an interagency committee that serves the president in overseeing the national security implications of foreign investment in the economy.[37] As China's economy and financial weight has grown, CFIUS has reviewed an increasing number of proposed acquisitions of American companies and infrastructure by Chinese entities. Many of these proposed mergers have received high levels of media and congressional attention, and most of the high-profile cases have ended in rejection or strong discouragement leading to abandonment of the deal. While the CFIUS process may have prevented individual cases of sensitive or illegal technology transfer, it could also have had the unintended effect of forcing Chinese actors to steal the data through espionage because of their inability to buy them. Recent legislation, signed by President Trump, is a substantial improvement to CFIUS, closing loopholes that the Chinese had been exploiting, and broadening the scope of the CFIUS authorities in important ways. The new law extends CFIUS review timeframes, increases the types of transactions subject to CFIUS' jurisdiction, makes certain notifications mandatory, and establishes a process for potentially expedited review and approval of certain transactions. The four new "covered transactions" include real estate deals near US national security facilities, deals involving "critical infrastructure" or "critical technologies," changes in ownership rights by a foreign investor, and any transaction designed to evade the CFIUS process. In exchange for all these additional burdens, the new law also helps companies by clarifying time limits for decisions and places important jurisdictional limits on the expansion of the law's scope.

APPENDIX 1

China's Influence Operations Bureaucracy

While recent months have brought increased attention to the United Front Work Department (UFWD), or united front activities, it is important to emphasize that this is but one of many institutions within the Chinese party-state involved in influence operations. As the accompanying graphic illustrates, the bureaucracy involved in extending China's global influence is large, complex, and specialized in function. Generally speaking, there are three types of bureaucratic organizations included in the chart: (1) policy coordination; (2) policy formulation and implementation; and (3) organizations with specialized functions.

As components of a Leninist party-state, CCP organizations have higher political status than government institutions. This has become even more pronounced under the party's general secretary Xi Jinping and following the bureaucratic reorganization announced after the March 2018 meeting of the National People's Congress. Generally speaking, party organs make policies, which are then implemented by state bureaucracies. There is *no* single organization overseeing the entirety of the country's influence operations abroad. The most important CCP organizations in the diagram are the Foreign Affairs Commission, the External Propaganda Leading Group/State Council Information Office, the CCP Propaganda Department, the CCP United Front Work Department, the CCP International Liaison Department, and united front departments inside the People's Liberation Army. Critical policies related

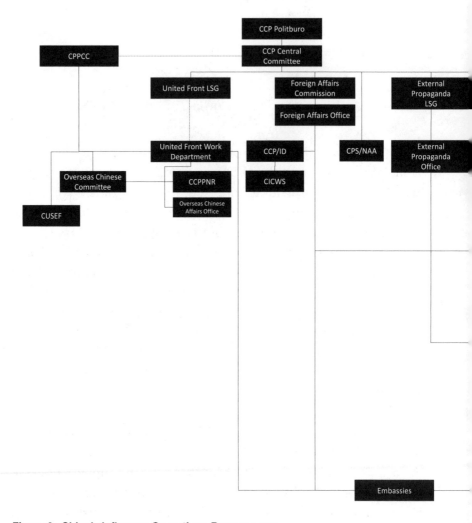

Figure 2: China's Influence Operations Bureaucracy

to foreign affairs are formulated in these bodies. The same organizations are also involved in coordinating the implementation of these policies.

The Policy-Making Process in the Chinese Party-State

The process is driven both by top leadership and functional bureaucracies. Policy formulation, which involves the generation of ideas and proposals, typically takes place in functional bureaucracies and specialized departments within these bureaucracies. In the process of policy formulation, one bureaucracy specializing in the functional or issue area (for example, propaganda) may take charge, but it also consults with other bureaucracies that may have a stake in the issue. The draft policy proposals are then forwarded to the Leading Small Groups (领导小组), which deliberate, vet, and sign off on the policy proposals before sending them to the politburo and the Politburo Standing Committee (PBSC) for a final decision. These Leading Small Groups, which range in size from five to a dozen members, are normally chaired by a politburo member and include a range of ministerial-level officials relevant to that functional policy area. Some meet at regular intervals (biweekly), whereas most convene on an ad hoc basis when necessary. In this formal, ministry- or department-initiated process, the ultimate decision-making authority lies with the Politburo Standing Committee.

At this level of policy formulation, of particular relevance to China's international influence activities are the External Propaganda Leading Group (对外宣传领导小组), which has a dual bureaucratic identity as the State Council Information Office (国务新闻办公室); the Central Committee Propaganda Department (中共中央宣传部); the Central Committee United Front Work Department (中共中央统战部); the Central Committee Foreign Affairs Commission (中共外事委员会);[1] and the Central Committee Education Leading Small Group (教育部). Although bureaucratically ranked slightly lower, the Ministry of Culture and Tourism, the Ministry of Education, the newly created Voice of China, and the Xinhua News Agency all exercise policy formulation and oversight roles in their functional domains.

There is also a parallel top-down policy process initiated by one of the top leaders on the Politburo Standing Committee (PBSC). As a rule, Xi Jinping, the CCP general secretary, has broad authority and may issue a brief directive on a matter he believes should receive extra attention or priority. (Typically, such directives are short comments he writes on reports that come across his desk.) Otherwise, only a PBSC member overseeing a particular portfolio can issue such directives on matters that fall into his or her area of responsibility. Such comments are then related to the functional bureaucracies and can lead to the formulation of a new policy, the modification of an existing policy, or other actions.

On the politburo and its seven-member PBSC, several members have direct responsibility for external affairs. As the chair of the Foreign Affairs Commission, Xi has overall authority on all aspects of China's foreign relations. Wang Huning, the PBSC member responsible for party affairs, ideology, and propaganda, is the top official with oversight of China's overseas propaganda (外宣) efforts, while politburo member and director of the CCP Propaganda Department Huang Kunming oversees all media organs and has day-to-day oversight of the entire propaganda system. Wang Yang, another PBSC member and the chairman of the Chinese People's Political Consultative Conference (CPPCC), has overall responsibility for the united front portfolio, although Sun Chunlan (the only female member of the twenty-five-person politburo and former director of the United Front Work Department from 2014 to 2017) may also continue to have some residual responsibilities as well, since her current portfolio includes education and culture. Additionally, You Quan, a member of the politburo secretariat, is now the new head of the UFWD, and he is in charge of the day-to-day work of the department. These leaders' views on particular issues carry a great deal of weight and can often result in significant policy initiatives or modifications.

Besides issuing brief policy directives via their comments on documents (known as 批示), top leaders can also communicate their ideas or orders in conversations or meetings with the ministers in charge of functional bureaucracies. Such ideas or orders can lead to actions at the implementation level or to the formulation of a new policy or the modification of an existing policy.

Policy Coordination

The Foreign Affairs Commission, which used to be called the Foreign Affairs Leading Small Group (est. 1956), is by far the most important of these organizations. The role of the commission is similar to that of the interagency "principals committees" in the US system. Its chairman is Xi Jinping, while Premier Li Keqiang and Vice President Wang Qishan serve as vice chairmen. Other PBSC members Wang Huning and Han Zheng are members. Le Yucheng, a vice minister of Foreign Affairs, is deputy director. Other members of the commission include the most senior leaders of the Chinese government: Yang Jiechi and the ministers of Foreign Affairs, State Security, Defense, Public Security, Commerce, the CCP's International Liaison Department, Taiwan Affairs Office, Hong Kong and Macao Affairs Office, Propaganda Department, External Propaganda Office, and Overseas Chinese Affairs Office.

The commission also has an attached "office," known as the Central Foreign Affairs Office (中央外办), which has a dedicated staff of approximately fifty (many of whom are seconded from the Ministry of Foreign Affairs, International Liaison Department of the CCP, other ministries, and the military). The director of this office is currently Yang Jiechi—a politburo member, former state councilor, and veteran diplomat. This body is the central coordinating body for China's foreign affairs—across all bureaucracies—on a daily basis.

While the Foreign Affairs Commission is the principal organization in the making and coordination of China's overall foreign policy, the United Front Leading Small Group and the External Propaganda Leading Small Group also have important—but somewhat lower—status in the Chinese hierarchy. They are led, respectively, by the Politburo Standing Committee member in charge of ideology and propaganda and the head of the United Front Work Department. The Leading Small Group for United Front Work is located inside the CCP's United Front Work Department and draws on UFWD personnel for staff work. The Leading

Small Group for External Propaganda is subordinate to the CCP Leading Small Group for Propaganda and Ideology and is required to seek guidance from the Foreign Affairs Commission, and it draws on the State Council Information Office (with which it has a dual role) for staff work. Both groups play an important role in the formulation of policy and coordination of implementation in their respective sectors.

Conferences

Another important instrument in the coordination of policy is the central or national conferences that are convened to formulate and announce new policy objectives and mobilize the bureaucracy to implement these policies. Some of these conferences are convened more frequently and are more important than others. Four central or national conferences are held to coordinate foreign policy and external influence operations: the Central Foreign Affairs Work Conference, the National Propaganda Work Conference, the Central United Front Work Conference, and the National Overseas Chinese Work Conference. These are large gatherings that last two to three days and are attended by key central, provincial, and local leaders, as well as various ministries and the Chinese military. These conferences serve to provide overall policy direction to cadres working in that bureaucratic system (系统) as well as to issue very specific annual plans for the coming year's activities.[2]

One measure of the importance of these conferences can be gauged by who gives the keynote speech. For example, Xi Jinping gave the keynote speeches at the Central Foreign Affairs Work Conference (2014 and 2018), the Central United Front Work Conference (2015), and the National Propaganda Work Conference (2013 and 2018). When Xi does not give the keynote speech, the politburo member in charge of that domain gives it. By contrast, the keynote speech at the National Overseas Chinese Conference in 2017 was given by Yang Jiechi, who was at that time a state councilor responsible for foreign affairs.

- The Central Foreign Affairs Work Conference is held at irregular intervals (2006, 2014, and 2018) to review Chinese foreign policy and announce new initiatives and objectives. It is attended by key

ministers, ambassadors, senior military officers, and local officials
responsible for foreign affairs.

- The Central United Front Work Conference, which used to be
  called the National United Front Work Conference, is also convened at irregular intervals (2000, 2006, and 2015). Both national
  and local officials responsible for religious, ethnic, and overseas
  Chinese affairs participate.

- Prior to 2013, the External Propaganda Work Conference was convened annually. But starting after that year, this conference has
  become part of the annual National Propaganda Work Conference.
  Officials in the propaganda sector from all over China attend these
  conferences.

- The National Overseas Chinese Work Conference has been held
  roughly every six years (2005, 2011, and 2017). Only national and
  local officials responsible for overseas Chinese affairs participate.

Hierarchy and Division of Labor

The CCP-affiliated organizations in our diagram that are involved in
making policies concerned with Chinese influence activities abroad enjoy
higher political status than those that execute these policies. What makes
the Chinese system notable is the division of labor, the specialization of
its bureaucracies, and the staffing of these bureaucracies with well-trained
and experienced professionals. Besides engaging their counterparts overseas, these bureaucracies either oversee or directly conduct influence
operations in their areas of specialization. While there exists *no* single
organization overseeing the entirety of China's influence activities abroad
(although if any one does have such sweeping purview, it is the Foreign
Affairs Commission), in the implementation of policies aimed to expand
Chinese influence abroad, there are two types of bureaucracies: general
purpose and specialized. The following institutional profiles include
many of the principal bodies involved in China's overseas influence
activities.

Ministry of Foreign Affairs

The Ministry of Foreign Affairs (MFA) is a typical general-purpose bureaucracy that serves as China's main interlocutor with foreign governments. But since most of its time is consumed by routine diplomatic activities, the foreign ministry itself does not play a significant role in influence operations overseas. The one area where it does is via its Department of Public Diplomacy (外交部公共外交司), which primarily oversees the MFA Spokesman's Office in Beijing, international media outreach, and China's embassy spokesmen abroad; international visitor programs; and "exchange" organizations, such as the Chinese People's Institute of Foreign Affairs (which bring a range of former officials and international affairs experts to China). Also, the MFA is important insofar as Chinese embassies abroad have representatives of the Ministry of Culture, the Xinhua News Agency, the CCP International Liaison Department, the Ministry of Education, and other bureaucratic bodies, each of which is involved in foreign influence activities.

United Front Work Department

The CCP United Front Work Department is a specialized CCP organization, one of four Central Committee departments.[3] Its principal mission is to build support for the CCP and its policies among domestic ethnic groups, religious groups, the eight so-called democratic parties (民主党派), the Chinese diaspora worldwide, and political, economic, and social elites in Hong Kong, Macao, and Taiwan. These united front activities have a long history dating to the CCP's pre-1949 rise to power. The main tasks and objectives of the CCP's united front activities outside of Greater China are laid out in Article 31 of the CCP Guidelines on United Front Work (中国共产党统一战线工作条例), issued in 2015—they target almost exclusively members of the Chinese diaspora, who are supposed to be encouraged to "contribute to the modernization and reunification of the motherland, advance the cause of opposing (Taiwanese) independence and promoting reunification, inherit and propagate China's outstanding culture, and promote the friendship between the Chinese people and the peoples of the other countries in the world."

Although the United Front Work Department has attracted much media attention, and the term "united front" has become a euphemistic one for many analysts writing about China's influence activities abroad, the scope of the UFWD's activities in China's external influence operations is actually limited. Its primary target audience is the Chinese diaspora in general, and its elite members in particular. The mission of engaging and influencing non–ethnic Chinese audiences, individuals, and foreign institutions is assigned to other specialized Chinese entities—such as the Chinese Academy of Social Sciences, the Ministry of Culture, the Ministry of Education, the Ministry of State Security (e.g., China Institutes of Contemporary International Relations), and other institutions that have well-trained professionals and long-standing ties with their counterparts overseas.

International [Liaison] Department

The CCP's International [Liaison] Department (中央联络部) (ID) is in charge of "party-to-party relations" (党际关系) and has the primary mission of cultivating foreign political parties and politicians around the world. This party organ has existed since before 1949 and was formerly charged with maintaining China's fraternal ties with other communist and socialist parties around the world, but in the wake of the Cold War, the CCP/ID drastically broadened its mandate to interact with virtually all political parties abroad (except fascist and racist parties). Today it claims to maintain ties with over 400 political parties in 140 countries, receives about 200 delegations, and dispatches about 100 delegations abroad every year. CCP/ID exchanges have provided an important prism through which the CCP and other organizations in China monitor the outside world and absorb lessons for China's own modernization. This kind of information gathering goes well beyond traditional intelligence collection (although, to be sure, the ID also engages in this activity).

Through its interactions with political parties all over the world, the CCP/ID serves an important function as a kind of "radar" for identifying up-and-coming foreign politicians before they attain national prominence and office. Having identified such rising stars, the CCP/ID brings them to China (usually on all-expenses-paid visits)—often offering them their first exposure to China and trying to make the best possible impression on them. Another key dimension of this function has been to expose CCP leaders at the provincial and subprovincial levels to the outside world—often for the first time. Many provincial party secretaries, governors, mayors, and other leading local cadres are taken abroad on ID delegations every year. The CCP/ID has also played a key diplomatic role in certain instances, such as providing a liaison dialogue channel between the United States and North Korea.

In addition, the ID performs a range of other functions:

- Administering "private sector" liaison organizations to facilitate contact with think tanks, NGOs, and individuals worldwide
- Collecting current intelligence and information on the foreign policies, domestic political scene and political parties, and societies in various nations worldwide
- Sending special study teams abroad to research important topics related to China's reforms
- Contributing to the work of Chinese embassies worldwide (usually monitoring domestic politics and liaising with domestic political parties, movements, and personages)
- Working with other CCP Central Committee departments and State Council ministries to facilitate their work overseas (e.g., assisting the United Front Work Department concerning Taiwan, the State Council Information Office/External Propaganda Leading Group concerning China's image abroad, or the National People's Congress on parliamentary exchanges)
- Arranging visits of central-level, provincial-level, municipal-level, and occasionally subprovincial-level CCP officials abroad
- Hosting foreign leaders, politicians, party officials, and ex-officials, as well as a range of foreign policy specialists, on tours of China

- Hosting the biannual World Political Parties High-Level Meeting and the annual CCP in Dialogue with the World meeting

As such, the ID performs extremely important roles overseas and is a key—but underappreciated and even unknown—instrument in China's international influence activities.

The State Council Information Office/External Propaganda Leading Group

The State Council Information Office/External Propaganda Leading Group (SCIO/EPLG) is the nerve center and leading organ in the sprawling system of China's international propaganda (对外外宣) work. It maps out the entirety of China's overseas "publicity" work, assigns different bureaucratic entities with specific tasks, fixes budgets for entities in this system, and convenes yearly meetings to implement the annual external propaganda plan (对外宣传计划). The SCIO is commonly known in Chinese both as the Guo Xin Ban (国新办) and Wai Xuan Ban (External Propaganda Office, 外宣办). The reason for the two names is because it straddles two bureaucratic systems—the party and the state. It is formally under the State Council, but it is also overseen by the Chinese Communist Party's External Propaganda Leading Group. This bureaucratic duality is what the Chinese describe as "one organ, two signboards" (一个机构两块牌子), a reference to the white placards that hang outside the gates of all Chinese institutions (in this case, giving the appearance of two different institutions inside but in reality only one). As such, the SCIO is the administrative office for the EPLG, playing a coordinating role in the media area similar to that performed by the Central Foreign Affairs Office (CFAO, 中央外办) for the Foreign Affairs Commission (中央外事委员会).

China's Influence Activities in Select Countries

This report has focused on the range of challenges the United States faces in an era of accelerating Chinese influence activities on multiple fronts. But this issue is hardly unique to the United States—indeed, China's influence activities now occur all around the world. In some instances, notably Australia, these activities appear to have proceeded much further than they have so far in the United States. In general, they seem more advanced in Asia and Europe, but there is also evidence of such activities in Africa and Latin America as well.

In order to explore some of the wider patterns that have emerged, this appendix offers brief summaries of the effects of such activities in eight countries: Australia, Canada, France, Germany, Japan, New Zealand, Singapore, and the United Kingdom. In each of these settings, the Chinese Communist Party (CCP) has refined its efforts through trial and error in order to exploit a critical asymmetry: China's communist party-state has established barriers to external political influence at home while, at the same time, seizing upon the openness of democratic systems overseas.

China seeks to make itself more palatable to democratic societies by using many of the customary vehicles of soft power—such as state-funded research centers, media outlets, university ties, and people-to-people exchange programs. These programs mimic the work of independent civil society institutions in a democracy, cloaking the extent to which the party-state controls these activities and genuine civil society is tightly repressed inside China. In conjunction with the dramatic expansion of Chinese economic interests abroad, the Chinese government has focused its influence initiatives on obscuring its policies and suppressing, to the extent possible, voices beyond China's borders that are critical of the CCP.[1] Targeting the media, academia, and the policy community, Beijing seeks to penetrate institutions in democratic states that might draw attention or raise obstacles to CCP interests, creating disincentives for any such resistance. Chinese economic activity is another important tool in this effort. Beijing is particularly skilled at using economic leverage to advance political goals in the realm of ideas, working through indirect channels that are not always apparent unless one examines Chinese business activities in conjunction with Beijing's other influence efforts.

Democracies worldwide are reckoning with the impact of "sharp power."[2] From Central Europe, where China has created the 16 + 1 Initiative, to sub-Saharan Africa and Latin America, where Chinese engagement in infrastructure and the media has grown discernibly in recent years, China's sharp power has come into view. A good deal more study is needed to understand the impact of these influence activities globally. Only with such understanding and comparative case studies can democratic societies craft responses that safeguard the integrity of their institutions while staying true to liberal democratic values.

AUSTRALIA

Australian journalists, scholars, officials, and political leaders have found themselves on the front lines of a global debate on how the CCP is working to covertly manipulate the political processes of democracies around the world. The Australian government has been the first to formulate a coherent and principled policy response. These efforts have had a catalyzing international impact. Randall Schriver, the Pentagon's senior official for Asia, said Australia has "woken up people in a lot of countries to take a look at Chinese activity within their own borders."[1] Hillary Clinton, the former New York senator and presidential candidate, said Australia (together with New Zealand) has sounded the alarm on "a new global battle."[2] Government leaders in New Zealand, Canada, and the United Kingdom have all been paying close attention to these growing Chinese activities. And yet, despite leading the way, effective implementation is far from assured in Australia. Sustaining a counter-interference strategy against the CCP—with its unrivaled resources and organization—will require an unprecedented degree of policy fortitude and political strategy from Australian political leaders on both sides of the parliamentary aisle as well as the support of business leaders and the general public.

The Australia conversation has mostly been led by enterprising journalists and aided by a handful of sinologists. It has been a healthy catalytic process in which security agencies have been communicating warnings to institutions at risk and politicians have been taking security agencies and credible media investigations seriously. The director-general of the Australian Security Intelligence Organization, Duncan Lewis, said the espionage and interference threat is greater now than at any time during the Cold War due to a greater number of foreign intelligence actors and the advent of cybertechnologies. He said foreign interference activities range from "a foreign power using local Australians to observe and harass its diaspora community here in our country through to the recruitment and co-opting of influential and powerful Australian voices to lobby our decision-makers."[3]

Much of the debate—particularly in its early stages—has been anchored in the community of Chinese Australians. Ethnic Chinese writers, entrepreneurs, and activists led the way in drawing the nation's attention to the party's efforts to suppress the diversity of their opinions through surveillance, coercion, and co-option. In 2005, Chinese defector Chen Yonglin exposed an enormous informant network that kept tabs on Chinese Australians, including Falun Gong practitioners, who defied the party line. In 2008, thousands of red-flag-waving students were mobilized to march on Canberra's Parliament to "defend the sacred Olympic torch" against pro-Tibet and other protestors as the torch wound its way to the Olympic ceremony in Beijing.[4] More recently, Chinese Australian journalists have laid a foundation of investigative reporting on the CCP's concealed links to Australian politics. Philip Wen, Beijing correspondent for the *Sydney Morning Herald*, showed how the party was "astroturfing" grassroots political movements to give the impression of ethnic Chinese support for Beijing's policies and leaders and to drown out its opponents. Over the past two years, Australian investigative journalists have documented a series of examples of Beijing-linked political donors buying access and influence, universities being co-opted as "propaganda vehicles," and Australian-funded scientific research being diverted to aid the modernization of the People's Liberation Army (PLA). Some of those reports showed how the CCP was using tools of coercion and co-option to manipulate deliberations of the Australian Parliament.

In 2017, CCP interference in Australian democratic processes became so brazen that party officials began to use their capability for interference as diplomatic leverage. The targets were bipartisan. The CCP reportedly leveraged the fact of its arbitrary power over Australian prisoners in China as it sought to persuade the Malcolm Turnbull government to ratify a controversial extradition treaty.[5] And Meng Jianzhu, then China's minister of public security, warned the Labor opposition leadership about the electoral consequences of failing to endorse the treaty. According to the *Australian* newspaper: "Mr. Meng said it would be a shame if Chinese government representatives had to tell the Chinese community in Australia that Labor did not support the relationship between Australia and China."[6]

In June 2017, a joint investigation by the Australian Broadcasting Corporation and Fairfax Media revealed that the Australian Security Intelligence Organization (ASIO) had warned the major political parties that two of Australia's most generous political donors had "strong connections to the Chinese Communist Party" and that their "donations might come with strings attached."[7] One of them leveraged a $400,000 donation in an attempt to soften the Labor Party line on the South China Sea. Most notoriously, an ambitious young Labor senator, Sam Dastyari, was shown to have recited Beijing's South China Sea talking points almost word for word immediately after the political donor had threatened to withdraw his money. Dastyari was also shown to have given counter-surveillance advice to the donor. As a result of these actions, Dastyari was forced to resign from Parliament. Again, the CCP was shown to be working both sides of the political aisle. The Liberal trade minister, Andrew Robb, was shown to have stepped directly from office into a consultancy job to the CCP-linked company that bought a controversial lease for the Port of Darwin. The contract showed Robb to be earning 880,000 Australian dollars per year (more than 600,000 US dollars plus goods and services tax) for unspecified services.[8]

Response and Counter-response

In December 2017, as the political attacks on Dastyari came to a head, Prime Minister Turnbull revealed that his coalition government had been "galvanized" by a classified report into foreign interference that he had commissioned in August 2016. Turnbull unveiled a new counter-foreign-interference strategy, which he said would be shaped by four principles. First, the strategy would target the activities of foreign states and not the loyalties of foreign-born Australians. As Turnbull put it, "Our diaspora communities are part of the solution, not the problem." Second, the strategy would be country-agnostic and not single out Chinese interference. Third, it would distinguish conduct that is "covert, coercive, or corrupting" from legitimate and transparent public diplomacy. And fourth, it would be built upon the pillars of "sunlight, enforcement, deterrence, and capability."[9]

At the same time, the prime minister introduced sweeping new legislation into Parliament. One bill introduced a wide-reaching ban on foreign political donations, including measures to prevent foreigners from channeling donations through local entities.[10] A second bill imposed disclosure obligations for those working in Australian politics on behalf of a foreign principal. This bill would capture many of the indirect methodologies of CCP intelligence and United Front Work Department (UFWD) operations that are not caught by the US Foreign Agents Registration Act. And a third tranche of legislation would close some large loopholes in the Australian criminal law by introducing tough but graduated political interference and espionage offenses.

Turnbull also introduced legislation to establish a new Department of Home Affairs, which, among other roles, would house a national counter-foreign-interference coordinator who would integrate intelligence and enforcement and coordinate policy development. On December 16, 2017, at the height of this debate—and days after Turnbull introduced the new laws—the coalition government passed a serious electoral test by winning a by-election in the Sydney seat of Bennelong. According to one opinion poll, two-thirds of voters support the foreign interference legislation, with just 11 percent opposed—in a seat that has one of the largest ethnic Chinese communities in the country.

And yet, despite this policy progress, strong evidence of electoral support, and favorable international recognition, the Turnbull government found the politics and the diplomacy to be heavy going. At one level this is not surprising. The CCP excels in using covert and deceptive means to work preexisting fault lines of open, democratic societies. It has shown itself prepared to use the levers of economic engagement as a tool of political coercion. And there is no precedent for a mid-sized, open, multicultural nation standing its ground against a rising authoritarian superpower that accounts for a large proportion of its migrants and one in every three of its export dollars.

After seizing the political and policy initiative in 2017, the Turnbull government went quiet over the first half of 2018. It faced pushback from powerful domestic lobbying groups arguing that the proposed legislation went too far. Media firms targeted the espionage law, charities the donations law, and universities the proposed transparency law. Further resistance was mounted by multicultural lobbyists who maintained that Australia's reputation as an inclusive society was challenged by mention of foreign government interference in community affairs. Prominent business leaders and academics with China contracts called for an end to "China-bashing."

China's embassy in Canberra also played a part, publicly intervening as if it were a champion of Chinese Australian communities to confront "racist bigotry" in Australia. China's government consistently portrayed the counter-interference policies and conversation as an attack on "China" and "Chinese people." And Beijing framed Canberra's efforts to defend its institutions as an attack on the bilateral relationship. As if to confirm its own judgment, Beijing was reported to have frozen ministerial and official meetings across a range of key portfolios. In the ensuing silence, some of the CCP's most potent narratives filled the vacuum. It was not clear that the Turnbull government could push through the most significant overhaul of counterintelligence legislation in forty years without explaining why it was necessary.

It took a series of further explosive media investigations and some unorthodox political interventions to regain control of the conversation and ensure bipartisan support for the legislation. The chair of the Joint Parliamentary Committee on Intelligence & Security, Andrew Hastie, named one of Australia's most generous political donors as a "co-conspirator" in a UN bribery investigation and linked the affair to covert interference. "In Australia it is clear that the Chinese Communist Party is working to covertly interfere with our media and universities and also to influence our political processes and public debates," Hastie told his committee, after receiving support from the deputy chair, Anthony Byrne. "And it's time we applied sunlight to our political system and a person who has featured prominently in Australian politics over the past decade."[11]

The counter-interference criminal legislation and the foreign influence transparency scheme both passed through Parliament on June 28. The Home Affairs legislation had passed through Parliament earlier in the year, with the counter-foreign-interference task force established in April 2018. This effectively elevated the importance of countering foreign interference to a similar status as countering terrorism.[12] At the time of writing, the legislation to ban foreign political donations has not passed through Parliament. And Turnbull himself has been replaced as prime minister. The new prime minister, Scott Morrison, appears to have opted for policy continuity.

The Turnbull government led the way in diagnosing the challenge, forging an internal consensus, and setting out a bold and coherent counterstrategy. Australia became the first country in the world to lay the foundations for a sustained and coherent counter-interference strategy.

But if Australia is going to reset the terms of its engagement with a superpower—holding China to its principle of noninterference and setting a precedent of sovereign equality that others might follow—then it will have to accept strains on the bilateral relationship. If the government is to successfully implement a transformational strategy to defend Australia's democratic processes and social cohesion, then it has to find politically sustainable ways of engaging the democratic process and publicly making the case.

CANADA

Canada has a long history of engagement with the PRC dating back to 1970. Substantial and rapidly expanding connections with China at multiple levels include human flows (migrants, tourists, students), trade (with a major and recurring imbalance in China's favor), and diplomatic interactions. There are roughly 160,000 PRC students in Canadian schools, about 70 percent of them in universities and colleges. Per capita, this is about three times as many as in the United States and roughly on par with Australia.

Canadian experiences with Chinese interference are less intense than those documented in Australia and New Zealand, although that is changing. As early as 1997, a leaked report by Canada's Security Intelligence Service of the Royal Canadian Mounted Police (RCMP) identified improper influence through community associations connected to Chinese intelligence agencies and efforts to award politically connected Canadians in high-level roles with Chinese entities.[1] Today, the view in Ottawa is that China is definitely trying to influence Canadian opinion and opinion makers but is not making much headway at present. At the federal level, the greatest concern with China has to do with the acquisition, often by legal means, of strategic Canadian assets such as oil sands or major companies.

As in other countries, Chinese state actors (the CCP International Liaison Department, commercial entities, media) have targeted political parties and politicians (with a few ongoing cases at the provincial and municipal levels that are being investigated by the RCMP), civil society (through Confucius Institutes and consular outreach), and academia (through the Chinese Students Association, China Scholarship Council supervision of student recipients, and pressure on Canadian China specialists). An informal survey of Canadian China professionals (political and business actors) and China specialists (research professionals) confirms some PRC state activity in all these realms. But no cases have yet reached the intensity or threat documented in Australia and New Zealand.

In large part, this difference in intensity is due to material factors: Canada is less dependent economically on China than Australia and New Zealand are, but it is smaller and less powerful than the United States. In short, while facing similar influence and interference efforts from China, Canada—like the United States—appears to have more effective mechanisms (diplomacy, election-funding transparency, foreign-investment regulations) than Australia and New Zealand. Indeed, in May 2018 Canada's security service produced a report warning of the extent of interference in New Zealand.[2]

Politics

The Liberal government elected in October 2015 is inclined to expand relations with China at the diplomatic and commercial levels, including with some form of bilateral free-trade agreement and deeper cooperation on global issues like climate change, counterterrorism, and peace-keeping. Yet, despite Asia's rising geoeconomic and geopolitical weight, Canada's strategic center of gravity remains heavily tied to the United States and the transatlantic world and to Western perspectives. There are significant disagreements in the public and within government about the possibilities, opportunities, limits, and risks of a deeper relationship with China.

In December 2018, Canada arrested an executive from the Huawei telecommunications company on an extradition request from the United States. The case sparked controversy in Canada, especially after China apparently retaliated by arresting two Canadians, one a former diplomat, on vague national security–related charges. The Canadian public seems to have been angered by the case and China's reaction.

Things weren't helped in February 2019 when members of the Chinese Students and Scholars Association, a group closely aligned with the Chinese government, shouted down and videotaped a Turkish human-rights activist during a speech she gave at McMaster University in apparent coordination with Chinese diplomats. That same month more than ten thousand people signed a petition trying to block a Tibetan woman from running for student president at the University of Toronto at Scarborough, because of her pro-Tibetan social media posts. China's state-run press had praised the campaign to silence her.

Media reports highlighting concerns over improper interference also include the following:

- In 2010, the director of Canadian Security Intelligence Service, Canada's national security agency, said at least two provincial cabinet members and other government officials were under the control of foreign countries (including China).[3] Facing political pressure, he later said none of the actions were "illegal" and that "foreign interference is a common occurrence in many countries around the world and has been for decades."[4]
- In 2016, Prime Minister Justin Trudeau was a subject of controversy for his attendance at cash-for-access dinners.[5] Among the attendees were Chinese billionaire Zhang Bin, who donated $1 million to the Pierre Elliott Trudeau Foundation. Also at the dinner was Liu Meng, a CCP official who was opening a Chinese Chamber of Commerce, a common united front organization, in the country.
- In 2017, a Conservative member of Parliament was denied a visa to visit China because she intended to raise questions about human rights.[6]
- In October 2017, the *Financial Times* acquired a united front teaching manual that praised the success of overseas Chinese candidates in Toronto elections and that stated, "We should aim to work with those individuals and groups that are at a relatively high level, operate within the mainstream of society and have prospects for advancement."[7]
- In December 2017, the *Globe and Mail* reported that two Conservative senators had set up a private consulting business with the intent of attracting Chinese investment to Newfoundland and Lab-

rador.[8] The paper also reported that the Senate's ethics watchdog was investigating an all-expenses-paid trip to China taken by three Conservative senators, including one involved in the consulting company.[9] (The paper had previously reported on thirty-six trips to China funded by arms of the Chinese government or business groups.)[10]

- In December 2017, Conservative senator Linda Frum called for an investigation into improper influence in Canada.[11] She alleged that laws banning direct foreign donations to political parties are sufficiently robust, but third-party groups—so long as they receive funds six months prior to the election—can use foreign money to influence voters.

Civil Society

In 2016, the *New York Times* reported about pressure on independent Chinese-language media in Canada.[12] In January 2018, a coalition led by Amnesty International submitted a confidential report to the Canadian government detailing harassment and digital disinformation campaigns and direct threats against Uighurs, Tibetans, Taiwanese, democracy advocates, and members of Falun Gong.[13]

Business

One of the emerging debates in Canada concerns the future of China's telecom giant Huawei, which is widely believed to have links with China's People's Liberation Army. Huawei has little significant business in the United States and was recently banned from participating in Australia's 5G wireless network project. Now Canada is debating that issue, despite the fact that the firm has established a vast network of relationships with all of Canada's major telecom carriers and Canada's leading research universities. Two former directors of the Canadian Security Intelligence Service—Richard Fadden and Ward Elcock—as well as John Adams, the former head of the Communications Security Establishment (CSE), told the *Globe and Mail* in August that Canada should also ban Huawei from supplying equipment for a 5G network.[14]

Universities

An example from academia suggests the efficacy of Canadian efforts to combat China's influence operations. At one West Coast Canadian university with large numbers of students from the PRC in undergraduate humanities and social science courses, where potentially divergent views of China and Chinese political behavior regularly form part of the curriculum, there has been no observation of the pressures documented in Australia, where professors are often openly criticized by Chinese students for proposing less-flattering ways of looking at China. However, at that university's for-profit "international transition program," which offers international students who did not qualify for admission the chance (for a fee) to prepare to meet entrance requirements, university administrators have generally failed to integrate the students who are overwhelmingly PRC Chinese with poor English ability into the broader campus community. The result is that, even without PRC consular pressure, there is a strong pro-PRC culture of "political correctness" that conforms to united front goals without the effort to promote it. It appears that social isolation is the driving factor in this case.

Conclusion

Much of China's influence activities in Canada are a legitimate extension of the public diplomacy in which all nations engage. The pressing issue is when and where China crosses the line between influence and interference. Canadian experience so far suggests more influence work than interference. However, there are clear examples where such influence has become interference. So far, it would appear that the key variable for the relatively low impact of Chinese state efforts (or proxies) turns out to be Canadian practice more than Chinese state efforts. That is, the internal diversity of the Canadian Chinese community blunts political efforts by any one political party (including the CCP). More generally, Canadian practices of multiculturalism, transparency, campaign financing rules, business regulation, and academic integrity are cultivated and fairly robust.

These experiences suggest the following solutions or best practices in the Canadian case, which largely parallel the broader report's findings:

- Make clear public statements of Canadian values—political, economic, social, and academic.
- Insist on reciprocity with Chinese actors in each domain of engagement.
- Identify what harms Canadian state, social, and community interests.
- Strengthen the practice of Canadian values of multiculturalism, open society, and integration.
- Share experiences in each sector to build capacity and promote best practices, particularly engaging the Canadian Chinese community.
- Train and make use of area specialists to better understand PRC intentions (just as the PRC relies on "Western" specialists).

FRANCE

France is the Western European country with the most favorable disposition toward China historically, dating back to the establishment of diplomatic relations in 1964. Yet, it is also the EU country where current public opinion toward China is the most negative, overtaking Italy in 2017. As in other countries, it is difficult to distinguish between the voluntary exposure to influence, due to the French seeking to benefit from China's rise, and active efforts by Beijing to exploit French vulnerabilities.

Both the left and right in France have supported close ties with China. The dual nature of these ties differs from those in other European countries, where for the most part the left has been critical of US policy in Asia and supportive of China and Vietnam. In France's case, it was the right, under Charles de Gaulle, which recognized China in January 1964 and criticized US policy during the Vietnam War. So, for example, in January 2014, an all-night celebration for the fiftieth anniversary of the recognition was held in Paris with funding largely from major French firms operating in China. But it also means that French state television of the 1960s often aired views favorable to the Cultural Revolution, while Maoism was influential inside the radical left. French diplomacy also has had its "China school," with leading figures such as Étienne Manac'h (a historical Gaullist) and Claude Martin (who recently published his memoirs under a title lifted creatively from a saying by Chairman Mao, *La diplomatie n'est pas un dîner de gala*, or "Diplomacy is not a dinner party").

Still, the shift in public opinion has been equally notable. Simon Leys wrote in French and spawned a critical tradition inside French sinology. The 1989 Tiananmen Square crackdown and a demonstration condoned by the French government on the eve of the G-7 Versailles Summit created a lasting row with the PRC (to which arms sales to Taiwan in the early 1990s can be traced). President Nicolas Sarkozy's stand on Tibet around the 2008 Olympics kindled an even more severe controversy with China, one that also left a trace inside French officialdom. Although diplomatic relations would be normalized in the ensuing years, this marked the beginning of a rebalancing of France's foreign policy in Asia. Today, France is a leading arms provider to Australia, Malaysia, Vietnam, India, Singapore, and—to a lesser degree—Japan. It is the leading country—and one of only two EU countries—participating in freedom of navigation naval operations in the South China Sea, albeit with more limited objectives than the United States. It has also taken the lead, with Germany and Italy, in calling for investment screening by the EU, a move that clearly targets Chinese attempts to obtain European high technology.

Diaspora

The Chinese diaspora in France is the largest in Europe, estimated to be between six hundred thousand and one million. Exact figures are not known, as ethnic or religious censuses are banned in France. The diaspora is not only large but diverse, including Hoa refugees from Indochina arriving in the late 1970s, Wenzhou immigrants, Dongbei workers, and, more recently, students and affluent Chinese. Wenzhou immigrants are notably apolitical, while Dongbei (northeast) people are closer to PRC traditions. Very few influential French of Chinese origins come from either of these two groups.

The PRC embassy in Paris and consulates in Marseilles and Strasbourg have increased China's outreach to the various Chinese communities in recent years. Notably, actions were taken to encourage and mobilize counterdemonstrations (largely from the student community) in Paris during the 2008 Olympics row, and to exploit the issue of crime against Asians (tourists or residents). In 2016, the death of a Chinese resident at the hands of the police spawned a very sudden and publicly condoned reaction in China itself, an echo and perhaps a reminder of the 2008 Olympics conflict. The PRC also has consulates in French Polynesia and on Reunion Island, with activities more directed to communities of Chinese origin that reside there.

Public figures from the second or third generation of immigrants are emerging slowly. The traditionally anticommunist sentiment in Paris's thirteenth district, populated by former refugees, has all but disappeared. The district's Socialist Party member of Parliament, a former advocate of Taiwan, switched his sympathies to the PRC before leaving politics in 2017. While France has always seen itself as a melting pot society—where even native languages dissolve over a generation—the economic attraction of China is clearly felt.

Police and judicial cooperation have also become an issue. In 2017, for the first time, a PRC citizen accused of corruption was extradited back to China; no public assurances were given regarding a possible death penalty. Another case erupted when Chinese public security officials made an unannounced visit to France to pressure a resident to return home and face charges.

Politics

For decades, China's National Day reception has been the most sought-after diplomatic reception in France, with queues often backing into the street. China's diplomatic buildings have in fact sprouted up around Paris, sometimes acquired from French government sites on sale. China has cultivated a stable of former French politicians. Of particular interest to China is former prime minister Dominique de Villepin, who is a frequent visitor to the country. He has regularly made positive remarks to Chinese state media and at other fora regarding the Belt and Road Initiative and Chinese cooperation with the EU. In 2018, he became a distinguished professor at the China Europe International Business School, and he now heads its advisory board.

Civil Society

A new generation of NGOs linking French and PRC members and sponsors has emerged, complementing the traditional role of business. Most prominent is the France-China Foundation, guided by an active French diplomat and presided over by current prime minister Edouard Philippe. With prominent PRC businessmen (such as Jack Ma) as cosponsors and old or new members of the French establishment (e.g., former prime minister Laurent Fabius and Cedric Villani, prominent mathematician and a member of Parliament since 2017), the foundation hosts social events, including at the Château de Versailles. Its strongest activity is a Young Leaders program that is patterned after the traditional Fondation France-Amérique. Other organizations include the Fondation Prospective et Innovation, headed by Jean-Pierre Raffarin, which awards a Wu Jianmin scholarship named after a former Chinese ambassador to France.

Business

France maintains a negative trade balance with China, and Chinese companies have not invested much in France compared to what they have poured into Germany, Italy, and the United Kingdom. Chinese investors reduced investments during the 2016–17 presidential campaign and have also met with informal refusals in some cases, such as Areva, the French nuclear company. The Chinese domestic market is set to save France's dairy industry, even creating a temporary shortage of butter for the first time since 1945. Still, complaints over too many purchases—or too many tourists, for that matter—are drowned out by the profits involved.

In mainland France, the Comité France-Chine of MEDEF, the French business union, has always been a prominent link, usually spearheaded by a prominent former French political figure (from Raymond

Barre to Valéry Giscard d'Estaing and Jean-Pierre Raffarin). A separate French-Chinese investment fund has also been created, headed by a former senior official in the Treasury department.

Until very recently, Sino-French activities were largely financed by major French firms operating in China, with EDF, the semipublic electricity company that cooperates on nuclear plants with China, being the most prominent. EDF has been criticized for its transfers of technology to China, which it justifies by its contracts in China and the United Kingdom with Chinese co-funding. This pattern of lobbying by the French themselves may be changing. Huawei now appears as a frequent donor, including for public conferences taking place in such prestigious locales as the French National Assembly or Senate.

Quiet Chinese investments with ownership below the 10 percent declaratory level, as well as in real estate, make for more diffuse influence. This is particularly true at the local level, where Chinese investors are eagerly sought and business intermediaries tend to mushroom. Many plans for industrial parks and regional airports have not materialized, however. The partial takeover of the Toulouse airport (home of Airbus and other aerospace firms) has been marred by the temporary arrest in China of the lead Chinese investor and by a search for quick profits.

Academia

In general, French academic and scientific institutions have welcomed Chinese students and researchers. The Commissariat à l'Énergie Atomique (CEA), the École Polytechnique, and the Paris Saclay cluster and science park are all active in working with Chinese counterparts. The Paris Saclay cluster and science park has signed agreements with Tsinghua University and its commercial and high-tech spin-offs, Qinghua Holdings and Qinghua Unigroup. The Fondation Franco-Chinoise pour la Science et ses Applications, cofounded by the French and PRC science academies, promotes stays in France for Chinese scientists. It does not list any Chinese sponsoring firm. Huawei has been a major donor to the Institut des Hautes Études Scientifiques, France's famous mathematics institution. The Fondation Victor Segalen is a partnership between a French business school, ESCP, and China's NDRC, and is sponsored by

Huawei and a roster of French firms. Among the recent spate of Belt and Road Initiative conferences, one at IRIS, a Paris-based think tank, was sponsored by the PRC embassy in France.

Media

The PRC now controls the only Chinese-language print media in France. Its TV channels (plus the Hong Kong–based Phoenix TV) are the only Chinese-language channels carried to France and its overseas territories. In the French-language media, China does not have a very strong position and the country's officials deplore what they believe is negative reporting by French reporters. The PRC has had more success with the publishing world, where several authors have appeared praising the Chinese model. The most noted example is François Jullien, a literature professor turned philosopher who emphasizes that China's thought is "perpendicular to ours." Jullien's work is popular among China-oriented businessmen. Michel Aglietta, an anticapitalist economist, promotes China's state-driven economy, while Philippe Barret, a former Maoist activist of the late 1960s turned government official and sovereigntist, published a book in 2018 titled ("Do not fear China").

GERMANY

China has so far made only a few conspicuous efforts to exert improper interference in German politics, society, and business.[1] Those that have occurred, however, deserve attention, and, coupled with the overwhelming resources dedicated to nominally legitimate influence activities, will demand a coherent counterstrategy over time.

Chinese influence activities in Germany seem sophisticated even though they currently do not appear very effective. The problem from the Chinese point of view is that German public opinion and its media are traditionally critical of the Chinese leadership. The Tiananmen Square massacre still plays an outsize role in the Germans' public perception of China as it fell in the same year that East Germany began to open up. Thus, instead of launching a PR campaign to play on German skepticism of the United States (for example), as China does elsewhere,

Chinese agencies have so far confined themselves to: (a) targeting younger persons—those who have a professional or academic interest in China; (b) weakening the EU and thus subverting a crucial foundation of Germany's influence; and (c) directing their major thrust at the one part of German society that has a clear interest in good German-Chinese relations and thus is susceptible to Chinese influence: the business community.

While this report has focused on distinguishing legitimate influence efforts from improper interference, it is important to acknowledge behavior that is unquestionably illegal. Most acts of espionage have not become public knowledge. Occasionally there are unconfirmed reports about cyberactivities and Chinese IT hardware containing devices enabling espionage. In December 2017, German authorities revealed that Chinese agents had used faked LinkedIn identities or avatars of Germans engaged with China to contact people in the political and media spheres.

Politics

Angela Merkel, the present chancellor, has a decidedly cool attitude toward China, although she has established mechanisms to work closely with China over the years. Possibly because of her experience of being raised in communist East Germany, Merkel clearly sees the challenges presented by China to democracy and a liberal society. Indeed, there's an argument to be made that with the retreat of the United States from human-rights issues, Germany has taken up the mantle as the strongest critic of China's human-rights practices. It was Merkel's government that won the release of Liu Xia, the widow of Nobel Peace Prize winner Liu Xiaobo. Thus, it makes sense that the Chinese Communist Party has opted to plant a seed within the German business elite with the hope that in a post-Merkel Germany, China's interests would be accommodated more than they are at present.

Germany is also an indirect target of China's efforts directed at the 16–1 group in Central Europe and within the EU. Among the sixteen Central and Eastern European countries (eleven of them EU member states) gathered in the 16–1 group, the expectation of Chinese investment has led to laxer application of EU rules on procurement and in some

cases to opposition to joint EU criticism of China (e.g., concerning
the South China Sea, human rights, and the Belt and Road Initiative).
Chinese "divide and rule" activities weaken the EU's China policy and
the EU's cohesion in general and thus affect Germany negatively.[2]

There have been limited conspicuous efforts to target specific politicians for cultivation, with two notable exceptions: former chancellor
Helmut Schmidt (now deceased) and former minister of economics
Philipp Roessler. Influence activities directed toward political parties
are negligible, apart from efforts to include them in events on the Belt
and Road Initiative and the recent commemoration of forty years of
the policy of Reform and Opening. There have been some attempts
to establish relations with the new right-wing party "Alternative für
Deutschland."

In 2016, the chair of the Human Rights Committee of the German
Parliament was told he would not be allowed to visit China with the rest
of the committee if he did not delete a report from his home page on
Tibetan flags being hoisted at German town halls. The committee
refused to go on the trip.

Academia

More than one hundred thousand Chinese nationals live in Germany,
most of them students. Intense exchanges take place between universities, research institutes, and think tanks, as well as between scholars in
many areas, in both the natural and social sciences. Similar to academics from other countries, several German researchers and academics
with a reputation of being critical toward the Chinese government
have been denied visas or access to interlocutors in China. China in
general targets junior scholars for cultivation. Contacts are initiated
from China with invitations to join research projects, apply for grants,
attend conferences, and write articles with the promise that they will
be published.

A notable instance of coercion occurred when the publishing company Springer Nature removed an estimated one thousand publications
from its internet catalog for China because their titles might not coin-
cide with official political positions of Beijing. So far, Springer has yet

to reverse its decision, unlike Cambridge University Press in a similar instance.

German universities host twenty Confucius Institutes (out of approximately 160 in all of Europe). Like their counterparts elsewhere, they invest more in gaining general sympathy in German civil society through cultural activities than in advancing an overtly political agenda (which does occur, although rarely). There are fifty-eight Chinese Students and Scholars Associations in Germany that are well organized and seemingly well funded.

Civil Society

Chinese officials regularly complain about the negative attitude toward China in the German public, proven by polls, but do not yet tackle the problem directly. Activities in the PRC by German NGOs and political foundations are increasingly confined in their activities, not only through China's new NGO law but also because former Chinese partners are reluctant to cooperate.

In a letter to the interior ministries of German federal states, the Chinese embassy requested that communities be asked not to hoist Tibetan flags on Tibet Day (March 10). In some cases, ministries complied, but in the majority of cases they did not. Almost none of the communities complied. The Chinese embassy in Berlin intervened with hotels where activities involving Taiwan (such as trade shows) flew the flag of the Republic of China. Probably in view of the costs incurred by canceling a contract with their Taiwanese partners, the addressees in general did not comply. In a similar incident, at the first of a series of tournaments between German third-league soccer clubs and Chinese soccer clubs, the Chinese coach demanded that spectators be forbidden from holding up Tibetan flags. The German soccer association's representative did not comply, and no more soccer matches of this sort have been held.

Business

Close relationships, often decades old, between various enterprises and business associations (including a newly established one on the Belt and Road Initiative) are nurtured by the Chinese embassy, consulates, and representatives from Beijing. The Chinese government provides financial and logistical support for events like the Hamburg Summit or Asia Pacific Days in Berlin. A long-standing practice has been to include CEOs of major enterprises in advisory boards of mayors of major Chinese cities and provinces (remuneration seems not to play a role).

The issue of "weaponized" investment is growing in importance. In 2016, Chinese companies spent 12.5 billion euros on investments in Germany—about as much as the total investment of the entire previous decade. The main targets have been successful technology companies. The blitz has subsided in the wake of greater political scrutiny beginning in 2017 and German efforts, along with those of the United Kingdom and France, to limit China's ability to buy, borrow, or steal leading European technology.

German enterprises in both China and Germany are major targets for information campaigns related to the Belt and Road Initiative. Enterprises generally respond positively although with circumspection (only 36 percent of German companies in China expect positive effects for their business). Especially large enterprises (e.g., Siemens) have played along and created their own "BRI Task Forces." Siemens CEO Joe Kaeser said in Davos in 2018 that the Belt and Road would become the "new WTO." Similar to instances elsewhere, when the Daimler company used a quote from the Dalai Lama on its Instagram account, it was confronted with massive protests in China's media and it apologized publicly— twice—to China. The city of Duisburg (one of the terminals of the trans-Eurasian railroads) in January 2018 reached a "strategic cooperation" agreement with Huawei to turn Duisburg into a "smart city." That entailed having Huawei build a "Rhine Cloud" to host Duisburg's data.[3]

Media

German media have, for decades, been the target of official and unofficial Chinese criticism that they are "anti-Chinese." China's state-run media have sought to make some inroads into the mainstream German press. *China Daily*'s advertisement supplement, *China Watch*, has been published in only one daily newspaper since readers protested its inclusion in another paper. In 2017, China's state-run Xinhua News Agency partnered with a German firm, the German Television News Agency, or DFA, to provide soft features about how important China is to Germany. Called "Nihao Deutschland," the program has been criticized as propaganda in the mainstream German press.[4]

Reaction

It is in business, the one area of tangible Chinese influence efforts, where pushback has begun in Germany. Chancellor Merkel and French president Emmanuel Macron have initiated discussions with businesses and the EU Commission on ways to establish stricter investment screening procedures and to push for more reciprocity for European firms in China. In April 2018, the second chamber of the German Parliament (representing the federal states) passed a resolution to lower the threshold at which the government may intervene in foreign direct investment projects in Germany. The measure was clearly targeted at China. As for the EU, the German government has supported language that criticizes the BRI concept for hampering free trade and putting Chinese companies at an advantage.[5]

Conclusion

Many of the coercive actions documented here are for the most part measures one might imagine German diplomats abroad also adopting. What raises questions are the size of China's activities and its objectives. China can wield massive resources in pushing its public diplomacy agenda. This can turn German and European partners into pawns. The outsize dimension of China's influence efforts can render them improper or even illegitimate. China's efforts on the investment side often involve draining technical know-how from German firms. On the political side, its support of Central European countries has been carried out with the aim of dividing the primary political organization of Europe, the EU. Neither of these can be regarded as proper and legitimate behavior between states.

The risk of Chinese interference in Germany is serious in the medium to long term, even though so far it is mainly an indirect one and German society by and large has proven sufficiently resilient. A preliminary recommendation on how to prevent the problem from becoming more serious would be to focus on more cohesion, exchange, and transparency among countries concerned, first of all within the EU. This will take time and effort, considering that some countries in Europe (such as a few Eastern European nations along with Greece) hope to use their support of China's political or technological goals to lure Chinese investment. Still, as a leader of Europe, Germany—along with France—needs to initiate a broad-based discussion among the public and the business community about the challenge presented by China's economy and political system and its objectives.

JAPAN

Japan would seem to be the perfect target for the Chinese party-state and its under-the-radar efforts to turn potential adversaries into benign friends. Japan has deep cultural and emotional ties with China, through history, language, and art, and a sense of Asian fraternity forged by their struggles to keep intrusive, overbearing Western powers at bay. Many in Japan also carry an enduring sense of remorse for their country's brutal subjugation of China in the opening half of the twentieth century. However, the kinds of covert Chinese influence operations that have come to light in countries like the United States, Canada, Australia, New Zealand, and parts of Europe—with one exception—are not easy to find in Japan.

A natural place to look for evidence of influence-peddling would be in Chinese support for the left-wing Japanese peace groups that have long investigated and published evidence of the Imperial Army's war atrocities in the 1930s and 1940s. Such Japanese research has been politically useful for China in buttressing its own efforts to chronicle the sufferings of its people during the conflict, as well as lending support to Beijing's tussling with Tokyo over how the history of the war should be managed and told.

But Japanese activists have never needed encouragement from China on this front. They lead homegrown movements with specific political targets in Japan itself, notably attacking the conservative establishment and defending the country's "peace constitution." These well-established groups, the origins of which lie in the Cold War splits of 1950s Japanese politics, have long been attacked from the right in Japan for being unpatriotic. But none has been linked credibly to Beijing's United Front Work Department. Nor is there evidence that they have been manipulated and managed by CCP-aligned or directed interests.

The Japanese Communist Party (JCP), which still retains a substantial electoral base, is little help to Beijing on the ground in Japan. The JCP was pro-Soviet through the Cold War and has no special affinity with Beijing.

Japan's cultural and institutional familiarity with China makes it, in different ways, less amenable to Chinese influence than it would appear to be at first blush. After all, Japan has absorbed much from China over many centuries, taking in what it wanted and adapting it to its own ends, and keeping out much else. On top of that, any notions of Asian solidarity have been subverted since the early twentieth century by war and politics and by the failure of the two countries to reach an equilibrium in the aftermath of Japan's defeat in 1945 and the victory of the Chinese communists in 1949.

Productive Back Channels

The opaque political cultures of both countries have shaped the way that bilateral relations are conducted. Aside from conventional diplomacy, leaders of the dominant political parties in China and Japan have extensively used back channels to establish understandings on sensitive issues, including the overt use of CCP organs, outside of normal state-to-state relations.

The Chinese People's Association for Friendship with Foreign Countries, headed by Li Xiaolin, the daughter of former Chinese president Li Xiannian, has long been a forum through which the two sides have conducted dialogues. The Friendship Association is effectively the public face of the CCP's UFWD. It is not covert and, for all the connotations conjured up in its name, it remains avowedly an arm of the party-state. In that respect, the Friendship Association remains a reliable conduit for passing messages between the two countries, especially at a time, as in recent years, when senior-level political exchanges have been fraught.

When bilateral relations froze in 2012 after the clash over the Senkaku/
Diaoyu Islands, it was a measure of how dangerous things became that
the back channels, or the "pipes," as the Japanese describe them, froze,
making diplomatic signaling difficult across the East China Sea.

Okinawa and Senkaku/Diaoyu Debates

The clearest case of covert meddling occurs far south of Tokyo in
Okinawa, the ancient island-kingdom that is geographically closer to
Taiwan than it is to the Japanese mainland. As late as 2015, prominent
Chinese were asserting that the Ryukyu Islands, which include Okinawa,
belonged as much to Beijing as they did to Japan. In large part, they
based their argument on the fact that the chain was once a Chinese
tributary state. The two countries still hotly contest this island chain,
known as Senkaku in Japan and Diaoyu in China. "I am not saying all
former tributary states belong to China, but we can say with certainty
that the Ryukyus do not belong to Japan," wrote Luo Yuan, a retired
and hawkish People's Liberation Army general.[1] Chinese scholars have
argued that Japan's annexation of the islands in 1879 was an invasion
and that the sovereignty of the island chain is thus open to question.
For the time being, the Chinese Foreign Ministry has not pressed this
issue.

Operating at arm's length from the government, a cabal of self-styled
Chinese patriots openly agitates for the Ryukyus (Senkaku/Diaoyu) to
be taken from Japan and to become part of China. The main group calls
itself the Organizing Committee for the Ryukyu Islands Special Administrative Region of the Chinese Race.[2] "The Chinese race does not fight
wars. The Chinese race only safeguards peace!," runs one pronouncement,
which was designed as an outreach to potential supporters on Okinawa.
"The Chinese race is relying on you. The Chinese race today relies on
you, and the Chinese race can rely on you."[3] Even more extreme is the
way that the group frames its assertion that the Ryukyus (Senkaku/
Diaoyu) should become part of China. "The Japanese people are a part
of the Chinese race and Japan is originally of Chinese blood," the group's
president, Zhao Dong, says in one posting.

Their appeals to a notion of Chinese brotherhood, combined with the fact the group writes in traditional Chinese characters, suggests that the main consumers of the Organizing Committee for the Ryukyus propaganda may not be on mainland China. Instead, the Organizing Committee may well be targeting supporters of the Kuomintang in Taiwan, where hardcore supporters of unification have become marginalized in mainstream politics, or overseas Chinese communities.[4]

It is of some significance that the same individuals who make up the Organizing Committee are also listed online as serving in CCP United Front Work Department positions in Hong Kong.[5] The Organizing Committee for the Ryukyus also has a robust online presence, with both a website and a Weibo (similar to Twitter) account.[6] It is worth noting, also, that the Hong Kong–based campaign to regain the Ryukyus has not won any overt or consistent support from Beijing.

But the Hong Kong patriots' campaign has the benefit of being aligned with anti-Japanese sentiment in Okinawa itself, where both political leaders and the local media are antagonistic toward Tokyo. The local discontent is directly related to the long-standing presence of tens of thousands of US military personnel stationed on the island and the ways in which they have interacted with the indigenous population.

For the CCP in Beijing, with an eye on the long game, building links between malcontents in Okinawa and patriots in Hong Kong could easily pay off in the future.

Countering Chinese Influence

The Japanese government has been at the forefront of attempts to counter Chinese efforts to gain influence throughout Asia. It maintains a robust, if under-the-radar, relationship with Taiwan. It has strong ties to Vietnam and it has attempted to modify China's influence over Cambodia and Laos, although to little effect. Japan has a close relationship with New Delhi that involves not simply trade but also security. Japan and India recently unveiled the Asia-Africa Growth Corridor as a way to compete with Chinese influence in Africa. Japan's ties to Australia are deep as well.[7] Japan's government was the source of the expression "Free and open Indo-Pacific" as a counterpoint to China's attempts to turn the Western Pacific (or at least the South China Sea) into a Chinese lake. Moreover, Japanese firms currently are outpacing Chinese firms in terms of infrastructure investment in Southeast Asia.

NEW ZEALAND

The issue of Chinese influence operations in New Zealand began to attract significant attention in September 2017 when Anne-Marie Brady, a professor at the University of Canterbury, published a detailed assessment of that country's experience in the weeks prior to national elections.[1]

China's influence operations in New Zealand are rooted in the same set of policies and institutions that guide its work globally, often proceeding outward from efforts targeted at the diaspora community. As has been observed elsewhere, influence operations in New Zealand have increased markedly since Xi Jinping became general secretary of the Chinese Communist Party. The Chinese government considers New Zealand an "exemplar of how it would like its relations to be with other states."[2] One unnamed Chinese diplomat even characterized relations between the two countries as similar to China's close ties with totalitarian Albania in the early 1960s.

New Zealand is of strategic interest to China for several reasons. As a claimant state in Antarctica, the country is relevant to China's growing ambitions in that territory. It manages the defense and foreign affairs of three other territories in the South Pacific. It is an ideal location for near-space research and has unexplored oil and gas resources. Most critically, as a member of the "Five Eyes" security partnerships with the United States, Australia, Canada, and the United Kingdom, New Zealand offers enormous possibilities for Chinese espionage.

New Zealand is particularly vulnerable to Chinese influence because it is a small state of 4.5 million people with strong trade ties to China. China is New Zealand's second largest trading partner and a critical market for two of its most important sectors, tourism and milk products. It should be noted that New Zealand has historically pursued closer ties with China than many other nations. What is changing is the willfulness with which China appears ready to exploit this dynamic and to subvert New Zealand's continued ability to independently shape its policy priorities.

Examples of improper influence in New Zealand include revelations that a member of Parliament concealed that he had been involved with Chinese military intelligence for fifteen years prior to immigrating to New Zealand; a New Zealand company found to be violating bans on exports to North Korea via its Chinese partner; and the almost complete domination of local Chinese-language media by pro-PRC outlets.

Chinese Diaspora

There are currently two hundred thousand ethnic Chinese in New Zealand, primarily concentrated in Auckland. During the Cold War, Chinese New Zealanders "were neither pro-CCP nor pro-PRC" and its community institutions were "proudly independent." Now, few activities are noticeably independent of Beijing.

In addition to its embassy in Wellington, Beijing coordinates its engagement with the diaspora through an Overseas Chinese Service Center, established in Auckland in 2014. The organization considered most closely connected with PRC authorities in New Zealand is the Peaceful Reunification of China Association of New Zealand, which was founded in 2000. Controlled by the United Front Work Department, it has encouraged bloc voting in the ethnic Chinese community, fundraising for friendly ethnic Chinese political candidates, and organizing of protests. The current leader of the association, a businessman in the food industry, also heads or has leadership roles in other united front organizations in New Zealand and has been publicly listed as an adviser to the Beijing Overseas Chinese Affairs Council.

Several current ethnic Chinese individuals active in New Zealand work "very publicly" with China's united front organizations in New Zealand.[3] In return they have benefited from fund-raising events held by the Peaceful Reunification Association, which has encouraged ethnic Chinese to vote for them. In the 2017 elections, a woman who led the New Zealand Chinese Students and Scholars Association was placed on the Labour Party's election slate, but the party did not receive enough votes for her to enter Parliament. Chinese individuals active in New Zealand politics have also attended Peaceful Reunification Association meetings, where they stated their intention to promote China's policies with respect to Tibet, promoted a think tank tied to the Belt and Road Initiative, and repeated slogans from Xi Jinping in local campaign materials.

Politics

In 2017, it was disclosed that Yang Jian, who to date remains a member of Parliament, concealed that he had been a student and teacher at two of China's military intelligence colleges for fifteen years before immigrating to New Zealand. He omitted this history on his English-language resume for his position at a New Zealand university, his permanent residency and citizenship applications, and his parliamentary position, but he disclosed it selectively to those speaking Chinese. Yang has acknowledged the veracity of these reports, including that he was a member of the Chinese Communist Party, but claims he ceased his affiliation after leaving the country in 1994. Since entering government, Yang "has been a central figure promoting and helping to shape the New Zealand National government's China strategy" and was a member of the Parliamentary Select Committee for Foreign Affairs, Defense, and Trade from 2014 to 2016, which would have given him privileged access to information.[4]

Chinese influence efforts targeted toward New Zealand politics transcend the diaspora community to include campaign contributions and the cultivation of relationships with former senior officials. Individuals with strong ties to united front organizations have donated several million dollars, primarily to the National Party. One such individual, who donated $112,000 to the National Party in 2017, is listed as an officer of no fewer than seven united front organizations.[5] Senior politicians who have secured high-profile roles in Chinese companies include a former party leader and members of Parliament who serve on the boards of the New Zealand affiliates of major Chinese banks. A former minister of finance serves on the board of a majority-Chinese-owned New Zealand dairy. In late September, a former prime minister who now represents an American company's interests in China attracted attention for the sale of property "well above market rates" to an undisclosed Chinese buyer. Local politicians have also been targeted.

Business

Chinese companies have also been instruments of interference in New Zealand. After acquiring a stake in a local telecom company in 2011, Chinese telecom giant Huawei went on to win the contract to build New Zealand's 4G wireless network in 2013. Huawei also established research partnerships and other investments in the country that may be leveraged for nonbusiness purposes. In another instance, New Zealand aeronautics company Pacific Aerospace in 2014 partnered with Beijing Automotive Group on the sale of planes to the Chinese market. In 2017, Pacific Aerospace was charged by New Zealand Customs with knowingly and illegally exporting parts to North Korea via its Chinese partner.

Universities

New Zealand has long-standing scientific cooperation agreements with China, most of which are benign. However, since China renewed an emphasis on civil-military research integration in 2015, New Zealand, like other countries hosting major research institutions, has been targeted for its potential to further these aims. New Zealand universities have partnerships with several Chinese universities linked to China's People's Liberation Army (PLA), including the PLA Institute of Military Culture (Massey); the National University of Defense Technology (Auckland, Massey); Northwestern Polytechnical University (Canterbury); Shenyang Aerospace University (UNITEC); and Xidian University (Otago, VUW). New Zealand regularly hosts doctoral students who were graduates of these universities and also hosts current students and staff on short-term fellowships. Some New Zealand academics have roles at PLA-linked universities. The potential for these relationships to be exploited requires a reevaluation of government policies on scientific exchange.[6]

Civil Society

Media are a key target of China's influence efforts. New Zealand's local Chinese-language outlets all have content cooperation agreements with China's Xinhua News Service, participate in annual media training conferences in China, have at times employed senior staff affiliated with the CCP, and have hosted CCP propaganda officials. CCP officials have given direct editorial instructions to Chinese-language media in New Zealand as part of the CCP's strategy to blend overseas content with that in the PRC. On television, a Chinese-language channel has removed Taiwanese programming from its network. Xinhua has also established its own television station.

With respect to English-language media, *China Daily* in 2016 established a partnership with the Fairfax newspapers in Australia and New Zealand. The Chinese embassy has sponsored the travel of journalists and politicians. In other instances, donors with close connections to the Chinese government have donated to organizations that provide research funding and subsidize journalist and youth visits to China, as well as exhibitions, book publications, and other activities that "promote a noncritical view of China."[7]

China's representatives in New Zealand also put considerable pressure on New Zealanders who speak up critically on China-related issues. Since the publication of her initial report on Chinese influence operations in the country, Anne-Marie Brady has experienced break-ins at her office and home, according to testimony before the Australian Parliament's Intelligence and Security Committee.[8]

Conclusion

New Zealand's government, unlike that of Australia, has taken few steps to counter foreign interference in its internal affairs. Charity fund-raising, which has been used by Chinese united front organizations to mask contributions, remains excluded from disclosure requirements. New Zealand's intelligence service still cannot investigate cases of subversion and foreign influence inside its political parties without the approval of the service's minister, whose political calculations may inhibit action. And media regulations remain inadequate to address improper influence by means other than outright ownership, which may also merit reform.

SINGAPORE AND ASEAN

Singapore is unique in that it is the only majority ethnic Chinese state outside of Greater China (Taiwan, Hong Kong, Macao). Singapore is also unique in Southeast Asia because its rigorous standards of governance and zero tolerance for corruption make it virtually impossible to bribe or openly suborn political leaders or opinion leaders.

In 2016–17, Singapore's generally friendly, smooth relationship with China took a downturn. The proximate cause was Singapore becoming country coordinator for China for the Association of Southeast Asian Nations (ASEAN). This post is held by ASEAN member states by rotation for a three-year term. China seemed to have convinced itself that the role entailed Singapore "coordinating" ASEAN's position on the South China Sea (SCS) territorial disputes in its favor. But China has long been unhappy with Singapore's clear and consistent position on the SCS. Singapore is not a claimant state to the South China Sea. The previous country coordinator was Vietnam, a claimant state whose relationship with China has been historically fraught. Chinese expectations of Singapore may have been unrealistically high, particularly after the Arbitral Tribunal on the case, brought by the Philippines against China, ruled against China's position in a verdict in July 2016.

China criticized Singapore's support for SCS disputes being resolved in accordance with international law as "taking sides." It objected to Singapore's leaders and officials even speaking on the SCS issue. When Singapore stood firm on its right to state its position on an issue of undoubted importance to the region, the Chinese influence apparatus was activated to pressure the government to change position. Singapore's experience in 2016–17 holds lessons for other ASEAN member states.

On the surface, China claims that it does not interfere in the internal affairs of other states. At the same time, it is led by a Leninist party that embraces the ideas of the united front as a key tactic. Translated into foreign policy, by its nature united front work involves lobbying, coercion, co-optation, and other influence operations—some of which are legitimate, others of which are not. China's self-declared role as the representative of all Chinese people around the world and its stated position that all Chinese are obliged to help China further complicate its position in Singapore, which is 76 percent Chinese.

This multifaceted and contradictory approach is deployed within an overarching narrative of China's inevitable and unstoppable rise and the United States' equally inevitable and absolute decline. This narrative and others are propagated by various means: WeChat with Chinese-speaking populations, social and mainstream media, whispering campaigns, business, clan, and cultural associations, and conventional agents of influence reporting to Chinese intelligence organizations, who cultivate what Lenin called "useful idiots."

A History of Influence

Chinese influence operations in Singapore are not a recent phenomenon. China's united front activities in the late 1950s and 1960s sought to export China's communist revolution to Southeast Asia and were part of an open political struggle. But even after China's proxies in the political contest were defeated, China continued to try to shape public opinion in Singapore. This attempt differed from the 2016–17 episode mainly in the means deployed, which reflected the technologies available at the time.

On May 15, 1971, the Singapore government announced the arrest and detention of three individuals under the Internal Security Act. The government press statement revealed that "officials of a communist intelligence service based in Hong Kong" had, between 1964 and 1968, given loans totaling more than 7 million Hong Kong dollars at the "ridiculously low interest rate of 0.1% per annum" to an ethnic Chinese businessman to start an English-language daily newspaper named the *Eastern Sun*.[1] The newspaper commenced publication in 1966. In return for the loans, the *Eastern Sun* was required not to oppose the PRC on major issues and to remain neutral on minor issues.

In 2004, China deployed intense pressure on Singapore when then deputy prime minister Lee Hsien Loong paid an unofficial visit to

Taiwan. The Chinese were trying to get Singapore to cancel the visit. Singapore adheres to a "One China Policy," but if China had succeeded, it would have forced a significant modification of Singapore's approach to Taiwan.

This was not the first unofficial visit by a Singaporean leader to Taiwan. Previous unofficial visits by even more senior Singaporean leaders had passed without incident. The 2004 visit conformed to the established pattern in form and substance of previous visits. But what the 2004 incident had in common with the 2016–17 episode was that both occurred at times of political transition in Singapore.

In 2004, it was clear that Lee Hsien Loong would replace Goh Chok Tong as Singapore's third prime minister. By 2016, Prime Minister Lee had made public his intention to step aside after the next general election (due by 2020) and let a younger generation of political leaders take over. The pressures deployed on both occasions may have been intended as tests of the resolve of new leaders and warnings to new leaders about what to expect unless they were more accommodating to China.

South China Sea

When Singapore became the ASEAN country coordinator in 2016, Chinese diplomats called upon Singapore to "explain" China's position on the SCS to other ASEAN countries, or to ensure that the issue was not raised in ASEAN forums, or, if raised, downplayed. Such démarches have been routine in all ASEAN countries for many years.

Simultaneously, messages targeting civil society and other sectors began to appear, most prominently on social media. The aim was to instill a fatalistic acceptance of the inevitability and desirability of a Chinese identity for multiracial Singapore and to get Singaporeans—and not just Chinese Singaporeans—to pressure the government to align Singapore's national interests with China's interests. In essence, they asserted:

- Unlike Lee Kuan Yew, who had died in 2015, the current Singapore leadership under Prime Minister Lee Hsien Loong did not know how to deal with China. Relations were so much better then.

- Singapore has no territorial claims in the SCS, so why was it siding with the United States against China?
- Surely, as a "Chinese country," Singapore should "explain" China's position to the others or stay neutral.

It is difficult to pin down the precise origins of such narratives, but they closely resemble arguments made in the Chinese media, in particular the *Global Times*. Omitted was the historical fact that Lee Kuan Yew was the only noncommunist leader who in the late 1950s and early 1960s went into a CCP-backed united front organization and emerged the victor. That drew a red line, which provided the basis on which Lee and his successors developed Singapore's relations with China. Also ignored was the fact that even though Singapore has no territorial claims on the SCS, that does not mean it has no interest there. And, most crucial of all, although the majority of Singaporeans are ethnic Chinese, Singapore is a multiracial country organized on the basis of meritocracy and it does not view itself as a monoracial state like China.

Still, many Singaporeans, only cursorily interested in international affairs, did not realize they were being fed oversimplifications and swallowed them, or played along for other reasons. Businessmen, academics, and others with interests in China were given broad hints that their interests might suffer unless Singapore was more accommodating, and they passed the messages to the Singapore government. The Belt and Road Initiative (BRI) was dangled as bait and the possibility of being excluded loomed as a threat, even though Singapore, as a highly developed country, did not need BRI infrastructure. Communist Party chairman Xi Jinping himself had asked Singapore to start a BRI-related project in Chongqing. Prime Minister Lee Hsien Loong was pointedly not invited to the BRI Summit held in Beijing in 2017, although Singapore was represented at a lower level. Appeals to ethnic pride were made to yet others.

The operation was effective. The pressures on the government were great. It was difficult to explain the nuances of the SCS issue or Singapore's relations with China to the general public.

Then Beijing went too far. In November 2016, nine Singaporean armored personnel carriers (APCs) en route home from an overseas military exercise were seized by China on the flimsiest of excuses.[2] Singaporeans immediately understood that this was naked intimidation. Even the leader of the opposition Workers' Party criticized China in Parliament. Beijing, by then increasingly concerned with the Trump administration, decided to settle. In January 2017, the APCs were released. The influence apparatus gradually stood down and relations returned to normal. Chinese leaders went out of their way to project friendliness. In late 2017, when news of Lee Hsien Loong being invited to the White House by President Trump became public, the prime minister was hastily invited to come to Beijing first, where he was received by Xi and other senior Chinese leaders.

Academia

Most of the means by which the Chinese narratives were spread in 2016–17 were *not* illegal. However, in August 2017, Huang Jing, an academic born in China who was teaching at the National University of Singapore's Lee Kuan Yew School of Public Policy, was expelled from Singapore and permanently banned from the country. The Ministry of Home Affairs (responsible for internal security and counterespionage) said in a statement announcing the expulsion that Huang had been "identified as an agent of influence of a foreign country" who had "knowingly interacted with intelligence organizations and agents of the foreign country and cooperated with them to influence the Singapore Government's foreign policy and public opinion in Singapore. To this end, he engaged prominent and influential Singaporeans and gave them what he claimed was 'privileged information' about the foreign country so as to influence their opinions in favor of that country. Huang also recruited others in aid of his operations."[3] The statement went on to say that Huang gave supposedly "privileged information" to a senior member of the school of public policy in order that it be conveyed to the Singapore government. The information was duly conveyed to very senior public officials who were in a position to direct Singapore's foreign policy. The intention, the statement said, was to use the information to cause the Singapore government to change its foreign policy. The statement concluded that Huang Jing's collaboration with foreign intelligence agents was "subversion and foreign interference in Singapore's domestic politics."

The Singapore government has not named the foreign country. In 1988, Singapore had expelled an American diplomat for interference in domestic politics. But it is generally accepted that Singapore's moves in Huang Jing's case were directed at China.

Implications for ASEAN

There has been no systematic study of Chinese influence operations in ASEAN member states. As a major economy contiguous to Southeast Asia, China will always naturally enjoy significant influence even in the absence of such operations. However, anecdotal evidence suggests that Singapore's experience is generally consistent across the region. The differences stem mainly from lax governance standards in other ASEAN member states and their lower level of development. Economic inducements and the greater dependence of these countries on Chinese investment, under the general rubric of the Belt and Road Initiative, seem to play a more prominent role.

A common factor is the focus on overseas Chinese communities. Such operations are leading China into sensitive territory in Southeast Asia, where the overseas Chinese are not always welcome minorities. China's navigation of these complexities has in many cases been clumsy. Malaysia provides a particularly egregious example that betrays a form of cultural and political autism. During the 2018 Malaysian general elections, the Chinese ambassador to Malaysia openly campaigned for the president of the Malaysian Chinese Association (MCA) in his constituency. This was a blatant violation of the principle of noninterference enshrined in Article 41 of the Vienna Convention on Diplomatic Relations. It exposed beyond the possibility of concealment what China really thinks of noninterference. The MCA president lost his seat.

This was not the only instance of insensitive behavior by Chinese diplomats in Malaysia. In 2015, the previous Chinese ambassador saw fit to make his way to Kuala Lumpur's Chinatown, where only days previously the police had to use water cannons to disperse a potentially violent anti-Chinese demonstration. There the Chinese ambassador delivered a speech that, among other things, pronounced the Chinese government's opposition to any form of racial discrimination, adding for good measure that it would be a shame if the peace of the area were to be disrupted by the ill intentioned and that Beijing would not stand idly by if anything threatened the interests of its citizens and Malaysia-China relations.

Under other circumstances, these sentiments would perhaps have passed unnoticed. But the timing and context laid the ambassador's remarks open to disquieting interpretations and drew a protest from the Malaysian government. The PRC foreign ministry spokesman defended the ambassador's action as "normal, friendly behavior." Undaunted, in another speech a day later, the Chinese ambassador said, "I would like to stress once more, overseas *huaqiao* and *huaren*, no matter where you go, no matter how many generations you are, China is forever your warm national home."[4]

Such behavior is not atypical in Southeast Asia. If other Chinese diplomats have behaved more prudently in their engagement of overseas Chinese communities in other ASEAN countries, it seems a matter of differences between individuals rather than policy. Since such behavior is patently not in China's interest, China may be beginning to believe its own propaganda. President Xi's concentration of power and insistence on greater party control seem to have created echo chambers where Chinese diplomats and officials probably report only what is in accordance with preexisting beliefs, resulting in situations where instructions are blindly given and followed.

This kind of behavior is not confined to countries where there are large overseas Chinese communities. Cultural autism or insensitivity is one of the self-created obstacles to the smooth implementation of the BRI that China is experiencing around the world. And as the media report on the problems, awareness spreads. This does not mean that countries will shun working with China. But countries are going to be increasingly cautious. They will push back when the terms of engagement are too onerous and they will seek to forge relationships with as many other major powers as possible.

Following the Malaysian elections, China is projecting friendliness toward Malaysia. But as with Singapore, this is a pause, not the end of the story. Since influence operations are embedded in the intrinsic nature of the Chinese state, they cannot be abandoned unless the nature of the Chinese state fundamentally changes. This is very unlikely.

UNITED KINGDOM

Unlike the United States, Australia, and New Zealand, the United Kingdom has had no significant all-encompassing debate over Chinese influence operations. When they have occurred, the debates tend to be confined to specific areas such as the media, academia, or the economy. The publication in February 2019 of a new report by the Royal United Services Institute (RUSI), a defense and security think tank, represents the first comprehensive consideration of the issue in a UK context.[1] As such, Britain's response to China's attempts to insinuate itself within Britain's critical infrastructure, universities, civil society, political system, and think tanks has been scattershot at best.

The United Kingdom has a complex political, economic, and historical relationship with China, which is a significant trading partner and an increasingly significant source of investment.[2] Especially since the official elevation of UK-China relations to Golden Era status in 2014 and the result of the 2016 Brexit referendum, the United Kingdom has become more open to Chinese influence.[3] Areas of vulnerability to improper interference include political and civil society actors as well as the media. Chinese firms are involved in strategic parts of the British economy, including telecommunications and nuclear power. The RUSI report notes that while the ethnic Chinese population stands at only 0.7%, a smaller proportion compared to the United States, Australia, Canada, and New Zealand, the United Kingdom is host to "more Chinese students . . . than the rest of Europe combined."[4]

Improper interference activities can be difficult to distinguish from acceptable influence via civil society exchange, public diplomacy, and commerce. Problem cases include not only Chinese cyberattacks on political organizations and think tanks but also willing collaboration and reluctant complicity. A report by the Global Public Policy Institute and the Mercator Institute for China Studies characterized the most important areas for Chinese influence operations as civil society and the media.[5] But others have noted that China's leverage over the UK economy is equally, if not more, important.

Politics

Since 2012, the UK governments under prime ministers David Cameron and Theresa May have progressively toned down criticism of China over human rights and Beijing's obligations toward the United Kingdom to respect the Sino-British agreement on Hong Kong. While this may be in part due to the United Kingdom's relatively weakening position, these changes have coincided with Chinese efforts to influence British foreign policy.

Influence activities by China have included not only apparent attempts to engage in cyberattacks on the Scottish Parliament and on think tanks specializing in international security issues with connections to government, but also reports of intimidating messages sent to politicians seen as enemies of China.[6] China has also denied UK politicians, such as members of the House of Commons Foreign Affairs Committee and the deputy chair of the Conservative Party's Human Rights Commission, Ben Rogers, access to Hong Kong to investigate human rights issues there.[7]

China has also acquired influence by offering jobs to former politicians, potentially creating dependencies. Former prime minister David Cameron is a case in point. Cameron distanced himself from the Dalai Lama in 2013 and embraced a Golden Era of UK-China ties in 2015 while still in office, positioning himself as China's best friend in Europe.[8] Once out of office, Cameron accepted a senior role in the UK-China Fund, a major infrastructure fund connected with China's Belt and Road Initiative.[9]

Academia and Civil Society

The Chinese government can exercise influence in the United Kingdom through a number of mechanisms: repression in China that affects China-related work, such as the new Foreign NGO Management Law; remote cybermonitoring; the creation of new institutions it controls; collaborations based on Chinese funding, with strings attached; control of Chinese nationals in the United Kingdom; and reporting on or pressuring domestic institutions and individuals in the United Kingdom. The targets of such influence activities include the communities these actors serve: students, clients, and the wider public.

Chinese scholars and students in the United Kingdom (some 170,000 as of March 2018) register with the Chinese Students and Scholars Association (CSSA) UK, which organizes political education events and is supposed to monitor its members in accordance with its "patriotic" mission.[10] Reportedly, students at some universities in the United Kingdom have also established Chinese Communist Party cells.[11] The use of the CSSA UK to monitor dissent among Chinese students in the United Kingdom is a direct violation of the principles of the United Kingdom's democracy. The RUSI report suggests that CSSAs were used to "drown out protesters" during premier Li Keqiang's 2014 visit to the country. In 2017, Durham University's CSSA barricaded a debate at which a Falun Gong supporter was to speak; the debating society was contacted by the embassy, asking that the speaking invitation be withdrawn and accusing the group of harming the bilateral Golden Era.[12]

Institutions created or managed by the Chinese authorities include the country's twenty-nine Hanban-managed Confucius Institutes as well as the new Peking University HSBC Business School Oxford Campus—the first overseas campus of a Chinese university. These institutions have triggered some concerns. They openly discriminate against certain groups, such as Falun Gong practitioners, who are excluded from employment, as North American cases have shown.[13] Reportedly, agreements with universities that host Confucius Institutes require adherence to

Chinese law according to Hanban policies and they are subject to non-disclosure agreements.[14] The concern that these institutions practice (self-)censorship is somewhat mitigated as long as the authorship of censored accounts is clear and robust and critical discussion takes place elsewhere in the United Kingdom.

Activities benefiting from Chinese funding or commercial ties with China are all the more concerning when Chinese influence is less easy to trace. It is impossible to tell, for example, if Huawei's donation to Chatham House's Asia-Pacific program will affect this venerable institution's independence and if UK universities' self-censorship on their Chinese campuses will bleed into their home bases.[15] It is clear, on the other hand, that funding provided to research students and researchers who come to the United Kingdom from China leads to self-censorship. The increased role of the China Scholarship Council, a PRC-funded grant provider, is therefore of great concern, as it clearly would not approve projects that might anger China's government.[16] UK-based publishing in China gives rise to concerns about censorship, as in the case of Cambridge University Press temporarily censoring the online version of its journal *China Quarterly* in China to accommodate government censorship requests.[17]

China's treatment of UK-funded educational institutions in China is also of concern in Britain. In June 2018, the University of Nottingham's campus in Ningbo removed its associate provost, Stephen Morgan, after he wrote an online piece criticizing the results of China's 19th National Party Congress.[18] Nottingham has previously given the appearance of buckling to Chinese pressure. In 2016, Nottingham abruptly shut its School of Contemporary Chinese Studies just as students were preparing for exams. The action led to the departure of its director, Steve Tsang, a China scholar known for his integrity and independence from Beijing. Sources close to the incident said that PRC pressure on the university played a direct role in the closure of the institute. Tsang is now the director of the China Institute at the School of Oriental and Africa Studies at the University of London.

Media

The UK media have long been important international sources of information and insight on China, reporting independently and critically. While independent reporting continues, Chinese official media have become more influential in the United Kingdom and internationally through their UK presence. Primarily, they have expanded their operations and reach. For example, the rebranded China Global Television Network Europe Ltd., headquartered in London, is seeking to increase activities, and *China Daily* now distributes its *China Watch* "supplement" as an advertisement inside the respected conservative newspaper the *Daily Telegraph*. (The RUSI report notes that while "detailed analysis is needed to determine whether the paper's editorial line has shifted . . . it is interesting to note that since 2016 *The Telegraph* has carried 20 signed articles by the Chinese ambassador to the UK, twice the number carried by the *Daily Mail*, the *Guardian*, and the *Financial Times* put together."[19]) The UK and Chinese governments have also concluded a Television Co-Production Agreement that provides a framework under which TV producers in both countries can share resources but have to respect "stipulations in the relevant Party's law and regulations."[20]

Given the United Kingdom's special historical relationship with Hong Kong, the central authorities' heavy influence on the Hong Kong media and the deterioration of media freedom in Hong Kong are of relevance in the United Kingdom, where the case of rising self-censorship at the *South China Morning Post*, for example, has been noted.[21] According to confidential reports, some journalists who have left Hong Kong for the United Kingdom have encountered intimidation attempts.

The effects of media-influencing activities taking place in the United Kingdom are hard to assess. Critical reporting continues, but the rise of commercial ventures transporting censorship into the United Kingdom looks set to continue too. For the moment, increasingly difficult access to information and insight in China, as a result of domestic repression, is at least as great a problem as attempts to influence or repress remotely in the United Kingdom.

The Economy

For years, the United Kingdom was a bit of an outlier in its openness to Chinese investment and its willingness to grant Chinese firms, even state-owned ones, access to its critical infrastructure. Nonetheless, there is now growing concern in London about China's ability to leverage its growing economic power into political influence and to use its riches to buy, borrow, or steal key Western technologies that sit at the heart of Western economies.

In partnership with France and Germany, the UK government has also introduced mechanisms to monitor and block Chinese takeovers of high-technology companies in sensitive sectors.[22] The three nations also support efforts to tighten EU-wide regulations to govern Chinese investment so that Chinese entities cannot exploit the weaker regulatory systems of some European countries to gain access to potentially sensitive technologies. It is unclear how the United Kingdom's Brexit plan will affect the stated desire of the UK government to ensure that critical technologies do not fall into Chinese hands.

For years, the Chinese telecom behemoth Huawei has provided broadband gear and mobile networks to its clients in Britain, which include British Telecom and Vodafone. And for years, Huawei executives used their substantial business opportunities in Britain as an example to counter allegations in the United States and other Western countries that Huawei was linked to the People's Liberation Army and therefore a security risk. Now it seems that Britain's government is having second thoughts. A government report issued in July 2018 noted that technical and supply-chain issues with equipment made by Huawei have exposed Britain's telecom networks to new security risks.[23] Earlier in 2018, Britain's cybersecurity watchdog warned telecommunications companies against dealing with the Chinese manufacturer ZTE, citing "potential risks" to national security.[24] ZTE was involved in widespread sanctions-busting in deals with Iran and North Korea.

Another area of growing concern is nuclear power. China General Nuclear Power—the main player in China's nuclear industry—is considering the purchase of a 49 percent stake in the United Kingdom's existing nuclear plants.[25] The nuclear power giant has already taken a 33.5 percent stake in the Hinkley Point C power station, which is being built with French technology. China experts in the United Kingdom such as Isabel Hilton, the CEO of Chinadialogue, have observed that in opening up its vital infrastructure to China, the United Kingdom was without parallel in the Western world. "No other OECD [Organisation for Economic Co-operation and Development] country has done this. This is strategic infrastructure, and China is a partner but not an ally in the security sense. . . . You are making a 50-year bet, not only that there will be no dispute between the UK and China but also no dispute between China and one of the UK's allies. It makes no strategic sense."[26]

Responses to Interference Activities

In addition to some limited pushback on Chinese economic moves, there are signs that the United Kingdom is slowly understanding the challenge presented by Chinese influence activities. UK media have continued to report pressure on journalists, the media, civil society, and those involved in politics. This reporting has been somewhat effective in correcting perceptions of the nature and functioning of Chinese governance. The media have also focused attention on how China monitors and obstructs the work of foreign reporters in China.

The political system has also begun to respond to some influence activities. At the domestic level, a parliamentary inquiry on the United Kingdom's relations with China, launched in 2015 and relaunched in 2017, has sought input on some of the issues discussed here.[27] A newly launched NGO, Hong Kong Watch, focuses on drawing attention to the United Kingdom's special responsibility toward Hong Kong. The Conservative Party Human Rights Commission has produced its own report on the deteriorating human rights situation in both China and Hong Kong and has organized inquiries and events on topics such as the United Kingdom's Confucius Institutes.[28] While the Foreign and Commonwealth Office presents the relationship with China as primarily collaborative, it is also conducting research on Chinese influence and interference activities.[29] At the international level, the United Kingdom has joined several open letters to signal its position on China's violations of human rights.[30]

Civil society has also sought to raise the Foreign NGO Management Law as well as to highlight intensified repression. By contrast, responses from academic institutions have so far been sporadic. For example, in 2011, the University of Cambridge disaffiliated CSSA Cambridge due to its undemocratic organization.[31] In 2017, international academics joined together to convince the Cambridge University Press to stop censoring its publications available in China.[32]

Among its recommendations, the RUSI report called for an intergovernmental effort to further study the issue and liaise with allies and important sectors, such as academia. Universities were called upon to establish a code of conduct "which places foreign interference under the umbrella of safeguarding academic freedom" and insist on greater transparency of funding. In politics, the report recommended that systems be developed to prevent "non-transparent financing of political activities" and "consider tightening" regulations governing ex-politicians and civil servants working for Chinese entities.[33]

Chinese-Language Media Landscape

Official and Semi-official Chinese-Language Media

By 2018, all of the major official Chinese media outlets had embedded themselves deeply into the communications and broadcasting infrastructure of the United States.

- CCTV or CGTN (English and Chinese), the semiofficial Hong Kong–based Phoenix TV, and a few Chinese provincial TV channels are available in add-on packages of two major satellite TV providers in the United States: DISH Network and DirecTV. CCTV channels (English and Chinese) are in the cable systems of all the major metropolitan areas of the United States.
- The major official Chinese TV networks, including CCTV and major Chinese provincial TV networks, and the quasi-official Phoenix TV, are all in the program lineups of Chinese TV streaming services that have become popular among Chinese communities in the United States. There are four major Chinese streaming services in the United States: iTalkBB Chinese TV (蜻蜓電視), Charming China (魅力中國), Great Wall (長城平台), and KyLin TV (麒麟電視). All these services carry the major official Chinese TV channels, including major provincial channels, and are accessible nationwide.

- The major official Chinese media organizations, CCTV (CGTN), Xinhua, the *People's Daily*, and *China Daily* (the only major official newspaper in English), have a heavy presence on all major social media platforms in the United States and have many followers. All these outlets use Facebook and Twitter and other platforms, even though those platforms are blocked in China.
- Quasi-official Phoenix TV (鳳凰衛視), a global TV network with links to the PRC's Ministry of State Security and headquartered in Hong Kong with branches around the world, including the United States, also has a substantial presence on all the major social media platforms in the United States.

PRC-Funded and PRC-Controlled Media Outlets

The Chinese Communist Party liaises with Chinese-language media mainly through the Overseas Chinese Affairs Office of the State Council (or Qiao Ban 侨办). The Qiao Ban holds an annual conference on Chinese-language media called the World Chinese Media Forum. These media outlets are registered in the United States by US citizens or permanent residents, but they might actually be owned by Chinese state-run companies.

The Overseas Chinese Affairs Office of the State Council of PRC (中國國務院僑務辦公室) appears to directly control the Asian Culture and Media Group (美國亞洲文化傳媒集團) in America, which has three media subsidiaries: SinoVision (美國中文電視), the *China Press* (*Qiaobao* or 僑報), and the *Sino American Times* (美洲时报). Sky Link TV (天下衛視) is another media outlet in the United States. Unlike SinoVision and *Qiaobao*, it is fully owned by Guangzhou Media American Co. Ltd. (美國廣視傳媒有限公司), which in turn is owned by GZ Television Media (广州影视传媒有限公司), a Chinese state-owned media outlet.

SinoVision

The group's main TV outlet is SinoVision. It operates two twenty-four-hour channels (one Chinese and one English), and it is on the program

Chinese Media Social Media Presence

(E) = English version; (C) = Chinese version

Platform	Official organizations and subscribers/followers				Quasi-official
	CCTV (CGTN)	Xinhua	*People's Daily*	*China Daily*	Phoenix TV (fully controlled by Chinese government)
Twitter	CCTV: 532K (E+C) CGTN: 7.19M (E)	11.8M (E) 11.6M (C)	4.54M (E) 221K (C)	1.8M (E)	7K (C)
Facebook	CCTV: 48.04M (E); 3.44M (C) CGTN: 58.28M (E) CGTN America: 1.2M (E)	46.92M (E)	43.15M (E) 171K (C)	35.17M (E)	14K (C)
YouTube	289K (C)	173K (E)	25K (E)	3K (E)	75K (C)
Instagram	550K (E)	111K (E)	696K (E)	23.5K (E)	N/A

lineups of cable systems Time Warner Cable-73, Verizon FiOS-26, CableVision-73, and RCN-80, covering about thirty million people. SinoVision's website (美国中文电视) ranks twelfth among all the Chinese websites in the United States. Its reporting hews closely to China's official media:

- Example 1: On June 27, 2017, the US Department of State, in its annual Trafficking in Persons Report 2017, put China at Tier 3, the lowest class. In reporting this news, SinovisionNet simply reposted comments from the official website of the Ministry of Foreign Affairs of China attacking the human-rights record of the United States.[1]
- Example 2: In March 2017, the US State Department published its 2016 Human Rights Report. SinovisionNet published two stories on this topic. One reported the reaction to the story by the Ministry of Foreign Affairs. The other story came from Xinhua, which was highly critical of the US human-rights situation. Sinovision-Net also published two reports by the Information Office of the State Council of China on America's human-rights record. It did not publish the State Department's human-rights report.[2]

- Example 3: On the tensions in the South China Sea, almost all the stories posted on SinovisionNet are from official Chinese media outlets and websites. They are naturally critical of US actions in that area.[3]

Qiaobao *and the* Sino American Times

Qiaobao, or the *China Press* (僑報), is the flagship pro-PRC newspaper published in the United States. Its website ranks forty-first among all the Chinese websites in the United States. *Qiaobao* was established in 1990. It is headquartered in New York City with branches in twelve major metropolitan areas of the United States. The *Sino American Times* (美洲时报) is a free paper and not a major media presence in the United States.

Independent Media

Over the course of the last decade, most of the independent Chinese-language media outlets in the United States have been taken over by businessmen sympathetic to the PRC.

- Duowei is another online source that was for years an independent Chinese-language media. It was purchased in 2009 by a pro-PRC Hong Kong businessman.
- Mingjing, or Mirror Media, a Chinese-language web presence based in Canada, was once considered independent of Beijing's control but has modified its reporting in recent years.
- BackChina (倍可亲), ranked as the fifth most popular Chinese website in the United States, was once a staunch critic of China like Duowei. But in 2017 its editors attended the ninth World Chinese Media Forum in China and its reporting became far more positive about the PRC.
- Sing Tao Newspaper Group was established in Hong Kong in 1938. In 2001, it was purchased by a pro-Beijing businessman.
- The *World Journal* (世界日报) was for years the premier Chinese-language paper in the United States. It, too, has softened its stance on the PRC in recent years.

- Ming Pao served the Hong Kong–immigrant community. It is another formerly independent newspaper that has fallen under Beijing's control.
- Boxun is a Chinese-language news site whose servers are located in North Carolina. It was founded by an immigrant from China. Its news is highly unreliable.
- The *Epoch Times* (大纪元), the Hope Radio, and New Tang Dynasty TV remain independent of PRC control. They are either owned or operated by adherents to the Falun Gong sect, which is banned in China. Their reporting on China is uneven.
- *Vision Times* was founded in 2001 as a website, SecretChina.com, and began publishing a free weekly newspaper in 2005.

DISSENTING OPINION

SUSAN SHIRK

Although I have no problem with the factual research that has gone into specific chapters of the report, I respectfully dissent from what I see as the report's overall inflated assessment of the current threat of Chinese influence seeking on the United States. The report discusses a very broad range of Chinese activities, only some of which constitute coercive, covert, or corrupt interference in American society and none of which actually undermines our democratic political institutions. Not distinguishing the legitimate from the illegitimate activities detracts from the credibility of the report. The cumulative effect of this expansive inventory that blurs together legitimate with illegitimate activities is to overstate the threat that China today poses to the American way of life. Especially during this moment in American political history, overstating the threat of subversion from China risks causing overreactions reminiscent of the Cold War with the Soviet Union, including an anti-Chinese version of the Red Scare that would put all ethnic Chinese under a cloud of suspicion. Right now, I believe the harm we could cause our society by our own overreactions actually is greater than that caused by Chinese influence seeking. That is why I feel I must dissent from the overall threat assessment of the report.

AFTERWORD

ORVILLE SCHELL AND LARRY DIAMOND

What makes this report timely and important is China's increasingly forward and aggressive posture on the global stage. Once largely a form of economic competition, China's recent turn to military and political rivalry with the United States has changed the whole equation of the bilateral relationship. If the United States is to fare well in this increasingly adversarial competition, Americans must have a far better sense than they now do about both the nature of the system and the values that underlie the People's Republic of China and the challenges Beijing's ambitious agenda of multifaceted outreach is beginning to pose for our country—especially our media, universities, think tanks, and other civil society institutions that make our society so unique, vibrant, and strong.

However, at the same time that we fortify ourselves against harmful outside interference, we must also be mindful to do no harm. In particular, we must guard against having this report used unfairly to cast aspersions on Chinese, whether Chinese American immigrants who have become (or are becoming) United States citizens, Chinese students, Chinese businesspeople, or other kinds of Chinese visitors, whose contributions to America's progress over the past century have been enormous.

Just because the Chinese Communist Party presumes that all ethnic Chinese (wherever they may reside) still owe some measure of loyalty "to the Chinese Motherland," *zuguo* (祖国), does not mean that they are collectively in possession of compromised loyalty to their adopted home or place of study. Our working group's findings do suggest that the leadership of the PRC has stepped up a new and well-funded campaign of influence seeking in the United States. However, this should not be viewed as an invitation to a McCarthy era–like reaction against Chinese in America. Rather, it is a summons to greater awareness of the challenges our country faces and greater vigilance in defending our institutions.

In helping to convene this working group on Chinese influence seeking in the United States (and elsewhere in the world), the intention of the task force on US–China Relations has been to limit the growing PRC challenge to American institutions and values, which is being played according to rules that are increasingly lacking in reciprocity. Developing strategies to counteract and protect our society when influence seeking becomes interference is the charge of this report, and perhaps the most effective defense is to strengthen our own democratic values and institutions. But at the same time, we would be naïve not to want to become more familiar with the full dimensions of Beijing's overseas ambitions, the state organs, and the resources now dedicated to "overseas propaganda," *waixuan* (外宣), and the less-than-transparent manner in which Chinese influence seeking is often carried out.

We reiterate: it is absolutely crucial that whatever measures are taken to counteract harmful forms of Chinese influence seeking not end up demonizing any group of Americans, or even visitors to America, in ways that are unfair or reckless.

NOTES

Introduction

1. Malcolm Turnbull, "Speech Introducing the National Security Legislation Amendment (Espionage and Foreign Interference) Bill 2017," December 7, 2017, https://www.malcolmturnbull.com.au/media/speech-introducing-the -national-security-legislation-amendment-espionage-an.
2. See CCP Central Committee Document No. 9: http://www.chinafile.com /document-9-chinafile-translation.
3. https://ustr.gov/countries-regions/china-mongolia-taiwan/peoples -republic-china.
4. National Endowment for Democracy, Sharp Power: Rising Authoritarian Influence, Washington, DC, December 2017, https://www.ned.org/wp -content/uploads/2017/12/Sharp-Power-Rising-Authoritarian-Influence -Full-Report.pdf.
5. Several other studies have recently been published concerning China's influence activities and united front work abroad, including: Alexander Bowe, "China's Overseas United Front Work" (Report of the US-China Economic and Security Review Commission, August 24, 2018), https://www.uscc.gov /sites/default/files/Research/China%27s%20Overseas%20United%20 Front%20Work%20-%20Background%20and%20Implications%20for %20US_final_0.pdf; Jonas Parello-Plesner, "The Chinese Communist Party's Foreign Interference Operations: How the US and Other Democracies Should Respond," Hudson Institute, June 2018, https://www.hudson .org/research/14409-the-chinese-communist-party-s-foreign-interference -operations-how-the-u-s-and-other-democracies-should-respond; Anastasya Lloyd-Damnjanovic, "A Preliminary Study of PRC Political Influence and

Interference Activities in American Higher Education," Woodrow Wilson Center Kissinger Institute on China and the United States, September 6, 2018, https://www.wilsoncenter.org/publication/preliminary-study-prc -political-influence-and-interference-activities-american-higher.

6. Throughout this report, we use the term "CCP," which stands for Chinese Communist Party. It is sometimes also referred to as the Communist Party of China (CPC).

Chapter One

1. Sources for the information and judgments in this chapter include: United States Congress, House Committee on Foreign Affairs, *Executive-Legislative Consultations over China Policy, 1978–1979* (Washington, DC: US Government Printing Office, 1980); Ramon Myers, Michel Oksenberg, and David Shambaugh, eds., *Making China Policy: Lessons from the Bush and Clinton Administrations* (Lanham, MD: Rowman & Littlefield, 2001); Harry Harding, *A Fragile Relationship: The US and China Since 1972* (Washington, DC: Brookings Institution, 1992); David M. Lampton, *Same Bed, Different Dreams: Managing US-China Relations, 1989–2000* (Berkeley: University of California, 2001); James Mann, *About Face: A History of America's Curious Relationship with China, from Nixon to Clinton* (New York: Knopf, 1999); Robert Sutter, *US-Chinese Relations: Perilous Past, Pragmatic Present* (Lanham, MD: Rowman & Littlefield, 2010); Nancy B. Tucker, *Strait Talk: United States-Taiwan Relations and the Crisis with China* (Cambridge, MA: Harvard University Press, 2009).

2. See website at http://www.china.org.cn/english/features/38189.htm.

3. See the institute's website at https://www.usasiainstitute.org/delegations /chin.

4. See the committee's website at https://www.ncuscr.org/content/congressional -committee-staff-delegation-china-1976.

5. Sources for this chapter rely on sources seen in note 1 and David Shambaugh, ed., *Tangled Titans* (Boulder, CO: Rowman & Littlefield, 2013); Robert Sutter, *US-China Relations: Perilous Past, Uncertain Present* (Boulder, CO: Rowman & Littlefield, 2018), 119–64.

6. Alexander Bowe, "China's Overseas United Front Work," US-China Economic and Security Review Commission, August 24, 2018, https://www .uscc.gov/Research/china's-overseas-united-front-work-background-and -implications-united-states.

7. Information from a participant on one trip to China arranged by Jimmy Wong.
8. Peter Mattis, "Contrasting China and Russia's Influence Operations," *War on the Rocks*, January 2018, https://warontherocks.com/2018/01/contrasting -chinas-russias-influence-operations.
9. See US Congress, House Ethics Committee, *Foreign Travel Paid for by a Foreign Government*, https://ethics.house.gov/travel-information/travel-paid -foreign-government (accessed October 5, 2018).
10. This chapter relies heavily on Gill Bates and Melissa Murphy, *Meeting the Challenges and Opportunities of China's Rise* (Washington, DC: CSIS, 2006), 6–12.
11. John Pomfret, "China's Lobbying Efforts Yield New Influence, Openness on Capitol Hill," *Washington Post*, January 9, 2010, http://www.washingtonpost .com/wp-dyn/content/article/2010/01/08/AR2010010803710.html?sid =ST2010010900293; Tim Reid and Susan Cornwell, "Exclusive: China Launches Lobbying Push on Currency Bill," *Reuters*, October 11, 2011, https://www.reuters.com/article/us-usa-china-lobbying/exclusive-china -launches-lobbying-push-on-currency-bill-idUSTRE79A76S20111012.
12. Reid and Cornwell, "Exclusive."

Chapter Two

1. As promised in the referenced sister-cities agreement.
2. Washington State China Relations Council, https://www.wscrc.org.
3. Michigan-China Innovation Center, https://www.michiganchina.org.
4. Maryland-China Business Council, http://www.mcbc.net.
5. Jennifer Burnett, "State Overseas Trade Offices, 2015," Council of State Governments, November 4, 2015, https://knowledgecenter.csg.org/kc /content/state-overseas-trade-offices-2015.
6. Asia Institute–Crane House, http://www.cranehouse.org.
7. China Institute in America, https://www.chinainstitute.org.
8. Washington also views "exchanges" with China as a form of public diplomacy that serves American interests, but it does not direct the activities of the American local governments and NGOs that do most of the work of engagement.
9. US-China People's Friendship Association, http://www.uscpfa.org/about .htm.
10. Anastasya Lloyd-Damnjanovic, "A Preliminary Study of PRC Political Influence and Interference Activities in American Higher Education,"

Woodrow Wilson Center Kissinger Institute on China and the United States, September 6, 2018, https://www.wilsoncenter.org/publication /preliminary-study-prc-political-influence-and-interference-activities -american-higher.

11. China General Chamber of Commerce–USA, https://www.cgccusa.org/en.

12. Donna St. George, "Holidays for All: Asian Students Ask for a Day Off on Lunar New Year," *Washington Post*, July 8, 2018, https://www.washingtonpost .com/local/education/holidays-for-all-asian-students-ask-for-a-day-off -school-on-lunar-new-year/2018/07/08/e7f3d004-7bf3-11e8-80be -6d32e182a3bc_story.html.

13. Rudolph Bell, "Chinese Continue to Eye SC for Investment," *Upstate Business Journal*, June 11, 2017, https://upstatebusinessjournal.com/chinese-continue -eye-sc-investment.

14. Tom Perkins, "How a Bizarre $300M 'Chinatown' Scandal Played Out in Ypsilanti, Beijing, and Wayne State," *Detroit Metro Times*, April 9, 2018.

15. United States Climate Alliance, https://www.usclimatealliance.org /governors-1.

16. Ben Bland, "L.A. Mayor Vows to Strengthen China Ties Despite Trade War Fears," *Financial Times*, July 31, 2018, https://www.ft.com/content /cee7c58a-9498-11e8-b67b-b8205561c3fe.

17. Esther Fung, "Chinese Reversing Big US Real Estate Buying Spree That Had Helped Boost Prices," *Wall Street Journal*, July 24, 2018, https://www .wsj.com/articles/chinese-real-estate-investors-retreat-from-u-s-as -political-pressure-mounts-1532437934.

Chapter Three

1. For a broad take on the issue of Chinese influence operations, see Peter Mattis, "An American Lens on China's Interference and Influence-Building Abroad," The Asan Forum, April 30, 2018, http://www.theasanforum.org/an -american-lens-on-chinas-interference-and-influence-building-abroad;for a more in-depth look at the individuals involved both on the Chinese and American sides, see Mark Eades, "China's United Front Seeks to Undermine US Support for Taiwan," *International Policy Digest*, September 11, 2017, https://intpolicydigest.org/2017/09/11/china-s-united-front-seeks-to -undermine-u-s-support-for-taiwan; "Florence Fang's '100,000 Strong Foundation': Education or Indoctrination?" Foreign Policy Association, May 27, 2016, https://foreignpolicyblogs.com/2016/05/27/florence-fangs -foundation-china-education-indoctrination.

2. http://www.chinaqw.com/node2/node2796/node2829/node3243/user object6ai5003.html.

3. See the United Front Work Department of the CCP Central Committee, http://www.zytzb.gov.cn/html/index.html.

4. The following US chapters of the China Council for the Promotion of Peaceful National Reunification carry some content: United States, http://www.zhongguotongcuhui.org.cn/hnwtch/bmz/mg/qmzgtch; one of the two Washington, DC, chapters, http://www.zhongguotongcuhui.org.cn/hnwtch/bmz/mg/hsdtch; one of the two New York chapters, O'Keeffe, www.zhongguotongcuhui.org.cn/hnwtch/bmz/mg/nyzgtch; one of the three Chicago chapters, http://www.zhongguotongcuhui.org.cn/hnwtch/bmz/mg/zjgtch; the west coast chapter, http://www.zhongguotongcuhui.org.cn/hnwtch/bmz/mg/mxzgtch; the San Francisco chapter, http://www.zhongguotongcuhui.org.cn/hnwtch/bmz/mg/jjswq; the Boston chapter, http://www.zhongguotongcuhui.org.cn/hnwtch/bmz/mg/bsdzgtch.

5. Zhongshen Wang, *Duiwai xuanchuan chulun* [Introduction to Foreign Propaganda] (Fuzhou: Fujian renmin chubanshe, 2000), 172.

6. Phila Siu, "The 'Down-to-Earth Liberal' Taking on China's Top Advisory Job," *South China Morning Post*, March 15, 2018, http://www.scmp.com/news/china/policies-politics/article/2137217/wang-yang-down-earth-liberal-taking-chinas-top-advisory.

7. Bethany Allen-Ebrahimian, "Chinese Cops Now Spying on American Soil," *The Daily Beast*, August 14, 2018. https://amp.thedailybeast.com/chinese-police-are-spying-on-uighurson-american-soil.

8. Kate O'Keeffe, Aruna Viswanatha, and Cezary Podkul, "China's Pursuit of Fugitive Businessman Guo Wengui Kicks Off Manhattan Caper Worthy of Spy Thriller," *Wall Street Journal*, October 23, 2017, https://www.wsj.com/articles/chinas-hunt-for-guo-wengui-a-fugitive-businessman-kicks-off-manhattan-caper-worthy-of-spy-thriller-1508717977.

9. Conversations with Chinese exiles and businessmen.

10. 吴锐成. "发挥侨务资源优势为建设文化强省服务." 广东侨. http://gocn.southcn.com/dzkw2010/hqyhr/1/201009/t20100907_116083.htm.

11. Frank Ching, "Beijing Seeks Loyalty from Ethnic Chinese with Foreign Passports," EJInsight, May 3, 2016, http://www.ejinsight.com/20160503-beijing-seeks-loyalty-from-ethnic-chinese-with-foreign-passports.

12. Wei Li, "梁冠军当选中华海外联谊会副会长," *The China Press*, October 11, 2013, http://ny.uschinapress.com/spotlight/2013/10-11/20536.html.

13. "中共走狗政协委员美东侨领梁冠军摊上大事," YouTube, August 14, 2017, https://www.youtube.com/watch?v=Dgu6FzlI1kA.

14. "36 位闽籍侨领受聘为十九大精神海外宣传员." 福建日报," November 24, 2017, http://news.163.com/17/1124/10/D40JLF68000187VG.html.

15. "美国华盛顿中国和平统一促进会," CCPPNR, February 28, 2012, http://www .zhongguotongcuhui.org.cn/hnwtch/bmz/mg/hsdtch/201309/t20130916 _4889986.html.

16. "北加州中国和平统一促进会声明：反独促统 再创新局," *People's Daily*, February 27, 2006, http://world.people.com.cn/GB/1029/42355/4146500.html.

17. See Chinese for Peaceful Reunification—Northern California, http:// www.cpu-nc.org.

18. Eades, "China's United Front."

19. "方李邦琴," China Overseas Exchange Association, http://www.coea.org.cn /472/2013/1017/246.html; 来自北加州反"独"促统的声音, CCTV, January 2, 2003, http://www.cctv.com/lm/523/51/75448.html.

20. The Chinese embassy also targets prominent Chinese Americans through the Committee of 100, an organization of the most elite Chinese Americans in the United States. Committee members report significant pressure from the Chinese consulate on committee members to toe the Party line. Some prominent committee members are openly sympathetic to the goals of the Chinese Communist Party. One of them is George Koo, who in addition to serving in a senior position on the committee is also listed as an "overseas director" of the China Overseas Friendship Association, based in Beijing.

21. "习近平主席在美过中秋与旅美华人华侨代表当面话家常 二十几位华人翘楚是谁," *USA Phoenix News*, September 27, 2015, http:// http://www.usaphoenixnews .com/newsshow-115662.html.

22. "美中交流要从娃娃抓起," *The China Press*, March 14, 2016, http://ny.uschina press.com/m/spotlight/2016/03-14/90681.html.

23. "列席今年全国政协会议的35 名海外侨胞都是谁?" *ChinaQW*, March 3, 2018, http://www.chinaqw.com/hqhr/2018/03-03/180466.shtml; "35 位海外列席代表受邀参加4位来自美国," *US-China Press*, March 2, 2018, http://www .uschinapress.com/2018/0302/1127148.shtml.

24. Conversations with overseas Chinese members of the CPPCC.

25. "第十次全國歸僑僑眷代表大會," Chinaql.org, September 1, 2018, http://www .chinaql.org/BIG5/n1/2018/0901/c421026-30265674.html.

26. "旧金山中国和平统一美洲高峰论坛," *China Review News*, November 3, 2013, http://220.194.47.118/doc/1028/4/2/1/102842102.html?coluid=93&kindid =10410&docid=102842102.

27. "华盛顿和统会召开座谈会," NACPU, May 17, 2017, http://nacpu.org/news /News2017/05172017nacpu.html.

28. Lia Zhu, "Reunification Gets Big Boost," *China Daily*, November 15, 2016, http://usa.chinadaily.com.cn/us/2016-11/15/content_27388427.htm; "美西和统会设宴欢迎民革中央代表团," *US-China Press*, August 15, 2016, http://www.uschinapress.com/2016/0815/1075554.shtml.

29. Interview with a Committee of 100 executive.

Chapter Four

1. This process is well documented in Cheng Li (ed.), *Bridging Minds Across the Pacific: US-China Educational Exchanges, 1978–2003* (Lanham, MD: Lexington Books, 2005).

2. "Places of Origin," Institute of International Education, 2017, https://www.iie.org/Research-and-Insights/Open-Doors/Data/International-Students/Places-of-Origin.

3. "For China's Elite, Studying Abroad Is de Rigueur," *Economist*, May 17, 2018, https://www.economist.com/special-report/2018/05/17/for-chinas-elite-studying-abroad-is-de-rigueur.

4. "For China's Elite," 2018.

5. Ibid.

6. "Destinations," Institute of International Education, 2017, https://www.iie.org/Research-and-Insights/Open-Doors/Data/US-Study-Abroad/Destinations.

7. A particularly useful survey of examples of China's interference on US campuses can be found in Anastasya Lloyd-Damnjanovic, *A Preliminary Study of PRC Political Influence and Interference Activities in American Higher Education* (Washington, DC: Woodrow Wilson International Center for Scholars Kissinger Institute on China and the United States, 2018), https://www.wilsoncenter.org/sites/default/files/prc_political_influence_full_report.pdf.

8. "About Confucius Institute/Classroom," Hanban, http://english.hanban.org/node_10971.htm.

9. Marshall Sahlins, "China U," *Nation*, October 30, 2013, https://www.thenation.com/article/china-u.

10. Elizabeth Redden, "Another Confucius Institute to Close," *Inside Higher Ed*, October 1, 2014, https://www.insidehighered.com/quicktakes/2014/10/01/another-confucius-institute-close; Joseph Baucum, "UWF Cuts Ties with Controversial Chinese-Affiliated Confucius Institute," *Pensacola News Journal*, February 7, 2018, https://www.pnj.com/story/money/business/2018/02/07/uwf-cuts-ties-chinese-run-confucius-institute-criticized-controversial-chinese-government-affiliated/312966002.

11. "Rubio Warns of Beijing's Growing Influence, Urges Florida Schools to Terminate Confucius Institute Agreements," Office of Senator Marco Rubio, February 5, 2018, https://www.rubio.senate.gov/public/index.cfm /2018/2/rubio-warns-of-beijing-s-growing-influence-urges-florida -schools-to-terminate-confucius-institute-agreements.

12. Jackie Wang, "Texas A&M System Cuts Ties," *Dallas Morning News*, April 5, 2018, https://www.dallasnews.com/news/higher-education/2018/04/05 /congressmen-urge-ut-dallas-texas-universities-cut-ties-chinas-confucius -institute.

13. Michael Martina, "Florida University Latest to Cut Ties . . ." *Reuters*, August 15, 2018, https://www.reuters.com/article/us-usa-china-education /florida-university-latest-to-cut-ties-with-chinas-confucius-institute -idUSKBN1L012Z.

14. 115th Congress, "John S. McCain National Defense Authorization Act of 2019," https://www.gpo.gov/fdsys/pkg/BILLS-115hr5515enr/pdf/BILLS -115hr5515enr.pdf.

15. Dore Feith, "Exploiting a Reputation: The Chinese Communist Party and Columbia's Brand," *Current*, Fall 2017, http://www.columbia-current.org /exploiting-a-reputation.html.

16. American Association of University Professors, "Partnerships with Foreign Governments: The Case of Confucius Institutes," June 2014, https://www .aaup.org/file/Confucius_Institutes_0.pdf.

17. "National Association of Scholars," Wikipedia, https://en.wikipedia.org /wiki/National_Association_of_Scholars.

18. Rachelle Peterson, "Outsourced to China: Confucius Institutes and Soft Power in American Higher Education," National Association of Scholars, https://www.nas.org/images/documents/confucius_institutes/NAS _confuciusInstitutes.pdf.

19. Statistic given in Bethany Allen-Ebrahimian, "Chinese Government Gave Money to Georgetown Chinese Student Group," *Foreign Policy*, February 14, 2014, http://foreignpolicy.com/2018/02/14/exclusive-chinese-government -gave-money-to-georgetown-chinese-student-group-washington-china -communist-party-influence.

20. Bethany Allen-Ebrahimian, "The Chinese Communist Party Is Setting Up Cells at Universities Across America," *Foreign Policy*, April 18, 2018, https:// foreignpolicy.com/2018/04/18/the-chinese-communist-party-is-setting-up -cells-at-universities-across-america-china-students-beijing-surveillance.

21. Allen-Ebrahimian, "The Chinese Communist Party."

22. Simon Denyer and Congcong Zhang, "Chinese Student Praised the 'Fresh Air of Free Speech' at a US College. Then Came the Backlash," *Washington*

Post, May 23, 2017, https://www.washingtonpost.com/news/worldviews/wp/2017/05/23/a-chinese-student-praised-the-fresh-air-of-free-speech-at-a-u-s-college-then-came-the-backlash.

23. Shaila Dewan, "Chinese Student in US Is Caught in Confrontation," *New York Times*, April 17, 2008, http://www.nytimes.com/2008/04/17/us/17student.html.

24. Emma Reynolds, "Tensions Rise as Chinese Government's Influence Infiltrates Aussie Universities," *News.com.au*, September 1, 2017, http://www.news.com.au/finance/economy/australian-economy/tensions-rise-as-chinese-governments-influence-infiltrates-aussie-universities/news-story/e7768b0bb1f5953a7608884527387372.

25. For example, to cite just two cases, in the last few years Wang Jianlin from Wanda is reported to have personally pledged substantial amounts to Harvard and Yale. SOHO China founders Pan Shiyi and Zhang Xin reportedly set up a $100 million scholarship fund for American universities in 2014 to facilitate attendance of underprivileged Chinese students, and they have already made substantial gifts to Harvard and Yale.

26. See the list of 18,467 foreign gifts to US institutions of higher education for the period 2011–17 accessible at https://studentaid.ed.gov/sa/about/data-center/school/foreign-gifts, accessed July 17, 2018.

27. Admissions officers at leading universities say this is an increasingly common practice.

28. "China Studies Program," Hanban, http://english.hanban.org/node_43075.htm.

29. This program, created in 2014, has been for short-term visits to China, but in 2018 has added a research grant component. See http://en.chinaculture.org/2016-07/21/content_845260.htm.

30. "About Us," China-United States Exchange Foundation, https://www.cusef.org.hk/about-us.

31. The CPPCC is a body through which the Communist Party liaises with China's eight so-called democratic parties. It comprises representatives of these parties as well as CCP members.

32. These activities are all listed in the CUSEF Annual Reports: https://www.cusef.org.hk/annual-reports.

33. Elizabeth Redden, "Thanks, but No Thanks," *Inside Higher Education*, January 16, 2018, https://www.insidehighered.com/news/2018/01/16/ut-austin-rejects-funding-chinese-government-linked-foundation.

34. It was assumed that the funding came from Chinese government funds.

35. Bethany Allen-Ebrahimian, "This Beijing-Linked Billionaire Is Funding Policy Research at Washington's Most Influential Institutions," *Foreign*

Policy, November 28, 2017, https://foreignpolicy.com/2017/11/28/this
-beijing-linked-billionaire-is-funding-policy-research-at-washingtons
-most-influential-institutions-china-dc.

36. "Paul Tsai China Center: About Us," https://law.yale.edu/china-center
/about-us.

37. Raymond Li, "Seven Subjects Off-Limits For Teaching, Chinese Universities Told," *South China Morning Post,* May 10, 2013, https://www.scmp.com
/news/china/article/1234453/seven-subjects-limits-teaching-chinese
-universities-told.

38. Emily Feng, "China Tightens Grip On University Joint Ventures," *Financial Times.* August 7, 2018, https://www.ft.com/content/dbb7b87e-99f7-11e8
-9702-5946bae86e6d.

39. Emily Feng, "China Closes A Fifth Of Foreign University Partnerships,"
Financial Times, July 18, 2018, https://www.ft.com/content/794b77e8-8976
-11e8-bf9e-8771d5404543.

40. See Sheena Chestnut Greitens and Rory Truex, "Repressive Experiences
Among China Scholars: New Evidence from Survey Data." Paper presented
at American Political Science Association, September 2018.

41. Perry Link, "China: The Anaconda in the Chandelier," *New York Review of
Books,* April 11, 2002, http://www.nybooks.com/articles/2002/04/11/china
-the-anaconda-in-the-chandelier.

42. See Glenn Tiffert, "Peering Down the Memory Hole: History, Censorship
and the Digital Turn," August 21, 2017, https://www.washingtonpost.com
/r/2010-2019/WashingtonPost/2017/08/23/Editorial-Opinion/Graphics
/Tiffert-Peering_down_the_memory_hole_2017.pdf.

43. "Chinese Companies Are Buying Up Cash-Strapped US Colleges," *Bloomberg,* March 21, 2018, https://www.bloomberg.com/news/articles/2018-03
-20/cash-strapped-u-s-colleges-become-targets-for-chinese-companies.

44. Karin Fischer, "Many Foreign Students Find Themselves Friendless in the
US," *Chronicle of Higher Education,* June 14, 2012, https://www.chronicle.com
/article/Many-Foreign-Students-Find/132275; "Do Years Studying in
America Change Chinese Hearts and Minds?" *Foreign Policy,* December 7,
2015, https://foreignpolicy.com/2015/12/07/do-years-studying-in-america
-change-chinese-hearts-and-minds-china-u-foreign-policy-student-survey.

Chapter Five

1. These include: The American Enterprise Institute, Asia Society, Carnegie
Endowment for International Peace, Brookings Institute, Center for American Progress, Center for Strategic and International Studies, Council on

Foreign Relations, International Peace Institute, Institute for China-American Studies, Kissinger Institute on China and the United States, and Stimson Center.

2. We have slightly revised the above discussion from our original report to reflect additional facts.

Chapter Six

1. He Qinglian has written the most detailed study of the Chinese-language media landscape in the United States. It is currently unpublished.

2. Anton Troianovski, "China Agency Nears Times Square," *Wall Street Journal*, June 30, 2010, https://www.wsj.com/articles/SB1000142405274870433 4604575339281420753918.

3. Min Xiong (熊敏), "新华社出海'踩油门,'" 21世纪经济报道, August 17, 2010, http://finance.eastmoney.com/news/1355,2010081790350313.html.

4. "At National Meeting on Propaganda and Ideological Work, Xi Jinping Stresses That It Is Necessary to Raise the Banner High, Win the Support of the People, Cultivate New Personnel, Invigorate Culture, Present a Good Image, and Urges to Better Accomplish the Mission and Task of Propaganda and Ideological Work Under the New Situation," Xinhua, August 22, 2018.

5. "Xi Jinping Delivers Important Speech at Central Conference on Work Relating to Foreign Affairs," Foreign Ministry of the PRC, November 29, 2014, http://www.fmprc.gov.cn/mfa_eng/zxxx_662805/t1215680.shtml.

6. "Xi Completes Media Tour, Stresses Party Leadership," Xinhua, February 19, 2016, http://www.xinhuanet.com/english/2016-02/20/c_135114528.htm.

7. "中国全面启动国家公关, 改善中国国际形象," 国际先驱导报, February 3, 2009, http://news.qq.com/a/20090203/000783.htm.

8. "中共 450 亿争夺话语权," 凤凰周刊, 2009 No. 7.

9. The Associated Press reports from some 80 bureaus, AFP from 110, and Reuters from 150.

10. EDI's CEO, James Su (鹰龍), has a long history of working with state-owned Chinese media. In 1994, Su helped CCTV begin its broadcasts through the US cable-TV network. In 2011, Su was honored as a cultural ambassador at the Second Global Chinese Broadcasting Awards in Beijing. Su is a regular guest of the Chinese consulate in Los Angeles and is routinely pictured with Chinese diplomats and officials.

11. Koh Gui Qing and John Shiffman, "Beijing's Covert Radio Network Airs China-friendly News Across Washington, and the World," Reuters, November 2, 2015, https://www.reuters.com/investigates/special-report/china-radio. Confirmed by Su in a 2015 interview with Reuters.

12. "What's Going On With the KDAY Sale?" *Radio Insight*, September 17, 2013. https://radioinsight.com/headlines/85091/whats-going-on-with-the-kday-sale/.

13. Yudhijit Bhattacharjee, "How the F.B.I. Cracked a Chinese Spy Ring," *New Yorker*, May 12, 2014, https://www.newyorker.com/news/news-desk/how-the-f-b-i-cracked-a-chinese-spy-ring.

14. "SoCal-Targeting Mexican AM Flipping to Chinese," Inside Radio, July 10, 2018, http://www.insideradio.com/free/socal-targeting-mexican-am-flipping-to-chinese/article_d5c425c0-840c-11e8-889e-df1a4cd5925c.html.

15. Interviews with sources close to the deal, and Bill Gertz, "Mexican Radio to Beam Chinese Propaganda," *Washington Free Beacon*, August 13, 2018, https://freebeacon.com/national-security/mexican-radio-beam-chinese-propaganda.

16. "Petition to Deny," US Federal Communications Commission, August 8, 2018, http://licensing.fcc.gov/myibfs/download.do?attachment_key=1487042.

17. Donnelle Eller, "China-Backed Newspaper Insert Tries To Undermine Iowa Farm Support For Trump, Trade War," September 24, 2018, https://www.desmoinesregister.com/story/money/agriculture/2018/09/24/china-daily-watch-advertisement-tries-sway-iowa-farm-support-trump-trade-war-tariffs/1412954002.

18. "China Foreign Trade and Economic Cooperation Gazette," Ministry of Commerce of the PRC, 2014, http://images.mofcom.gov.cn/bgt/201408/20140813101828934.pdf.

19. Chris Buckley, "China Gives Communist Party More Control Over Policy and Media," *New York Times*, March 21, 2018, https://www.nytimes.com/2018/03/21/world/asia/china-communist-party-xi-jinping.html.

20. Xin Zhou, Choi Chi-yuk, and Nectar Gan, "Xi Jinping to Shake Up Propaganda, Censorship Chiefs as China's Image Abroad Suffers," *South China Morning Post*, July 26, 2018, https://www.scmp.com/news/china/policies-politics/article/2156921/china-reshuffles-propaganda-cyber-administration-chiefs.

21. The group's current chairman of the board, Cen Gong (岑工), moved from Beijing to the United States in the 1990s. Previously, Cen had served as a deputy director of the Overseas Chinese Affairs Office of the PRC.

22. Xie Yining (谢一宁).

23. You Jiang, "游江. "游江：美国《侨报》跨区域发展面临的机遇和挑战," *China News*, August 17, 2015, http://www.chinanews.com/kong/2015/08-17/7472496.shtml. *Qiaobao* is headed by its president, You Jiang (游江), and general editor, Zheng Yide (郑衣得). You Jiang graduated from People's University in the late 1980s.

24. Bethany Allen-Ebrahimian, "Beijing Builds Its Influence in the American Media," *Foreign Policy*, December 21, 2017, https://foreignpolicy.com/2017 /12/21/one-of-americas-biggest-chinese-language-newspapers-toes -beijings-party-line-china-influence-united-front.

25. An example would be Fan Dongsheng, who in 1999 served as *Qiaobao*'s president and editorial director. Before coming to the United States, Fan worked for the China News Service and had established two magazines funded by the State Council's Overseas Chinese Affairs Office. "范东升的 BLOG." Personal website, February 3, 2011, http://fan-dongsheng.blog .sohu.com.

26. "美国中文电视首席记者反腐更艰难," Boxun, January 16, 2011, https://www .boxun.com/news/gb/china/2011/03/201103130653.shtml.

27. http://www.chinanews.com/kong/2015/08-17/7472496.shtml.

28. Baozhu Yu (虞宝竹), "中国新闻社社长郭招金专访," 人民网—中华新闻报, August 31, 2007, http://media.people.com.cn/GB/40606/6198886.html.

29. The colorful Sally Aw Sian—known as the Tiger Balm Lady.

30. Charles Ho (何柱國).

31. You Jiang.

32. You Jiang, 游江. "游江：美国《侨报》跨区域发展面临的机遇和挑战," *China News*, August 17, 2015, http://www.chinanews.com/kong/2015/08-17/7472496 .shtml.

33. Ruicheng Wu (吴锐成), "发挥侨务资源优势为建设文化强省服务," 广东侨. 网, http://gocn.southcn.com/dzkw2010/hqyhr/1/201009/t20100907_116083 .htm.

34. He Qinglian estimates that 70 percent of Canada's thirty Chinese-language papers, almost all of Australia's twenty papers, and 80 percent of Japan's thirty papers received PRC funds.

35. Dawei Zhang (张大卫), "宣传和推动反独促统是海外华文媒体的光荣使命," 第三 届世界华文传媒论坛学术集锦. 世界华文传媒网, September 22, 2005.

36. "Yu Pun-hoi," Wikipedia, https://en.wikipedia.org/wiki/Yu_Pun-hoi.

37. He Pin.

38. "Chinese-American Journalist Says Wife Kidnapped by China," Associated Press, January 17, 2018, https://www.cbsnews.com/news/china-wife-chinese -american-journalist-chen-xiaoping. The businessman is identified in this story as Guo Wengui.

39. "首届华文传媒论坛将如期开幕 (The First Forum on the Global Chinese Language Media Opens as Scheduled)," China News Service, September 14, 2001, http://www.fcm.chinanews.com.cn/2001-09-14/2/91.html.

40. Kaiqi Yang, "78位海外华文媒体负责人聚北京研修 (78 Executives of Overseas Chinese Language Media Gather in Beijing for Seminar)," China News

Service, May 11, 2015, http://www.chinanews.com/hr/2015/05-11/7267777 .shtml.

41. "北京奥组委在纽约召开华文媒体见面会 刘淇出席," 新华网, November 2, 2007, http://news.xinhuanet.com/sports/2007-11/02/content_6998448.htm.

42. Qiaosu Zhang, "中国新闻社海外中心 (the China News Service Overseas Center)," Xinhua, November 2, 2007, http://news.xinhuanet.com/zgjx/2007 -11/02/content_6998084.htm.

43. Interview with Peter Wang, publisher of New York edition of *Vision Times*.

44. "美国《文学城》网站 CEO：想给重庆开一个关注"较闭'的栏目," *China Daily*, September 17, 2011, www.chinadaily.com.cn/dfpd/chongqing/2011-09-17 /content_3809264.html.

45. Interview with Wayne Lin, owner of Wenxue City.

46. Chi Zhang, "WeChatting American Politics: Misinformation, Polarization, and Immigrant Chinese Media," Tow Center for Digital Journalism, April 19, 2018, https://www.cjr.org/tow_center_reports/wechatting-american -politics-misinformation-polarization-and-immigrant-chinese-media .php.

47. This has led some like Zhang to question whether or not WeChat is at least tacitly supporting the creation of fake news about the United States.

48. Dongsheng Yan (翟东升), "外宣工作脱困," IT 经理世界, July 5, 2006, http:// www.ceocio.com.cn/12/93/148/165/6876.html.

49. Haiming Li, *My 35 Years in CCTV* (China Democracy & Rule of Law Publishing House, Beijing, 2013).

50. James Peck.

51. Youyi Huang (黄友义), "时代的创新." 中国网, November 2, 2009, http://www .china.com.cn/culture/zhuanti/wwj60n/2009-09/02/content_18450217 .htm.

52. Charlotte GAO, "Foreign Journalists in China Say Life Increasingly Harder in 2017," *Diplomat*, February 3, 2018, https://thediplomat.com/2018/02 /foreign-journalists-in-china-say-life-increasingly-harder-in-2017.

53. Craig S. Smith, "*The New York Times* vs. The 'Great Firewall' of China," *New York Times*, March 31, 2017, https://www.nytimes.com/2017/03/31 /insider/the-new-york-times-vs-the-great-firewall-of-china.html.

54. Barbara Demick, "The *Times*, Bloomberg News, and the Richest Man in China," *New Yorker*, May 5, 2015, https://www.newyorker.com/news/news -desk/how-not-to-get-kicked-out-of-china.

55. Interview with VOA staff.

56. As head of this VOA service, Sasha Gong pared down the budget for *Cultural Odyssey* and reapproved funding for more hard-hitting pieces on mod-

ern Chinese history and a program, *History's Mysteries*, was started. With its reports on the famine during the Great Leap Forward, the suppression of the Falun Gong religious sect of 2001, and the June 4th crackdown on pro-democracy protesters of 1989, the program became popular among viewers in China. However, Gong's time at the head of the service ended in 2017, after she and VOA management had a falling-out over an interview VOA was doing with Chinese billionaire dissident Guo Wengui.

Chinese authorities have used both a charm offensive and tougher tactics to deal with both VOA and Radio Free Asia. China's retaliation goes far beyond trying to block their transmissions into China. Security officials from the PRC government have been involved in a campaign of intimidation against some VOA and RFA staffers and their family members. In early 2018, relatives of some Uighur reporters on Radio Free Asia were detained by Chinese authorities in Xinjiang province. VOA's Mandarin service has approximately one hundred employees. Although many of them write under pseudonyms, it appears that Chinese state security knows who they are. Five Chinese staff members interviewed for this report said that while visiting family in China they had been contacted by representatives from state security who have impressed upon them the necessity to change how they have reported on China. In one case, a young woman who is in the United States on a journalist visa and who does not yet have American citizenship was threatened with imprisonment during a visit last year to China if she did not reveal the names of her editors. She did so. In some cases, those affected have contacted the security department at the Broadcasting Board of Governors. In other cases, worried about potential Chinese retribution against family members still in China, they have not.

57. Interview with FCC official.
58. Kate O'Keeffe and Aruna Viswanatha, "Justice Department Has Ordered Key Chinese State Media Firms to Register as Foreign Agents," *Wall Street Journal*, September 18, 2018, https://www.wsj.com/articles/justice-department -has-ordered-key-chinese-state-media-firms-to-register-as-foreign-agents -1537296756?mod=hp_listc_pos4.
59. Jack Stubbs and Ginger Gibson, "Russia's RT America Registers as 'Foreign Agent' in US," Reuters, November 13, 2017, https://www.reuters.com /article/us-russia-usa-media-restrictions-rt/russias-rt-america-registers -as-foreign-agent-in-u-s-idUSKBN1DD25B.
60. O'Keeffe and Viswanatha, "Justice Department."

Chapter Seven

1. "Trade in Goods with China," US Census Bureau, July 2018, https://www
.census.gov/foreign-trade/balance/c5700.html.

2. "Chinese Investment Monitor," Rhodium Group, http://cim.rhg.com/inter
active/china-investment-monitor. Accessed September 3, 2018.

3. Evan A. Feigenbaum, "Is Coercion the New Normal in China's Economic
Statecraft?" Carnegie Endowment for International Peace, July 25, 2017,
http://carnegieendowment.org/2017/07/25/is-coercion-new-normal-in
-china-s-economic-statecraft-pub-72632; Greg Levesque, "China's Evolving Economic Statecraft," *Diplomat*, April 12, 2017, https://thediplomat
.com/2017/04/chinas-evolving-economic-statecraft.

4. Ben Bland, Tom Hancock, and Bryan Harris, "China Wields Power with
Boycott Diplomacy," *Financial Times*, May 3, 2017, https://www.ft.com
/content/c7a2f668-2f4b-11e7-9555-23ef563ecf9a.

5. "CGCC Participates in Public Hearing on Section 301 Investigation of
China and Voices for the Legal Rights and Interests of Chinese Enterprises
in the United States," China General Chamber of Commerce–U.S.A.,
October 10, 2017, https://www.cgccusa.org/en/cgcc-participates-in-public
-hearing-on-section-301.

6. "CGCC-D.C. and Chinese Embassy Host Roundtable Discussion with
China's Ministry of Commerce," China General Chamber of Commerce–
U.S.A., November 6, 2017, https://www.cgccusa.org/en/cgcc-d-c-and
-chinese-embassy-host-roundtable-discussion-with-chinas-ministry-of
-commerce.

7. "CGCC Hosts 2017 'Lunch & Learn' Series No. 5: Understanding Labor
and Safety Issues in the US & Get Prepared for Natural Disasters and
Emergencies," China General Chamber of Commerce–U.S.A., November 6, 2017, https://www.cgccusa.org/en/cgcc-hosts-2017-lunch-learn-series
-no-5-understanding-labor-and-safety-issues.

8. "CGCC Promotes State-Province Economic and Trade Cooperation
between China and US - Alaska and Missouri Governors' Trip to China,"
China General Chamber of Commerce–U.S.A., October 6, 2017, https://
www.cgccusa.org/en/cgcc-promotes-state-province-economic-and-trade
-cooperation-between-china-and-us-alaska-and-missouri-governors-trip
-to-china.

9. Organizations that can reasonably be considered part of united front activ-
ities include (official English translations where available): American-
Chinese Commerce Development Association (美国华人工商业联合会);
America-China Enterprise Chamber of Commerce (美中企业总商会); China

Enterprise Council (洛杉矶中资且也协会); American Chinese National Chamber of Commerce (美国华人总商会); American One Belt, One Road Chamber of Commerce (美国一带一路总商会); America Beijing Chamber of Commerce (美国北京总商会); US-Hebei Chamber of Commerce (美国河北总会上); Chongqing-Sichuan Chamber of Commerce (庆川渝同乡总商会); American Fujianese Business Association (美国福建商会); US-China Guangdong Chamber of Commerce (每种广东商会); US California-Hebei Chamber of Commerce (美国加州河北商会); US-China Chamber of Commerce (美国总商会); US-Henan Business Alliance Association (美国河南联合总商会); US-Inner Mongolia Chamber of Commerce (美国内蒙古总商会); US-Jiangsu General Chamber of Commerce (美国江苏总商会); US-Jiangxi Chamber of Commerce (美国江西总商会); US-Macau Chamber of Commerce (美国澳门总商会); US-Minjiang Chamber of Commerce (美国闽江总商会); US-Northwest China Chamber of Commerce (美国大西北总商会); American Shandong Chamber of Commerce (美国山东总商会); US-Shanghai Chamber of Commerce (美国上海总商会); US-Shanxi Chamber of Commerce (美国山西总商会); US-Shanxi Jin Chamber of Commerce (美国山西晋商会); Eastern US-Shenzhen Chamber of Commerce (美国东深圳总商会); US-Tianjin Chamber of Commerce (美国天津总商会); US Silicon Valley—Tianjin Chamber of Commerce (美国硅谷天津总商会); Chinese Chamber of Commerce in Washington State (华盛顿州中国总商会); US-Wenzhou General Chamber of Commerce (美国温州总商会); Zhejiang Chamber of Commerce USA (美国浙江商会) [San Francisco]; and US-Zhejiang General Chamber of Commerce (全美浙江总商会) [Los Angeles]; Los Angeles Hunan Chamber of Commerce (洛杉矶湖南总商会), likely rebranded from US-Changsha Chamber of Commerce (美国长沙总商会).

10. Several of these groups conduct outreach to elected officials. Summaries of Chinese New Year and other galas regularly mention the presence of American officials or their representatives. The Philadelphia-based Shenzhen Chamber's New Year's party included a city council member and a county commissioner. A member of the House of Representatives from California has appeared at several events hosted by different organizations, including a January 2018 forum organized by the Wenzhou chamber that was subsequently featured prominently on the website of another united front organization, the All America Chinese Youth Federation. In another instance, the former mayor of a California city attended a meeting hosted by a chamber welcoming a visiting Overseas Chinese affairs official from Hebei province. There is no reason to believe that any of these politicians are aware of the groups' interactions with the Chinese party-state. See "美东深圳总商会、美东深圳联谊会携手中美交流协会举办中秋敬老联欢晚会," 东南网, September 29,

2017, http://usa.fjsen.com/2017-09/29/content_20192454.htm; Richard Ren, "美国温州总商会举办华人商会合作论坛 凝聚海外华商力量," All America Chinese Youth Federation, January 27, 2018, http://www.aacyf.org/?p=8242; "河北海外联谊会代表团到访湾区, 加州河北商会举办座谈会热烈欢迎." 美国加州河北商会 (Silicon Valley-Hebei Chamber), November 21, 2017, https://mp.weixin.qq.com/s/Xt1CII2rsFsUsIiuLHr9tw.

11. For example, in the United States, the Jiangsu chamber's launch event in California was attended by a vice chair of the Provincial Standing Committee; a Shenzhen chamber's launch event, also in California, was joined by Lin Jie of Guangdong Province's united front department; and in 2016, the California-based Guangdong chamber itself hosted a provincial Overseas Chinese Affairs department secretary. In China, the America-China Enterprise Chamber of Commerce met a provincial united front official in Fujian in September 2017; a US-based Zhejiang chamber was received in Hangzhou by a provincial CPPCC vice chair who manages Overseas Chinese work; and the leader of the Inner Mongolia chamber met with that province's Overseas Chinese Association chair in 2016. See "美国江苏总商会成立." Chinese American Federation. March 15, 2017. http://chinese-usa.org/新闻活动/新闻集锦/172-美国江苏总商会成立.html; "参加美国美东深圳总商会, 美东深圳联谊会领导班子就职仪式." 美篇. September 28, 2016. https://www.meipian.cn/6m9vy0p; "广东省侨办书记一行抵洛 侨胞热忱欢迎." US-China Guangdong Chamber of Commerce. Accessed September 12, 2018. www.uscgcc.com/showactivity.asp?id=795; "美中企业总商会福建交流中心成立大会在厦门举行." 东南网. September 20, 2017. http://usa.fjsen.com/2017-09/20/content_20152181.htm; "全美浙江总商会一行拜访浙江侨联 欲在浙落地高新项目." 中国侨网. November 4, 2017. http://www.chinaqw.com/jjkj/2017/11-04/167171.shtml; "于忠霞的商业密码." US News Express. September 2, 2017. http://www.usnewsexpress.com/archives/35405.

12. Sherry Fei Ju and Charles Clover, "China's Diplomacy Budget Doubles under Xi Jinping," *Financial Times*, March 6, 2018, https://www.ft.com/content/2c750f94-2123-11e8-a895-1ba1f72c2c11.

13. Thilo Hanemann and Daniel H. Rosen, "New Neighbors 2017 Update: Chinese FDI in the United States by Congressional District," Rhodium Group, April 24, 2017, https://rhg.com/research/new-neighbors-2017-update-chinese-fdi-in-the-united-states-by-congressional-district.

14. Hanemann and Rosen, "New Neighbors."

15. Michael S. Schmidt, Keith Bradsher, and Christine Hauser, "US Panel Calls Huawei and ZTE 'National Security Threat'," *New York Times*, October 8, 2012, http://www.nytimes.com/2012/10/09/us/us-panel-calls-huawei-and-zte-national-security-threat.html.

16. Danielle Cave, "The African Union Headquarters Hack and Australia's 5G Network," *Strategist*, July 13, 2018, https://www.aspistrategist.org.au/the -african-union-headquarters-hack-and-australias-5g-network.

17. Nick McKenzie, "China's ZTE Was Built to Spy and Bribe, Court Documents Allege," *Sydney Morning Herald*, June 1, 2018, https://www.smh.com .au/business/companies/china-s-zte-was-built-to-spy-and-bribe-court -documents-allege-20180531-p4ziqd.html.

18. Stu Woo, Dan Strumpf, and Betsy Morris, "Huawei, Seen as Possible Spy Threat, Boomed Despite US Warnings," *Wall Street Journal*, January 8, 2018, https://www.wsj.com/articles/huawei-long-seen-as-spy-threat-rolled -over-u-s-road-bumps-1515453829.

19. Jeff Stein, "Why the US Is Investigating the Chinese Ownership of a CIA- Linked Insurance Company," *Newsweek*, September 27, 2016, http://www .newsweek.com/wright-usa-fosun-group-insurance-company-china -476019.

20. Lachlan Markay, "Embattled Chinese Telecom Giant ZTE Hired Trump Campaign Veteran," *Daily Beast*, June 1, 2018, https://www.thedailybeast .com/embattled-chinese-telecom-giant-zte-beefs-up-lobbying-muscle.

21. "HNA Group Names Israel Hernandez as Head of International Corporate Affairs," *PR Newswire*, https://www.prnewswire.com/news-releases/hna -group-names-israel-hernandez-as-head-of-international-corporate -affairs-300627805.html.

22. Author's analysis of OpenSecrets data.

23. "Exhibit A to Registration Statement," US Department of Justice, August 9, 2017, https://www.fara.gov/docs/6452-Exhibit-AB-20170809-1.pdf.

24. "Client Profile: Summary, 2017," Open Secrets, https://www.opensecrets .org/lobby/clientsum.php?id=D000068897&year=2017. Accessed March 9, 2018.

25. Wanhua Chemical joined the American Chemistry Council, which has spent over $40 million over the 2012, 2014, and 2016 election cycles. Alibaba joined the American Legislative Exchange Council, a group known for its success in effectively ghostwriting legislation in legislatures nationwide. These associations, which operate as nonprofit 501(c)(6) corporations, are not subject to detailed disclosure requirements, making it difficult to ascertain whether the funds contributed by foreign members are being used for political purposes. Similarly, 501(c)(4) social welfare organizations, while limited to spending no more than half of their expenditures on political activities, do not have to disclose the names of their donors, making it possible for foreign donors, who are prevented from making political contributions, to conceal their involvement. See Fang Lee, "Chinese State-Owned

Chemical Firm Joins Dark Money Group Pouring Cash into US Elections," *Intercept*, February 15, 2018, https://theintercept.com/2018/02/15/chinese -state-owned-chemical-firm-joins-dark-money-group-pouring-cash-into -u-s-elections/; Fang Lee and Nick Surgey, "Chinese Corporation Alibaba Joins Group Ghostwriting American Laws," *Intercept*, March 20, 2018, https://theintercept.com/2018/03/20/alibaba-chinese-corporation-alibaba -joins-group-ghostwriting-american-laws/; Belinda Li, "Avoiding China-gate 2.0," *Kleptocracy Initiative*, April 10, 2017, http://kleptocracyinitiative .org/2017/04/avoiding-chinagate-2-0.

26. Lee Fang, "Gary Locke, While Obama's Ambassador to China, Got a Chinese Tycoon to Buy His House," *Intercept*, August 3, 2016, https://the intercept.com/2016/08/03/gary-locke-ambassador-to-china-house-sale -chinese-tycoon.

27. Fang, "Gary Locke."

28. "Donor Lookup," *Open Secrets*, https://www.opensecrets.org/donor-lookup /results?name=&cycle=&state=&zip=&employ=HNA+Group&cand=; Ibid. https://www.opensecrets.org/donor-lookup/results?name=&cycle=&state =&zip=&employ=HNA+Innovation+Finance&cand=. Accessed March 9, 2018.

29. Michelle Ye Hee Lee, Anu Narayanswamy, Emily Rauhala, and Simon Denyer. "Invitations Offer Wealthy Chinese Access to President Trump at Fundraiser," *Washington Post*, May 25, 2018, https://www.washingtonpost .com/politics/invitations-offer-wealthy-chinese-access-to-president -trump-at-fundraiser/2018/05/25/3bc6a8ae-5e90-11e8-a4a4-c070ef53f315 _story.html?utm_term=.5e994d591961.

30. Fang Lee, "Chinese Law Firm to Merge with American Firms, Employ Howard Dean, Newt Gingrich," *Intercept*, May 21, 2015, https://theintercept .com/2015/05/21/newt-gingrich-joins-lobbying-firm-merging-howard -deans-law-firm-major-chinese-law-firm.

31. "People search results," Dentons, https://www.dentons.com/en/our-pro fessionals/people-search-results?locations=%7b01b010ec-b912-4de3-ad35 -c18d31d3db87%7d&IsSeeFullTeam=1. Accessed February 28, 2018.

32. Matthew Campbell, "A Chinese Casino Has Conquered a Piece of America," *Bloomberg Businessweek*, February 15, 2018, https://www.bloomberg.com /news/features/2018-02-15/a-chinese-company-has-conquered-a-piece-of -america.

33. Rebecca Beitsch, "Lawmakers Look to Curb Foreign Influence in State Elections," *PBS Newshour*, March 12, 2017, https://www.pbs.org/newshour /politics/lawmakers-look-curb-foreign-influence-state-elections.

34. Laura Vozella and Simon Denyer, "Donor to Clinton Foundation, McAuliffe Caught Up in Chinese Cash-for-Votes Scandal," *Washington Post*, September 16, 2016, https://www.washingtonpost.com/local/virginia-politics /clinton-foundation-mcauliffe-donor-caught-up-in-chinese-cash-for -votes-scandal/2016/09/16/bfb3b8fc-7c13-11e6-ac8e-cf8e0dd91dc7_story .html.

35. "Factual and Legal Analysis," Federal Election Commission, November 9, 2017, http://eqs.fec.gov/eqsdocsMUR/17044432226.pdf.

36. "Corruption Perceptions Index 2017," *Transparency International*, February 21, 2018, https://www.transparency.org/news/feature/corruption_perceptions _index_2017.

37. Koh Gui Qing, "China Banks Miss Out on US Investment Banking Bonanza," *Reuters*, April 26, 2017, https://www.reuters.com/article/us-china -banks-wallstreet/china-banks-miss-out-on-u-s-investment-banking -bonanza-idUSKBN17S0DL.

38. Douwe Miedema, "US Fed Raps China Construction Bank over Money Laundering," *Reuters*, July 22, 2015, https://www.reuters.com/article/us-fed -banks-chinaconstruction/u-s-fed-raps-china-construction-bank-over -money-laundering-idUSKCN0PV1P920150722.

39. Greg Farrell, "China's AgBank Fined $215 Million for Hiding Transactions," *Bloomberg*, November 4, 2016, https://www.bloomberg.com/news /articles/2016-11-04/chinese-bank-fined-215-million-for-lax-controls-by -new-york.

40. Henny Sender, "Fed Finds 'Serious Deficiencies' at China's ICBC," *Financial Times*, March 14, 2018, https://www.ft.com/content/75f6c914-273b-11e8 -b27e-cc62a39d57a0.

41. Matthew Miller, "Chinese State Entities Argue They Have 'Sovereign Immunity' in US," *Reuters*, May 11, 2016, https://www.reuters.com/article /us-china-usa-companies-lawsuits/chinese-state-entities-argue-they-have -sovereign-immunity-in-u-s-courts-idUSKCN0Y2131.

42. While outside of this report's focus on Chinese influence in the United States, the authors believed it important to highlight how China also leverages foreign corporations to legitimize and defend its core interests. Starting in 2018, joint ventures operating in China have been pressured to allow internal Communist Party cells an explicit role in decision making, including investment plans and personnel changes. This is but one of the most explicit signals of Chinese efforts to control foreign enterprises in an effort to legitimize and defend its rule and other core interests, such as its claim to sovereignty over Taiwan. While companies must follow the laws of the

jurisdictions in which they operate, China uses the extraordinary combination of its enormous market and its authoritarianism to enforce compliance with laws and norms that deviate from practice elsewhere. Companies' decisions to comply not only affect their financial success within China, but they can also serve to legitimize these practices internationally.

China's government directs significant attention toward American technology companies in an effort to control the flow of information in Chinese society. Many of these companies' services in China are blocked outright or are subject to intrusive national security reviews or other regulatory obstacles. Regardless, many American companies redouble their attempted engagement with the Chinese government. But in doing so, they not only become subject to the restrictions on Chinese technology users, but they also help to legitimize China's vision for "cyber-sovereignty," an issue that has become an important ongoing global governance debate. In some cases, they may even be inadvertently advancing China's goals for military technological superiority. American technology CEOs, including those from Google, Apple, and Cisco, are prominent attendees at the World Internet Conference. At one installment of the conference, a Chinese anti-terrorism expert argued that Beijing should increase its pressure on foreign internet companies such as Twitter, which he argued should be punished for tweets that "defame the party, Chinese leaders, and related national strategies." Facebook has been notably solicitous of the Chinese government in an effort to enter the Chinese market, reportedly developing a tool that could be used by a third party to censor content. Despite being blocked in China, Facebook nonetheless generates significant advertising revenues from Chinese companies seeking to reach foreign consumers. As it seeks to reenter the Chinese market, Google's willingness to facilitate that country's national artificial intelligence (AI) priorities stand in contrast to its decision to end limited AI cooperation with the US Department of Defense. In June 2018, Tsinghua announced that Google's AI chief would serve as an adviser to that university's new center for artificial intelligence research. The company is already involved in research at Peking University and the University of Science and Technology of China, among others. Artificial intelligence is a declared strategic priority for the Chinese government with significant military implications. The Chinese government is actively coordinating the efforts of not just its universities but also nominally private companies such as Baidu. Commenting on Google's AI China Center, at which several hundred engineers are employed, former deputy defense secretary Bob Work has stated, "Anything that's going on in that center is going to be used" by the Chinese military. In the summer of 2018, it was reported that Google was considering reentering the Chinese market with a censored search engine, but Chinese government officials have discounted the prospect and many of Google's own employees have expressed opposition.

China also seeks to enlist foreign corporations to reinforce its so-called "core interests" in ways that have influenced what they feel comfortable saying even outside of China. In early 2018, for example, foreign companies, particularly in the travel industry, were targeted for listing Hong Kong, Taiwan, Macau, and Tibet as separate entities on their websites rather than as sovereign parts of China. The Civil Aviation Administration of China sent letters to international airlines demanding that any references to these destinations except as part of China be removed from their materials and websites. In May, the Trump administration declared the Chinese government's order to airlines to be "Orwellian nonsense and part of a growing trend by the Chinese Communist Party to impose its political views on American citizens and private companies" with which they might not necessarily agree. At the direction of the American government, the airlines initially and collectively declined to follow Beijing's orders, as the US government considered the issue a diplomatic matter to be resolved between governments. However, when China declined to negotiate with the US government over the issue, by July the airlines partially met Beijing's demands by referring only to cities.

Targeting foreign companies' speech extends beyond Taiwan to China's fraught relationship with its ethnic minorities. At Marriott, an employee responsible for managing the company's social media accounts unwittingly "liked" a tweet by a pro-Tibet group and was fired as a result of the backlash. The company's website and app were blocked in China for one week, at unknown financial cost. Daimler, the German car manufacturer, was similarly forced to apologize for posting a reference to the Dalai Lama, the exiled Tibetan spiritual leader, on social media. In the latter two cases, the companies were targeted even though the social services on which they were posting were blocked inside China. See Michael Martina, "Exclusive: In China, the Party's Push for Influence inside Foreign . . ." *Reuters*, August 24, 2017, https://www.reuters.com/article/us-china-congress -companies/exclusive-in-china-the-partys-push-for-influence-inside-foreign -firms-stirs-fears-idUSKCN1B40JU; Chun Han Wong and Eva Dou, "Foreign Companies in China Get a New Partner: The Communist Party," *Wall Street Journal*, October 29, 2017, https://www.wsj.com/articles /foreign-companies-in-china-get-a-new-partner-the-communist-party -1509297523; Simon Denver, "Command and Control: China's Communist Party Extends Reach into Foreign Companies," *Washington Post*, January 28,

2018, https://www.washingtonpost.com/world/asia_pacific/command-and
-control-chinas-communist-party-extends-reach-into-foreign-companies
/2018/01/28/cd49ffa6-fc57-11e7-9b5d-bbf0da31214d_story.html; Yoko Kubota
and Tripp Mickle, "Apple CEO to Attend State-Run Internet Conference
in China," *Wall Street Journal*, December 2, 2017, https://www.wsj.com
/articles/apple-ceo-to-attend-state-run-internet-conference-in-china
-1512178941; Paul Mozur, "China Presses Its Internet Censorship Efforts
across the Globe," *New York Times*, March 2, 2018, https://www.nytimes
.com/2018/03/02/technology/china-technology-censorship-borders
-expansion.html; Emily Parker, "Mark Zuckerberg Is Determined to
Launch His Social Network in China, Whatever It Takes," *MIT Technology
Review*, October 18, 2016, https://www.technologyreview.com/s/602493/mark
-zuckerbergs-long-march-to-china; Alyssa Abkowitz, Deepa Seetharaman,
and Eva Dou, "Facebook Is Trying Everything to Re-Enter China—and
It's Not Working," *Wall Street Journal*, January 30, 2017, https://www.wsj
.com/articles/mark-zuckerbergs-beijing-blues-1485791106; Mike Isaac,
"Facebook Said to Create Censorship Tool to Get Back into China," *New
York Times*, November 22, 2016, https://www.nytimes.com/2016/11/22
/technology/facebook-censorship-tool-china.html; George P. Slefo, "Report:
China, Despite Ban, Is Facebook's Second-Largest Ad Market," *Ad Age*,
May 15, 2018, http://adage.com/article/digital/china-facebook-s-largest-
market/313524/; Daisuke Wakabayashi and Scott Shane, "Google Will
Not Renew Pentagon Contract That Upset Employees," *New York Times*,
June 1, 2018, https://www.nytimes.com/2018/06/01/technology/google
-pentagon-project-maven.html; Kyle Wiggers, "Tsinghua University Plans
to Open AI Research Center in China, Names Google's AI Chief as Advisor," VentureBeat, June 29, 2018, https://venturebeat.com/2018/06/28
/tsinghua-university-plans-to-open-ai-research-center-in-china-names
-googles-ai-chief-as-advisor/; Sydney Freedberg, "Google Helps Chinese
Military, Why Not US? Bob Work," *Breaking Defense*, July 6, 2018,
https://breakingdefense.com/2018/06/google-helps-chinese-military
-why-not-us-bob-work/; James Palmer and Bethany Allen-Ebrahimian,
"China Threatens US Airlines over Taiwan References," *Foreign Policy*,
April 28, 2018, http://foreignpolicy.com/2018/04/27/china-threatens-u
-s-airlines-over-taiwan-references-united-american-flight-beijing;
Chris Buckley, "'Orwellian Nonsense'? China Says That's the Price of
Doing Business," *New York Times*, May 6, 2018, https://www.nytimes
.com/2018/05/06/world/asia/china-airlines-orwellian-nonsense.html;
Matthew Miller, "Exclusive: China Shuns US Request for Talks on Air-
line Website . . ." *Reuters*, June 28, 2018, https://www.reuters.com/article/us

-usa-trade-china-airlines-exclusive/exclusive-china-rejects-u-s-request-for
-talks-on-airline-website-dispute-idUSKBN1JO0JP; Demetri Sevastopulo,
"White House Presses US Airlines to Resist Beijing over Taiwan," *Financial Times*, June 5, 2018, https://www.ft.com/content/74498d14-68cb-11e8
-b6eb-4acfcfb08c11; Wayne Ma, "Marriott Employee Roy Jones Hit
'Like.' Then China Got Mad," *Wall Street Journal*, March 3, 2018, https://
www.wsj.com/articles/marriott-employee-roy-jones-hit-like-then-china
-got-mad-1520094910; Paul Mozur, "China Presses Its Internet Censorship Efforts across the Globe," *New York Times*, March 2, 2018, https://
www.nytimes.com/2018/03/02/technology/china-technology-censorship
-borders-expansion.html; Wayne Ma, "Delta, Zara and Medtronic Join
Marriott in Beijing's Doghouse After Location Gaffes," *Wall Street Journal*,
Dow Jones & Company, January 12, 2018, https://www.wsj.com/articles
/delta-zara-and-medtronic-join-marriott-in-beijings-doghouse-after
-location-gaffes-1515755791.
43. Paul Weisskopf, "Backbone of the New China Lobby: US Firms," *Washington Post*, June 14, 1993, https://www.washingtonpost.com/archive/politics/1993
/06/14/backbone-of-the-new-china-lobby-us-firms/ed135802-77fd-4a2f
-b9aa-7e7a78df96a8.
44. Lingling Wei and Yoko Kubota, "China's Xi Tells CEOs He'll Strike Back at US," *Wall Street Journal*, June 25, 2018, https://www.wsj.com/articles
/chinas-xi-tells-ceos-hell-strike-back-at-u-s-1529941334.
45. Alexander Hammer, "The Size & Composition of US Manufacturing Off-
shoring in China," US International Trade Commission, https://www.usitc
.gov/publications/332/executive_briefings/sizecompositionebot.pdf.
46. Author analysis of Bloomberg data, February 23, 2018. The Bloomberg data is subject to company disclosures, which means these figures undercount total exposure to China. For instance, General Electric and Walmart earn about 6 percent and 3 percent of revenues, respectively, from China according to news reports, but these do not appear in filings detected by Bloom-
berg. Similarly, General Motors reports income of $2 billion from its China joint venture, equivalent to 20 percent of adjusted operating income. Boeing in 2016 disclosed that 10.9 percent of its revenues came from China.
Richard Blackden, "GE Warns of Slowing China Sales and Slump in Oil Prices," *Financial Times*, January 22, 2016, https://www.ft.com/content
/29315f70-c10a-11e5-9fdb-87b8d15baec2; "Wal-Mart Needs to Grow Over-
seas, and China's the Big Prize," *Chicago Tribune*, June 1, 2016, http://www
.chicagotribune.com/business/ct-walmart-china-20160601-story.html; "Q4
2017 Results," General Motors, February 6, 2018, https://media.gm.com
/content/dam/Media/gmcom/investor/2018/feb/GM-2017-Q4-Earnings

-Deck.pdf; "Annual Report," Boeing Company, 2016, http://s2.q4cdn
.com/661678649/files/doc_financials/annual/2016/2016-Annual-Report
.pdf.

47. In 2017, Steve Wynn, then CEO of an American casino that derives a sig-
nificant portion of its revenues from the Macau Special Administrative
Region, reportedly delivered a request on behalf of the Chinese government
to the American president that a Chinese dissident be deported from the
United States and sent back to China. Kate O'Keeffe, Aruna Viswanatha,
and Cezary Podkul, "China's Pursuit of Fugitive Businessman Guo Wengui
Kicks Off Manhattan Caper Worthy of Spy Thriller," *Wall Street Journal*,
October 23, 2017, https://www.wsj.com/articles/chinas-hunt-for-guo
-wengui-a-fugitive-businessman-kicks-off-manhattan-caper-worthy-of
-spy-thriller-1508717977; Lingling Wei and Yoko Kubota, "China Warns
of Corporate Casualties as Trade War Brews," *Wall Street Journal*, Dow
Jones & Company, June 15, 2018, https://www.wsj.com/articles/trade-fight
-squeezes-u-s-companies-working-in-china-1529082957.

48. In October 2018, the *New York Times* reported that Chinese intelligence services were especially monitoring the president's interactions with prominent American businesspersons. The Chinese government has then sought
to channel messages, including via Chinese businessmen, to those individuals with the aim that Beijing's views would "eventually be delivered to the
president by trusted voices." The report added that US intelligence officials
believed that the president's associates "were most likely unaware of any
Chinese effort." Matthew Rosenberg and Maggie Haberman, "When
Trump Phones Friends, the Chinese and the Russians Listen and Learn,"
New York Times, October 24, 2018, https://www.nytimes.com/2018/10/24/us
/politics/trump-phone-security.html.

49. http://www.xinhuanet.com/english/2018-01/31/c_136939098.htm.

50. Ben Fritz, "Overseas 2017 Box-Office Results Offset US, Canada Slump,"
Wall Street Journal, April 4, 2018, https://www.wsj.com/articles/overseas
-2017-box-office-results-offset-u-s-canada-slump-1522868354.

51. Aynne Kokas, *Hollywood Made in China* (University of California Press,
2017), 28–29.

52. Kokas, *Hollywood*, 33.

53. Tatiana Siegel, "Richard Gere's Studio Exile: Why His Hollywood
Career Took an Indie Turn," *Hollywood Reporter*, April 18, 2017, https://
www.hollywoodreporter.com/features/richard-geres-studio-exile-why
-his-hollywood-career-took-an-indie-turn-992258. To mitigate the risk
that future business in China would be harmed because of its production of *Kundun*, a movie about the Dalai Lama, Disney in 1997 hired

Henry Kissinger. Also see Bernard Weinraub, "At the Movies; Disney Hires Kissinger," *New York Times*, October 10, 1997, https://www.nytimes.com/1997/10/10/movies/at-the-movies-disney-hires-kissinger.html.

54. Charles Clover and Matthew Garrahan, "China's Hollywood Romance Turns Sour," *Financial Times*, December 26, 2017, https://www.ft.com/content/d5d3d06e-de8b-11e7-a8a4-0a1e63a52f9c.

Chapter Eight

1. See William Hannas, James Mulvenon, and Anna Puglisi, *Chinese Industrial Espionage* (London: Routledge, 2013).

2. For the best analysis of Made in China 2025, see *Made in China 2025: Global Ambitions Built on Local Protections*, US Chamber of Commerce, 2017, https://www.uschamber.com/sites/default/files/final_made_in_china_2025_report_full.pdf.

3. "The IP Commission Report: The Report of the Commission on the Theft of American Intellectual Property," National Bureau of Asian Research, May 2013, http://www.ipcommission.org/report/IP_Commission_Report_Update_2017.pdf.

4. For his comments on costs, see AEIVideos. "Gen. Alexander: Greatest Transfer of Wealth in History," YouTube, July 9, 2012, https://www.youtube.com/watch?v=JOFk44yy6IQ.

5. All analysis and data are taken directly from the official Thousand Talents Program website: http://www.1000plan.org.

6. "The Recruitment Program of Global Experts," Thousand Talents, http://www.1000plan.org/qrjh/section/2?m=rcrd.

7. All analysis and data are taken directly from the official Thousand Talents Program website: http://www.1000plan.org.

8. See Triway International website: http://www.triwayinc.com. Note that the term "S&T" is missing from the site's English-language version.

9. Northern California Global Trade Assistance Directory, 2000–2001. About 10 percent of SCEA's members are from Taiwan.

10. "China-US Joint Research Center for Ecosystem and Environmental Change," University of Tennessee Knoxville, http://jrceec.utk.edu/about.html.

11. "China-US Joint Research Center."

12. Ibid.

13. Wei Zhou (周偉), "我国企业对外直接投资战略分析" ("Analysis of China's Strategy for Corporate Foreign Direct Investment"), 科技进步与对策, *Science & Technology Progress and Policy*, 11, no. 56 (2004).

14. With gratitude to Robert Skebo Sr. (personal communication) for pointing this out.

15. Zhaozhi Zeng (曾昭智), Niu Zhengming (牛争鸣), and Zhang Lin (张林), "利用专利文献促进科技创新" ("Using Patent Resources to Promote Scientific and Technological Innovation"), in 技术与创新管理, *Technology and Innovation Management* 6 (2004): 46–48.

16. Meide Cai (蔡美德), Du Haidong (杜海东), and Hu Guosheng (胡国胜), "反求工程原理在高职课程体系创新中的应用" ("Using the Principle of Reverse Engineering for Innovation in High-Level Knowledge Processes and Systems"), 科技管理研究, *Science and Technology Management Research* 7 (2005).

17. Can Peng (彭灿), "基于国际战'联盟的模仿创新" ("Imitative Innovation Based on International Strategic Alliances"), 科研管理, *Science Research Management* 2 (2005): 23–27.

18. Ying Zhang (张莹) and Chen Guohong (陈国宏), "跨国公司在中国的技术转移问题及对策分析" ("Analysis of the Problem of Technology Transfer of Multinational Corporations in China and Measures for Dealing with It"), 科技进步与对策, *Science & Technology Progress and Policy* 3 (2001): 134.

19. For example, see Brett Kingstone, *The Real War Against America* (Specialty Publishing/Max King, 2005).

20. Lingling Wei and Bob Davis, "How China Systematically Pries Technology from US Companies," *Wall Street Journal*, September 26, 2018, https://www.wsj.com/articles/how-china-systematically-pries-technology-from-u-s-companies-1537972066.

21. "US Competitiveness Ranking Continues to Fall; Emerging Markets Are Closing the Gap," World Economic Forum, September 7, 2011, http://www.weforum.org/news/us-competitiveness-ranking-continues-fall-emerging-markets-are-closing-gap.

22. "Foreign Agents Registration Act," US Department of Justice, https://www.justice.gov/nsd-fara.

23. See 18 US Code § 209, available at: https://www.law.cornell.edu/uscode/text/18/209.

24. "Homeland Security: Performance of Information System to Monitor Foreign Students and Exchange Visitors Has Improved, but Issues Remain," General Accounting Office, GAO-04-69, June 2004, http://www.gao.gov/new.items/d04690.pdf. SEVIS was mandated by the Illegal Immigration Reform and Immigrant Responsibility Act (IIRIRA) of 1996 and augmented by the USA Patriot Act of 2001, Enhanced Border Security and Visa Entry Reform Act of 2002, and the Cyber Security Research and Development Act of 2002.

25. "Student and Exchange Visitor Information System General Summary Quarterly Review," US Immigration and Customs Enforcement, April 1, 2011, https://www.ice.gov/doclib/sevis/pdf/quarterly_rpt_mar2011.pdf.

26. Matthew Gruchow, "FBI Gets Access to SEVIS," *Minnesota Daily*, September 22, 2004, http://www.mndaily.com/nuevo/2004/09/22/fbi-gets-access-sevis.

27. "Homeland Security: Performance of Information System to Monitor Foreign Students and Exchange Visitors Has Improved, but Issues Remain," General Accounting Office, GAO-04-69, June 2004, http://www.gao.gov/new.items/d04690.pdf.

28. For the authoritative FAQ on deemed exports, see "Deemed Exports FAQs," US Department of Commerce, https://www.bis.doc.gov/index.php/policy-guidance/deemed-exports/deemed-exports-faqs.

29. "Deemed Export Controls May Not Stop the Transfer of Sensitive Technology to Foreign Nationals in the US," US Department of Commerce Office of Inspector General, Final Inspection Report No. IPE–16176—March 2004.

30. "Revisions and Clarification of Deemed Export Related Regulatory Requirements," *Federal Register*, May 31, 2006, https://www.gpo.gov/fdsys/pkg/FR-2006-05-31/pdf/E6-8370.pdf.

31. "Export Controls: Agencies Should Assess Vulnerabilities and Improve Guidance for Protecting Export-Controlled Information at Universities," General Accounting Office, GAO-07-70, http://www.gao.gov/new.items/d0770.pdf.

32. "Export Control Reform Initiative: Strategic Trade Authorization License Exception," *Federal Register*, June 16, 2011, https://www.bis.doc.gov/index.php/documents/product-guidance/231-sta/file.

33. *Federal Register*, "Export Control."

34. "President Obama Announces First Steps toward Implementation of New US Export Control System," White House Office of the Press Secretary, December 9, 2010, https://obamawhitehouse.archives.gov/the-press-office/2010/12/09/president-obama-announces-first-steps-toward-implementation-new-us-expor.

35. White House Office, "President Obama."

36. Ibid.

37. James K. Jackson, "The Committee on Foreign Investment in the United States," CRS Report RL33388, Congressional Research Service, July 29, 2010, http://www.fas.org/sgp/crs/natsec/RL33388.pdf.

Appendix 1

1. This body was upgraded from leading small group status in March 2018.
2. These plans are normally classified and only circulated within the Chinese bureaucracies, but occasionally they find their way into the public domain. See, for example, State Council Information Office, "Summary of China's External Propaganda Work in 2013 (中国对外宣传工作 2013年综述)," in *China Journalism Yearbook* [中国新闻年鉴 2014], ed. Chinese Academy of Social Sciences Journalism Institute (Beijing: Zhongguo Shehui Kexue Chubanshe, 2014), 63–66.
3. See Alexander Bowe, "China's Overseas United Front Work: Background and Implications for the United States," US-China Economic & Security Review Commission, August 24, 2018; James Kynge et al., "Inside China's Secret 'Magic Weapon' for Worldwide Influence," *Financial Times*, October 26, 2017, http://www.ft.com/content/fb2b3934-b004-11e7-beba-5521c 713abf4; Anne-Marie Brady, "Magic Weapons: China's Political Influence Activities under Xi Jinping," Wilson Center Kissinger Institute on China and the United States, September 18, 2017, https://www.wilsoncenter.org /article/magic-weapons-chinas-political-influence-activities-under-xi -jinping.

Appendix 2

1. Sarah Cook, "The Long Shadow of Chinese Censorship: How the Communist Party's Media Restrictions Affect News Outlets Around the World," Center for International Media Assistance, October 22, 2013, accessed October 11, 2018, http://www.cima.ned.org/wp-content/uploads/2015/02 /CIMA-China_Sarah%20Cook.pdf.
2. Juan Pablo Cardenal, Jacek Kucharczyk, Grigorij Mesežnikov, and Gabriela Pleschová, *Sharp Power: Rising Authoritarian Influence* (Washington, DC: National Endowment for Democracy, December 2017), accessed October 11, 2018, https://www.ned.org/wp-content/uploads/2017/12/Sharp-Power -Rising-Authoritarian-Influence-Full-Report.pdf.

Australia

1. Peter Hartcher, "Australia Has 'Woken Up' the World on China's Influence: US Official," *Sydney Morning Herald*, February 27, 2018, accessed October 11, 2018, https://www.smh.com.au/politics/federal/australia-has

-woken-up-the-world-on-china-s-influence-us-official-20180226-p4z1un
.html.

2. Ben Doherty and Eleanor Ainge Roy, "Hillary Clinton Says China's Foreign Power Grab 'A New Global Battle,'" *Guardian* (UK), May 8, 2018, accessed October 11, 2018, https://www.theguardian.com/us-news/2018/may/08/hillary-clinton-says-chinas-foreign-power-grab-a-new-global-battle.

3. "Advisory Report on the National Security Legislation Amendment," Parliament of Australia, June 7, 2018, accessed October 11, 2018, https://www.aph.gov.au/Parliamentary_Business/Committees/Joint/Intelligence_and_Security/EspionageFInterference/Report/section?id=committees%2Freportjnt%2F024152%2F25708.

4. Rob Taylor, "Chinese Rally in Australia to Guard Olympic Flame," Reuters, April 15, 2008, accessed October 11, 2018, https://www.reuters.com/article/idUSSYD3301.

5. Greg Sheridan, "Malcolm Turnbull's Chinese Double: Dishonour and Defeat," *Australian* (New South Wales), March 30, 2017 (requires subscription), https://www.theaustralian.com.au/opinion/columnists/greg-sheridan/turnbulls-chinese-double-dishonour-and-defeat/news-story/55fbe920041a5f5ff7ec04b818085631.

6. Primrose Riordan, "China's Veiled Threat to Bill Shorten on Extradition Treaty," *Australian* (New South Wales), December 4, 2017 (requires subscription), https://www.theaustralian.com.au/national-affairs/foreign-affairs/chinas-veiled-threat-to-bill-shorten-on-extradition-treaty/news-story/ad793a4366ad2f94694e89c92d52a978.

7. "Power and Influence: The Hard Edge of China's Soft Power," Australian Broadcasting Corporation, June 5, 2017, expired December 7, 2018, accessed October 11, 2018, http://www.abc.net.au/4corners/power-and-influence-promo/8579844.

8. Nick McKenzie and James Massola, "Andrew Robb's Secret China Contract: Money for Nothing," *Sydney Morning Herald*, December 6, 2017, accessed October 11, 2018, https://www.smh.com.au/politics/federal/andrew-robbs-secret-china-contract-money-for-nothing-20171205-gzzaq5.html.

9. Malcolm Turnbull, "Speech Introducing the National Security Legislation Amendment (Espionage and Foreign Interference) Bill 2017," December 7, 2017, accessed October 11, 2018, https://www.malcolmturnbull.com.au/media/speech-introducing-the-national-security-legislation-amendment-espionage-an.

10. The debate in Australia has evolved considerably since 2009, when prime minister Kevin Rudd proposed campaign-finance-reform legislation that would have rendered foreign-sourced political donations illegal, and Turnbull (as opposition leader in Parliament) declined to support the legislation. Rudd has argued that this legislation would have mitigated some of the more problematic behaviors regarding foreign influence that have since occurred. Others, however, maintain that the ban would not have stopped the bulk of CCP-backed donations, which are channeled through Australian residents and citizens, and that the more important reform was to ensure greater transparency in identifying foreign agents. For Rudd's critique, see his February 24, 2018, column in the *Australian*, http://kevinrudd.com/portfolio-item /kevin-rudd-writes-in-the-australian-chairman-mals-new-mccarthyism.

11. Simon Benson, "Chau Chak Wing Identified by FBI in UN Bribery Case, Andrew Hastie Says," *Australian* (New South Wales), May 23, 2018, accessed October 11, 2018, https://www.theaustralian.com.au/national-affairs/chau -chak-wing-identified-by-fbi-in-un-bribery-case-andrew-hastie-says /news-story/e062198e1d3d7ec76b3a7a394c3b2543.

12. Simon Benson, "Crack Unit to Ward off Spy Attacks," *Australian* (New South Wales), April 25, 2018 (requires subscription), https://www.theaustralian .com.au/national-affairs/national-security/crack-unit -to-ward-off-threats -from-espionage/news-story/8409b24c8595bee1bc27e9927f05fbd5.

Canada

1. "Chinese Intelligence Services and Triads Financial Links in Canada," Royal Canadian Mounted Police and Canadian Security Intelligence Service, June 24, 1997, accessed October 11, 2018, http://www.jrnyquist.com /sidewinder.htm.

2. Steven Chase and Robert Fife, "CSIS Report Warns of Chinese Interference in New Zealand," *Globe and Mail* (Toronto), May 31, 2018, accessed October 11, 2018, https://www.theglobeandmail.com/politics/article-csis -report-warns-of-chinese-interference-in-new-zealand.

3. Sarah Boesveld, "Government Infiltrated by Spies, CSIS Boss Says," *Globe and Mail* (Toronto), May 1, 2018, accessed October 11, 2018, https://www .theglobeandmail.com/news/politics/government-infiltrated-by-spies-csis -boss-says/article4392618.

4. Petti Fong, "CSIS Head Backtracks on Allegations of Foreign Influence over Canadian Officials," *Star* (Toronto), June 23, 2010, accessed October 11, 2018, https://www.thestar.com/news/canada/2010/06/23/csis_head _backtracks_on_allegations_of_foreign_influence_over_canadian _officials.html.

5. Robert Fife and Steven Chase, "Trudeau Attended Cash-for-access Fundraiser with Chinese Billionaires," *Globe and Mail* (Toronto), April 7, 2017, accessed October 11, 2018, https://www.theglobeandmail.com/news/politics/trudeau-attended-cash-for-access-fundraiser-with-chinese-billionaires/article32971362.

6. Joanna Smith, "Candice Bergen: China Denied My Travel Visa, Liberals Were No Help," *Canadian Press*, September 29, 2017, accessed October 11, 2018, http://www.cbc.ca/news/politics/china-travel-visa-bergen-1.4314000.

7. James Kynge, Lucy Hornby, and Jamil Anderlini, "Inside China's Secret 'Magic Weapon' for Worldwide Influence," *Financial Times* (London), October 26, 2017, accessed October 11, 2018, https://www.ft.com/content/fb2b3934-b004-11e7-beba-5521c713abf4.

8. Robert Fife and Steven Chase, "Two Conservative Senators' Business Venture Linked to China," *Globe and Mail* (Toronto), December 15, 2017, accessed October 11, 2018, https://www.theglobeandmail.com/news/politics/two-conservative-senators-business-venture-linked-to-china/article37340503.

9. Robert Fife, Steven Chase, and Xiao Xu, "Senate Ethics Watchdog Probes China Trip by Three Conservative Senators," *Globe and Mail* (Toronto), December 7, 2017, accessed October 11, 2018, https://www.theglobeandmail.com/news/politics/senate-ethics-watchdog-probes-china-trip-by-three-conservative-senators/article37232605.

10. Robert Fife, Steven Chase, and Xiao Xu, "Beijing Foots Bill for Canadian Senators, MPs to Visit China," *Globe and Mail* (Toronto), December 1, 2017, accessed October 11, 2018, https://www.theglobeandmail.com/news/politics/beijing-foots-bill-for-visits-to-china-by-canadian-senators-mps/article37162592.

11. Terry Glavin, "Glavin: Learn from Australia—We Should Beware of Chinese Influence-peddling," *Ottawa (Ontario) Citizen*, December 13, 2017, accessed October 11, 2018, http://ottawacitizen.com/opinion/columnists/glavin-learn-from-australia-we-should-beware-of-chinese-influence-peddling.

12. Dan Levin, "Chinese-Canadians Fear China's Rising Clout Is Muzzling Them," *New York Times*, August 27, 2016, accessed October 11, 2018, https://www.nytimes.com/2016/08/28/world/americas/chinese-canadians-china-speech.html.

13. Tom Blackwell, "'Don't Step Out of Line': Confidential Report Reveals How Chinese Officials Harass Activists in Canada," *National Post* (Toronto), January 5, 2018, accessed October 11, 2018, https://nationalpost.com/news/world/confidential-report-reveals-how-chinese-officials-harass-activists-in-canada-there-is-a-consistent-pattern.

14. Robert Fife, Steven Chase, and Ian Bailey, "Trudeau Won't Say If Canada Will Follow Australia, US in Blocking Huawei from Big Projects," *Globe and Mail* (Toronto), August 28, 2018, https://www.theglobeandmail.com /politics/article-pm-trudeau-hazy-on-whether-canada-will-join-allies-to -ban-chinas.

Germany

1. The recent reports by ECFR and Merics/GPPI list some of them, but mainly deal with Europe in general: Francois Godement and Abigael Vasselier, "China at the Gates: A New Power Audit of EU-China Relations," European Council on Foreign Relations, December 1, 2017, accessed October 11, 2018, http://www.ecfr.eu/publications/summary/china_eu_power_audit7242; and Thorsten Benner, Jan Gaspers, Mareike Ohlberg, Lucrezia Poggetti, and Kristin Shi-Kupfer, "Authoritarian Advance: Responding to China's Growing Political Influence in Europe," MERICS, February 2018.
2. Then foreign minister Sigmar Gabriel on August 30, 2017, in a speech asked China to respect the "One Europe Principle" as much as it demands Europeans respect the "One China Principle."
3. Achim Sawall, "Duisburg und Huawei Starten die Rhine Cloud," Golem .de, June 11, 2018, accessed October 11, 2018, https://www.golem.de/news /du-it-duisburg-und-huawei-starten-die-rhine-cloud-1806-134892.html.
4. "'Nihao Deutschland' Zeigt Deutschen China," *Hamburger Abendblatt*, August 8, 2017, accessed October 11, 2018, https://www.abendblatt.de /kultur-live/tv-und-medien/article211511923/Nihao-Deutschland-zeigt -Deutschen-China.html.
5. Dana Heide, Till Hoppe, Klaus Stratman, and Stephan Scheur, "EU Ambassadors Band Together Against Silk Road," *Handelsblatt*, April 17, 2018, accessed October 11, 2018, https://global.handelsblatt.com/politics /eu-ambassadors-beijing-china-silk-road-912258.

Japan

1. Justin McCurry, "China Lays Claim to Okinawa as Territory Dispute with Japan Escalates," *Guardian* (UK), May 15, 2013, https://www.theguardian .com/world/2013/may/15/china-okinawa-dispute-japan-ryukyu.
2. Ryukyu Network, Organising Committee for the Special Administrative Region of the Chinese Race, accessed October 11, 2018, http://www.ryukyu -china.com.
3. "中華民族琉球特別自治区」の正体は . . . 中国共産党中央統一戦線工作部," *Japan+*, November 10, 2015, accessed October 11, 2018, http://japan-plus .net/952.

4. Taiwanese newspapers have already covered the Organizing Committee in a rather disparaging fashion: "Pushing Japan to Hand Back the Ryukyus: Chinese People Draw up an International Lawsuit," "促日歸還琉球 中國人擬告上國際法庭" *Liberty Times* (Taiwan), August 2, 2016, accessed October 11, 2018, http://news.ltn.com.tw/news/world/paper/1017100.

5. "China Brilliant Cause Investment Group CCTV International News Introduction," *Yanzhao Nightly/Shijiazhuang Daily*, accessed October 11, 2018, http://www.hnqxgs.com/yzwbfz/2196344.html.

6. "Organising Committee for the Ryukyu Islands Special Administrative Region of the Chinese Race," *Weibo*, accessed October 11, 2018, https://www.weibo.com/u/1931192953?is_hot=1.

7. Daniel Moss, "As China Steps Up, Japan Isn't Stepping Aside," Bloomberg, July 10, 2018, accessed October 11, 2018, https://www.bloomberg.com/view/articles/2018-07-10/japan-reasserts-influence-as-china-rises.

New Zealand

1. Anne-Marie Brady, "Magic Weapons: China's Political Influence Activities under Xi Jinping," Kissinger Institute on China and the United States, September 18, 2017, accessed October 11, 2018, https://www.wilsoncenter.org/article/magic-weapons-chinas-political-influence-activities-under-xi-jinping. Also see Anne-Marie Brady, "Looking for Points in Common While Facing Up to Differences," Small States and the New Security Environment, November 14, 2017, accessed October 11, 2018, https://www.canterbury.ac.nz/media/documents/research/Looking-for-points-in-common-while-facing-up-to-differences.pdf.

2. Brady, "Magic Weapons."

3. Ibid.

4. Ibid.

5. Ibid.

6. Anne-Marie Brady, "University Links with China Raise Questions," *New Zealand Herald*, July 13, 2018, accessed October 11, 2018, https://www.nzherald.co.nz/nz/news/article.cfm?c_id=1&objectid=12086974.

7. Brady, "Magic Weapons."

8. Matt Nippert, "University of Canterbury Professor Anne-Marie Brady Concerned Break-ins Linked to Work on China," *New Zealand Herald*, February 16, 2018, accessed October 11, 2018, http://www.nzherald.co.nz/nz/news/article.cfm?c_id=1&objectid=11995384.

Singapore and ASEAN

1. "Singapore Government Statement," Government of Singapore, May 15, 1971, http://www.nas.gov.sg/archivesonline/data/pdfdoc/SGPress_3_15.5.71.pdf.
2. Jermyn Chow, "SAF Armoured Vehicles Seized in Hong Kong Port, Mindef Expects Shipment to Return to Singapore 'Expeditiously,'" *Straits Times* (Singapore), November 24, 2016, accessed October 11, 2018, https://www.straitstimes.com/asia/se-asia/9-saf-armoured-vehicles-seized-at-hong-kong-port.
3. "Cancellation of Singapore Permanent Residence (SPR) Status—Huang Jing and Yang Xiuping," Singapore Ministry of Home Affairs, August 6, 2017, accessed October 11, 2018, https://www.mha.gov.sg/newsroom/press-release/news/cancellation-of-singapore-permanent-residence-(spr)-status—huang-jing-and-yang-xiuping.
4. Shannon Teoh and Eunice Au, "KL Wants Chinese Envoy to Explain Remarks," *Straits Times* (Singapore), October 2, 2015, accessed October 11, 2018, https://www.straitstimes.com/asia/se-asia/kl-wants-chinese-envoy-to-explain-remarks.

United Kingdom

1. Charles Parton, "China-UK Relations: Where to Draw the Border Between Influence and Interference," Royal United Services Institute, February 2019, https://rusi.org/publication/occasional-papers/china-uk-relations-where-draw-border-between-influence-and.
2. $9.6 billion in the United Kingdom according to Godement and Vasselier, "China at the Gates."
3. "New Phase in Golden Era for UK-China Relations," Government of the United Kingdom, December 15, 2017, accessed October 11, 2018, https://www.gov.uk/government/news/new-phase-in-golden-era-for-uk-china-relations.
4. Charles Parton, "China-UK Relations."
5. Benner et al., "Authoritarian Advance."
6. Paul Hutcheon, "China Accused of Being Behind Recent Cyber Attack on Scottish Parliament," *Herald* (Scotland), September 16, 2017, accessed October 11, 2018, http://www.heraldscotland.com/news/15540166.China_accused_of_being_behind_recent_cyber_attack_on_Scottish_Parliament; Gordon Corera, "UK Think Tanks Hacked by Groups in China, Cyber-Security Firm Says," BBC, February 26, 2018, accessed October 11, 2018, http://www.bbc.co.uk/news/uk-43172371.

7. George Parker, "British MPs Banned from Hong Kong Visit," *Financial Times* (UK), November 30, 2014, accessed October 11, 2018, https://www.ft.com/content/08919562-78ba-11e4-b518-00144feabdc0; Tom Phillips and Benjamin Haas, "British Conservative Party Activist Barred from Entering Hong Kong," *Guardian* (UK), October 11, 2017, accessed October 11, 2018, https://www.theguardian.com/world/2017/oct/11/british-conservative-party-activist-benedict-rogers-hong-kong.

8. Lucy Hornby, James Kynge, and George Packer, "'Golden Era' of UK-China Trade Links in Peril," *Financial Times* (UK), January 26, 2018, subscription required, https://www.ft.com/content/cb552198-02c0-11e8-9650-9c0ad2d7c5b5.

9. "Summary of Business Appointments Applications—Rt Hon David Cameron," Advisory Committee on Business Appointments, Government of the United Kingdom, February 28, 2018, accessed October 11, 2018, https://www.gov.uk/government/publications/cameron-david-prime-minister-acoba-recommendation/summary-of-business-appointments-applications-rt-hon-david-cameron; Emily Feng, "David Cameron Takes Senior Role in China Infrastructure Fund," *Financial Times* (UK), December 16, 2017, subscription required, https://www.ft.com/content/07a05ac2-e238-11e7-97e2-916d4fbac0da.

10. "Chinese Embassy Concerned as Lasting UK University Strike Affects Students," *Xinhua* (China), March 1, 2018, accessed October 11, 2018, http://www.xinhuanet.com/english/2018-03/01/c_137006815.htm.

11. Bethany Allen-Ebrahimian, "The Chinese Communist Party Is Setting Up Cells at Universities Across America," *Foreign Policy*, April 18, 2018, accessed October 11, 2018, https://foreignpolicy.com/2018/04/18/the-chinese-communist-party-is-setting-up-cells-at-universities-across-america-china-students-beijing-surveillance.

12. Charles Parton, "China-UK Relations."

13. James Bradshaw and Colin Freeze, "McMaster Closing Confucius Institute over Hiring Issues," *Globe and Mail* (Toronto), May 11, 2018, accessed October 11, 2018, https://www.theglobeandmail.com/news/national/education/mcmaster-closing-confucius-institute-over-hiring-issues/article8372894.

14. Rachelle Peterson, "Outsourced to China: Confucius Institutes and Soft Power in American Higher Education," National Association of Scholars, April 2017, accessed October 11, 2018, https://www.nas.org/images/documents/confucius_institutes/NAS_confuciusInstitutes.pdf; Daniel Sanderson, "Universities 'Sign Chinese Gagging Clause,'" *Times* (London), September 5, 2018, accessed October 11, 2018, https://www.thetimes.co.uk/article/universities-sign-chinese-gagging-clause-q7qz7jpf3.

15. "Chinese Power 'May Lead to Global Academic Censorship Crisis,'" *Times Higher Education* (London), December 7, 2017, accessed October 11, 2018, https://www.timeshighereducation.com/news/chinese-power-may-lead -global-academic-censorship-crisis#survey-answer.

16. For example, King's College London increased its CSC PhD scholarships tenfold "in recent years." King's College London, July 12, 2017, accessed October 11, 2018, https://www.kcl.ac.uk/newsevents/news/newsrecords /2017/12-December/King's-China-scholarship-programme-expands -tenfold.aspx.

17. Tom Phillips, "Cambridge University Press Censorship 'Exposes Xi Jinping's Authoritarian Shift,'" *Guardian* (UK), August 20, 2017, accessed October 11, 2018, https://www.theguardian.com/uk-news/2017/aug/20 /cambridge-university-press-censorship-exposes-xi-jinpings-authoritarian -shift.

18. Emily Feng, "China Tightens Party Control of Foreign University Ventures," *Financial Times* (UK), July 2, 2018, accessed October 11, 2018, https://www.ft.com/content/4b885540-7b6d-11e8-8e67-1e1a0846c475.

19. Charles Parton, "China-UK Relations."

20. "Exploratory Memorandum on the Television Co-production Agreement between the Government of the United Kingdom of Great Britain and Northern Ireland and the People's Republic of China," accessed October 11, 2018, https://assets.publishing.service.gov.uk/government/uploads/system /uploads/attachment_data/file/649774/EM_UK_China_TV.pdf.

21. Tom Phillips, "Mysterious Confession Fuels Fears of Beijing's Influence on Hong Kong's Top Newspaper," *Guardian* (UK), July 25, 2016, accessed October 11, 2018, https://www.theguardian.com/world/2016/jul/25/south -china-morning-post-china-influence-hong-kong-newspaper-confession.

22. Bates Gill and Benjamin Schreer, "The Global Dimension of China's Influence Operations," *Strategist*, Australian Strategic Policy Institute, April 11, 2018, accessed October 11, 2018, https://www.aspistrategist.org.au/global -dimension-chinas-influence-operations.

23. Jack Stubbs, "Exclusive: Britain Says Huawei 'Shortcomings' Expose New Telecom Networks Risks," Reuters, July 19, 2018, accessed October 11, 2018, https://www.reuters.com/article/us-huawei-security-britain-exclusive /exclusive-britain-says-huawei-shortcomings-expose-new-telecom-networks -risks-idUSKBN1K92BX.

24. "China's ZTE Deemed a 'National Security Risk' to UK," *Guardian* (UK), April 17, 2018, accessed October 11, 2018, https://www.theguardian.com /technology/2018/apr/17/chinas-zte-a-national-security-risk-to-uk-warns -watchdog.

25. Zoe Wood, "China Looking to Buy Stake in UK Nuclear Plants, Say Reports," *Guardian* (UK), July 8, 2018, accessed October 11, 2018, https://www.theguardian.com/environment/2018/jul/08/china-interested-majority-stake-uk-nuclear-power-stations-reports.

26. Adam Vaughan and Lily Kuo, "China's Long Game to Dominate Nuclear Power Relies on the UK," *Guardian* (UK), July 26, 2018, accessed October 11, 2018, https://www.theguardian.com/environment/2018/jul/26/chinas-long-game-to-dominate-nuclear-power-relies-on-the-uk.

27. "UK Relations with China Inquiry," Parliament of the United Kingdom, June 8, 2017, accessed October 11, 2018, https://www.parliament.uk/business/committees/committees-a-z/commons-select/foreign-affairs-committee/inquiries1/parliament-2015/inquiry; "New Inquiry: China and the International Rules-based System," Parliament of the United Kingdom, November 21, 2017, accessed October 11, 2018, https://www.parliament.uk/business/committees/committees-a-z/commons-select/foreign-affairs-committee/news-parliament-2017/china-inquiry-launch-17-19.

28. "The Darkest Moment: The Crackdown on Human Rights in China, 2013-16," Conservative Party Human Rights Commission, June 2016, accessed October 11, 2018, http://conservativehumanrights.com/reports/submissions/CPHRC_China_Human_Rights_Report_Final.pdf.

29. Foreign Office of the United Kingdom, "Why Does China Matter to the UK?" YouTube, November 29, 2017, accessed October 11, 2018, https://www.youtube.com/watch?v=YWwBDB1KPeY.

30. Godement and Vasselier, "China at the Gates."

31. "Chinese Students & Scholars Association Disaffiliated from University," *Varsity* online, December 3, 2011, accessed October 11, 2018, https://www.varsity.co.uk/news/4166.

32. James A. Millward, "Open Letter to Cambridge University Press about Its Censorship of the China Quarterly," *Medium*, August 19, 2017, accessed October 11, 2018, https://medium.com/@millwarj/open-letter-to-cambridge-university-press-about-its-censorship-of-the-journal-china-quarterly-c366f76dcdac.

33. Charles Parton, "China-UK Relations."

Appendix 3

1. "美国务院欲将中国人权状况调为最差等级 外交部回应," SinoVision, June 27, 2017, http://news.sinovision.net/politics/201706/00411546.htm.

2. "中国国新办发布《2016年美国的人权纪录." SinoVision, March 9, 2017, http://news.sinovision.net/politics/201703/00401996.htm; "中国外交部就美国人权报告涉华内容等答问," SinoVision, March 6, 2017, http://news.sinovision.net/politics/201703/00401682.htm.

3. "航行自由≠ 军事行动自由 中方驳斥对南海问题误读," SinoVision, February 19, 2018, http://news.sinovision.net/politics/201802/00431582.htm; "过年也不消停？美国航母"卡尔森"号春节前南海巡航," SinoVision, February 13, 2018, http://news.sinovision.net/politics/201802/00431309.htm.

WORKING GROUP PARTICIPANTS

This report grew out of a series of discussions over the past year and a half at the Hoover Institution, Sunnylands, and George Washington University in which the following scholars participated:

Robert Daly is director of the Kissinger Institute on China and the United States at the Woodrow Wilson International Center for Scholars.

Larry Diamond is senior fellow at the Hoover Institution and at the Freeman Spogli Institute for International Studies at Stanford University.

Elizabeth Economy is the C. V. Starr Senior Fellow and director for Asia Studies at the Council on Foreign Relations.

Gen. Karl Eikenberry (Ret.) is the Oksenberg-Rohlen Fellow, director of the US-Asia Security Initiative, and faculty member at Stanford University's Shorenstein Asia-Pacific Research Center.

Donald Emmerson is director of the Southeast Asia Program and senior fellow emeritus at the Freeman Spogli Institute for International Studies, Stanford University.

Francis Fukuyama is the Mosbacher Director of the Center on Democracy, Development, and the Rule of Law, and Olivier Nomellini Senior Fellow at the Freeman Spogli Institute for International Studies, Stanford University.

Bonnie Glaser is senior adviser for Asia and director of the China Power Project at the Center for Strategic and International Studies.

Kyle Hutzler is an MBA candidate at the Stanford Graduate School of Business.

Markos Kounalakis is a foreign affairs columnist for the McClatchy newspapers and Visiting Fellow at the Hoover Institution.

Winston Lord is a former US ambassador to China and former assistant secretary of state for East Asian and Pacific affairs.

Evan Medeiros is the Penner Family Chair in Asian Studies at the Georgetown University Walsh School of Foreign Service.

James Mulvenon is general manager at SOS International.

Andrew J. Nathan is the Class of 1919 Professor of Political Science at Columbia University.

Minxin Pei is the Tom and Margot Pritzker '72 Professor of Government and George R. Roberts Fellow at Claremont McKenna College.

Jeffrey Phillips is the policy director at The Annenberg Foundation Trust at Sunnylands.

John Pomfret is a *Washington Post* journalist and author.

Orville Schell is the Arthur Ross Director of the Center on US-China Relations at Asia Society.

David Shambaugh is Gaston Sigur Professor of Asian Studies, Political Science & International Affairs and director of the China Policy Program at the Elliott School of International Affairs, George Washington University.

Susan Shirk is research professor and chair of the 21st Century China Center at the University of California–San Diego's School of Global Policy & Strategy.

Robert Sutter is professor of practice of international affairs at the George Washington University Elliott School of International Affairs.

Glenn Tiffert is a visiting fellow at the Hoover Institution.

Ezra Vogel is the Henry Ford II Professor of the Social Sciences Emeritus at Harvard University.

Christopher Walker is vice president for studies and analysis at the National Endowment for Democracy.

International Associates

Timothy Garton Ash is a senior fellow at the Hoover Institution and professor of European studies at the University of Oxford.

Anne-Marie Brady is professor at the University of Canterbury and a global fellow at the Woodrow Wilson Center in Washington.

Timothy Cheek is director of the Institute of Asian Research, Louis Cha Chair in Chinese Research, and professor of history at the University of British Columbia.

John Fitzgerald is an emeritus professor in the Center for Social Impact at Swinburne University of Technology.

John Garnaut is a political risk consultant to the Australian government and private sector and was senior advisor to former prime minister Malcolm Turnbull.

Francois Godement is the director of the European Council on Foreign Relations Asia and China Program.

Bilahari Kausikan is a former permanent secretary of the Singapore Ministry of Foreign Affairs.

Richard McGregor is a senior fellow at the Lowy Institute and a journalist.

Eva Pils is a professor of law and director of doctoral studies at the Dickson Poon School of Law, King's College London.

Volker Stanzel is vice president of the German Council on Foreign Relations and former German ambassador to China and Japan.

The views expressed in this publication are solely those of the participants in the workshop and do not necessarily reflect the views of the staff, officers, or Board of Overseers of the Hoover Institution or the participants' affiliated institutions. The convening organizations of this project have no affiliation with the United States government.

INDEX

AAUP (American Association of University Professors), 55
Adams, John, 173
Afghanistan war, 24
Africa, 163, 164, 189
Aglietta, Michel, 180
Agricultural Bank of China, 132
airlines, Chinese government pressure on, 243
Albania, 190
Alexander, General Keith, 140, 145
Alibaba, 61, 83, 129, 239n25
All America Chinese Youth Federation, 237n10
All-China Federation of Overseas Chinese, 9
All-China Federation of Returned Overseas Chinese, 47
America–China Enterprise Chamber of Commerce, 238n11
American Enterprise Institute, 230n1
American Foreign Policy Council, 84
American Pacific International Capital (APIC), 130
Amnesty International, 173
"anaconda in the chandelier" syndrome, 63
Apple corporation, 242
artificial intelligence (AI), 242
ASEAN (Association of Southeast Asian Nations), 195, 197, 200–2
Asia-Africa Growth Corridor, 189
Asian affairs specialists, 18
Asian Culture and Media Group, 106, 120

Asia-Pacific Exchange Foundation (aka Far East Studies Institute), 21
Asia Society, 60, 230n1
ASIO (Australian Security Intelligence Organization), 165, 166
Aspen Institute, 24
assembly, freedom of, 6
Association to Promote China Unification, 40, 45
Australia, 11, 44, 58, 130, 163, 164–67, 171; Chinese-language media in, 233n34; "Five Eyes" security partnerships and, 190; Japan's relationship with, 189; response to Chinese influence activities, 167–70, 252n10

BackChina website, 214
Baidu, 242
Bank of China USA, 125
banks, Chinese, 132
Barret, Philippe, 180
BBC (British Broadcasting Corporation), 121
Beijing Olympics (2008), 102, 112, 165, 176, 177
Belt and Road Initiative, 16, 178, 180, 192, 200, 201; "BRI Task Forces," 184, 185; Germany and, 182, 183, 184; Singapore and, 198; UK–China relations and, 203
Better Hong Kong Foundation (BHKF), 21
Biden, Joe, 135
Bloomberg News, 117, 131
Boggs, Patton, 24